# PRAISE FOR THIS WORK:

*"The best thing I've learned regarding both my personal and professional life...Very powerful and insightful. I hope to be a better human being as a result... It was a moving experience for me... Very important to my development as a person, husband, father, manager, leader... A valuable learning experience, one that I will never forget... It made me step back and challenge how I handle certain situations and how I see and deal with certain individuals... Priceless... Valuable... Very eye-opening... Uplifting... Overdue... Inspirational... Fundamental, yet critical... Infinite possibilities... Insightful and will be useful for a long, long time...Very relevant in my personal life and professional career. Listening is very powerful... What I needed in my life... It was wonderful and a new experience for me... I will never forget it... A rewarding experience that I will share with my wife and child... Opened my eyes to look at myself. There's more to us than we exactly know."*

**Direct quotes from workshop participants:**
*Nashville, TN and Atlanta, GA*

*"What a tremendous job you have done for us. In my 23 years in management, you are the best investment the Social Security Administration has ever made in management development. I am a better person because of your work and hopefully that translates into being a better leader."*

**Harris N. Gibbs, District Manager,**
**United States Social Security Administration:**
*Orlando, FL*

*"Chalmers is one of the most thought-provoking speakers that I have heard while being a TEC member. The possibilities are endless in terms of take-home value... I feel this information needs to be shared with anyone who will listen...Valuable and useful for both business and personal application... ... Meaningful to all, very appropriate for both business and personal relationships... This was one of the few presentations to our group that I cared to have on tape for future reference...*

*Excellent and thought-provoking, this was a very insightful and inspirational presentation... Open, genuine, real, authentic, down-to-earth grasp of material... ... Best 'relational' seminar for business CEOs... Thanks for the mind change... Strong insights into language and its use, power and impact... Very helpful with listening, body language, moods and beliefs... Information and content were very valuable and practical...Easy to grasp and can be implemented immediately...I see its future use clearly... Really had my attention and I will apply this within our organization... Well presented, a real eye-opener... He sent me away with a list of things to think about and implement... Chalmers' message was very appropriate for our company."*

**Direct quotes from CEO's and members of Vistage International,
an international association of CEO's:**
*Philadelphia, PA; San Francisco, CA; Naples, FL; Rochester, NY;
Indianapolis, IN; Columbus, OH; Boston, MA*

*"I can tell you without reservation that your unique message on leadership and life is unparalleled. What a great experience this has been. You've helped hundreds of managers to become better leaders. Keep up the good work."*

**B.J. Hughes, District Manager,
United States Social Security Administration:**
*Clearwater, FL*

*"This body of work directly enhances an organization's ability to create and maintain clear and coordinated action, as well as to sustain healthy and productive workplace relationships. What I have learned working with Chalmers continues to have profound impact on me, both professionally and personally. His insights and distinctions are supporting me to move to a higher order of self-awareness and personal accountability, helping me achieve the results I desire as a manager, husband and father."*

**Dave Pendery, Director—Human Resources Information Strategy,
The Coca-Cola Company,**
*Atlanta, GA*

# Language
## and the pursuit of
# Happiness

A new foundation
for designing your life,
your relationships & your results

**new
possibilities
press**

naples florida

# New Possibilities Press

8805 Tamiami Trail North, Suite #A-311
Naples, FL  34108
chalmersb@comcast.net • Fax: 239-593-3275

**Library of Congress Cataloging-in-Publication Data**
Library of Congress control number: 2004101156
Brothers, Chalmers.
Language and the prusuit of happiness: a new foundation for designing your life,
your relationships and your results/Chalmers Brothers.

ISBN 10: 0-9749487-0-5
ISBN 13: 978-0-9749487-0-6

Printed in the United States of America

*Edited by: James Mayo*
*Cover design and illustrations by: Chameleon Communications, L.L.C.*
*Produced by: New Possibilities Press*

for

*Betsy*

*Rachael*

*Ben*

*&*

*Caroline*

# CONTENTS

# FOREWORD

Welcome. The book you are beginning is not a typical "self-help" or "self-improvement" book, although it can certainly support you in helping yourself and improving yourself in a number of ways. In a bigger way, this is also an introduction to an emerging way of thinking, a new way of understanding ourselves, our language and our ways of learning, growing and relating to each other. It's also in this larger light that I invite you to move through these pages.

We are living in extraordinary times, and are facing changes and challenges in virtually every aspect of our lives. The nature of the transformation that humanity is currently living through demands that we re-examine and quite possibly change our fundamental assumptions in every single area of life. And as we know very well, this is an enormous task for multiple reasons.

First of all, we don't live our assumptions as assumptions, we live them as "that's the way things are." This forces us to go through a reflective process that is not only intellectually challenging but also emotionally demanding. We must first identify our assumptions that are hidden in the transparency of living. Then we must confront the reality that the remainder of our thinking is resting on these assumptions. This confrontation—being forced to revise many realms of our understanding—can make us feel like we're in a free fall.

Secondly, the simple idea that "truths" that I have known all my life can be superseded by other beliefs is, to say the least, threatening. Therefore, we fall into the tendency to oppose change, to seek refuge in some unquestionable and final truth. The fundamentalist in us is awakened.

In times like these, when assumptions of all kinds in many different domains of our thinking are called to critical examination, social unrest, governmental repression, religious cultism, crime, terrorism, and mental illness increase. But also we witness the creation of new disciplines and practices, and the expansion of possibilities in a wide range of fields. In other words, "nothing vast comes to human territory without bringing its shadows with it."

Throughout history, we have had some assumptions that have been particularly resistant to change, remaining engraved in our common sense for millennia. *This is the case for the fundamental assump-*

*tions we have about human language as a descriptive consensual code and as a passive phenomenon.* In these assumptions, language was limited to describing what we perceived or felt or what we thought about things, but had nothing to do with those "things" themselves. Speaking did not change anything; language was passive, fundamentally separated from action. And the inability to change these particular assumptions has resulted in a great cost for humanity: *we have not been able to tap consistently into one of the most powerful self-transformational forces available to us.* The assumptions have always held that we could *describe* and *analyze* ourselves but, bottom line, we couldn't *change* ourselves. We have lived in a kind of inherent resignation, essentially transparent to us.

This began to change during the "linguistic revolution" that took place in philosophy at the beginning of the last century. The English philosopher J.L. Austin began a critical revision of those assumptions. Today, we realize that language is not only a descriptive phenomenon, as unquestionably it is, but it is also a _generative_ and _active_ one. Our language is an essential element in constituting each of us as the unique observer we are, in creating the "me" who sees what I see and the "you" who sees what you see. Through the power it grants us to make distinctions, and by enabling us to make things happen, we are able to design ourselves as well as to alter the world in which we participate.

The last great philosopher who claimed the transformative power of language before Austin and other "philosophers of language" had been Heraclitus, at the end of the sixth century before Christ. He claimed that "Logos," the word, was the basis of all that existed and was the force that transformed chaos into order. After him, language was never again thought of as generative and creative until the beginning of the last century.

I have been an "ontological coach" for over twenty years. I know the power of language not from an intellectual approach but from recurrent encounters with people who attend my programs in pursuit of a _learning_ that goes beyond gathering information or conquering effective action. They attend out of a disturbing and also freeing realization: there must be a _learning that transcends the traditional kind of learning_—a learning that aims beyond the descriptive informational approach and beyond the utilitarian goal of effective action. They realize that those may be important steps at some level but, ultimately, they are insufficient to deal with their quest for **effective living**. And here, language is of the essence.

So what connections can we make between language and living? Between language and being? Between language and happiness? Let's start by realizing that we live in language in the same way that fish live in water: it is transparent to us. It's not that we don't know that we speak and listen, but rather we are unaware that language is *shaping* the world as we see it. When we see the sky after an astronomer shares with us distinctions about celestial bodies, we are able to see what we were unable to see before that conversation. We see galaxies, planets, and satellites where before there were only a bunch of "stars." This happens to us all the time when we engage in conversations with people who share with us distinctions we did not have before. Why do those things appear to be obviously there now but were not there a few seconds ago? How much am I unable to observe because I lack distinctions? What might I be missing? How does all of this affect my possibilities for action if, of course, I can't intervene in a world I don't see?

We also live with the illusion that *we have conversations* when, in reality, most of the time *our conversations have us*. It takes a strong process of reflection to escape from our conversational inertia with all of its limiting consequences. We belong to historical discourses, old cultural and societal narratives and interpretative traditions that have a hold on us. Waking up to that fact generates a freedom that's unimaginable before the experience! The way to happiness requires a process of initiation, a reflection that allows us to see that most of the time what we call "my thinking" is nothing more that a historical burp. And to notice that the claim "that's the way I am" isn't rooted in any biological or psychological facts. Instead, these point more to our having participated in a lifelong interpretive path that we did not personally or consciously choose. As Heidegger would say, it's more accurate to say that we find ourselves "thrown" into the particular conversations we're living in. Becoming aware of this opens the door to a new way of learning, a new set of choices, an entirely different set of possibilities.

Finally, let me say that language lives braided with emotions. Language is never isolated, never separated from the world of moods and emotions. There is no such thing as unemotional thinking or unemotional conversing. Our every internal and external conversation is already coming from a particular emotional space, as well as holding the built-in potential to impact and change the emotional state of others. Emotions are predispositions for action; that is, they have the result of pre-disposing us *toward* certain actions and *away* from others. And, as we have already learned, language is action. It's clear that our moods and emotions are tremendously important in shaping and creating "the world we have in front of us," as well as our ability to adapt, change and learn. They are tightly connected to language in some obvious and not-so-obvious ways. A new understanding of language is essential for managing our moods and emotions, as well as for more effectively designing our personal and professional relationships.

And in times like these, a new way of understanding language may very well be essential for bringing about more effective and more beneficial ways of relating, living, learning and solving problems—at a multitude of levels. If all of this interests you, I am glad you have this book in your hands. You are about to initiate a wonderful voyage into a world that often will challenge your common sense understanding and your views about beginning a new kind of learning. I invite you to stick with it. It's worthwhile all the way.

*Julio Olalla*
Boulder, Colorado
April, 2004

# INTRODUCTION

Let's have a conversation—and maybe a *different* conversation—about happiness. That's what I'm up to here. The fact that you've even picked up this book, given it's title, to me is a hopeful indication that we're both interested in at least exploring this topic a bit! The notion of *exploring* is a perfect way of describing what I believe to be the best way to move through this book. Not the physical type of exploring, like pioneers crossing the plains, but exploring in a different sense. Exploring in the sense of setting out on a path, not knowing exactly where you're going to end up, and being willing to at least start the journey anyway. Exploring as moving into and through some uncharted territory, and opening yourself up to learning about it. And exploring as being willing to temporarily suspend what you know about something, because you're aware that doing so is a pre-requisite for being truly open to new (and presently invisible) possibilities and opportunities. In these sorts of ways, my invitation to you is to come exploring with me. I believe explorers of all types take risks, though of very different sorts. And explorers of all types make discoveries, sometimes entirely different than those which were anticipated. *One of my goals in this book is to be able to show you how the discoveries you will make on this journey are absolutely worth the risk-taking that's required to get there.* So let's start out broadly, with a bit of a historical perspective on this topic. This can serve to set the stage for our conversation, for what I want to share with you, and for what I hope will lead to some of those unanticipated discoveries.

From the U.S. Declaration of Independence we read: *"We hold these truths to be self-evident, that all men are created equal, that they are endowed by their Creator with certain inalienable Rights, that among these are Life, Liberty and the pursuit of Happiness."* [1]

Many years ago, the philosopher Aristotle pointed to what he saw as the universal nature of this pursuit when he said: *"Happiness is the meaning and the purpose of life, the whole aim and end of human existence."* [2]

Another philosopher, William James, suggested much the same when he said: *"How to gain, how to keep, and how to recover happiness is, in fact—for most men, at all times—the secret motive for all they do, and for all they are willing to endure."* [3]

And the Dalai Lama, in his 1999 book *Ethics for the New Millennium*, offers his perspective which, to me, is also a solid place from which to begin. He says: *"For my part, meeting innumerable others from all over the world and from every walk of life reminds me of our basic sameness as human beings. Indeed, the more I see of the world, the clearer it becomes that no matter what our situation, whether we are rich or poor, educated or not, of one race, gender, religion or another, we all desire to be happy and to avoid suffering. Our every intended action, in a sense our whole life—how we choose to live it within the context of the limitations imposed by our circumstances—can be seen as our answer to the great question which confronts us all: 'How am I to be happy?'"* [4]

Clearly, this is a big issue for a great many of us... and apparently has been for quite a long time. People today continue to search for answers to this question in an incredible variety of ways. In this book I share with you a way of understanding that brings truly unique and unprecedented possibilities to this equation. It is at once broad enough to touch and include virtually every other approach out there, and yet has roots deep enough to serve as a solid platform for each of us to use at home and at work, everywhere we go and in everything we do for the rest of our lives. This I know: it changed mine. And I believe it can change yours, too.

**This book is built entirely around the following 2 major claims:**

1. **A new understanding of language provides a new foundation, a new starting point, a new set of options and a new set of tools for those of us seeking to design more happiness and fulfillment into our lives.**

2. **This new way of understanding language is directly connected to a new way of understanding ourselves, a new way of understanding human beings... and it is here that things get really interesting!**

The approach I will share with you may in some ways seem counterintuitive, going against the grain of what you may have grown up believing and thinking about yourself and how you end up producing the results you produce in your life. And in other ways, I believe, it will resonate with you as a different type of "common sense," as it points to things you have known all along but somehow may not have been using in your everyday life. In any event, I promise that this can allow you to *see* a great many things differently and *do* a great many things differently, *at a level at which seeing and doing things differently matters a great deal.*

In this book, I will share with you a different and powerful way of thinking and observing. I will show you how a new way of understanding *language* unlocks a new way of understanding yourself, your relationships, your effectiveness and your results—*in a tremendously wide variety of areas.* I will show you ways in which your language is directly connected to your ability to design your own life and manage your own moods. And at many places along the way, I will invite you to speculate with me, to consider "what if..." questions for yourself and to "try on" a different set of glasses through which to look at yourself, your relationships, your moods and your life. After all, that's what this type of exploring's all about.

❋　❋　❋

For our purposes, let's define happiness in a simple way. Moving forward, when we say happiness, we'll be talking about one or both of the following:

- Peacefulness
- Productivity.

(I also like Ingrid Bergman's definition of happiness. She says: *"Happiness = good health and a bad memory!")*

***Within these pages, we'll say that achieving Happiness = achieving some balanced combination of Peacefulness and Productivity.***

<u>Peacefulness</u> includes the *qualitative* side, the subjective nature of your experience as you do what you do. It includes your emotional space, the degree to which you experience (or don't experience!) suffering or dissatisfaction in an ongoing way. And <u>productivity</u> includes the *quantitative* side, the objective getting-things-done side, the making-a-contribution, real-world, tangible results side. Happiness, as used within these pages, involves *both*. What I'll be sharing with you on the following pages is directly applicable to *both* your ability to achieve peacefulness, as well

ii-3

as to your ability to be productive, in all areas of your life. The goal for a great many of us is to create a *balance that works*—and this we will call happiness.

The claim of this book is that a *new understanding of language* provides an incredibly powerful foundation from which to achieve this balance. This new approach is directly and immediately valuable in three primary areas:

- Our personal lives–for us as individuals
- Our relationships–personal and professional; and
- Our effectiveness in any leadership roles that we assume in our lives.

It's my goal to have you *see new possibilities* for yourself, as you go through the following pages, within each of these three areas. This is where it all starts—because seeing new possibilities is always the first step toward producing new results.

❋ ❋ ❋

Let's start with what we see around us. In America and the industrialized West, large numbers of people have achieved and acquired a great deal—nice, comfortable homes, central air and heat, enough food to eat, adequate clothing, a reduction in some physical ailments and diseases, education, careers, activities, country club memberships, material and social "success"—and yet somehow, many of us report that we're not happy, not fulfilled, not producing certain important results we want to be producing. What's going on?

We may have had, when we were younger, a mental picture of what we thought it would take to make us satisfied, peaceful, productive, happy. And now, when we've actually achieved and acquired these things, we find something missing and we say we're not happy. This situation is widespread in our society today—have you noticed? Do you find yourself here from time to time? Many of us have. Today there are literally millions of people "living the good life" reporting that they are extremely "stressed out" and "overwhelmed," and that they have been this way for quite awhile now. What's going on here? *And more importantly: Is there a way that we may design our lives so that they include real balance, satisfaction, peace, effectiveness... that is, happiness?*

The Dalai Lama and many others who have traveled extensively have come to a similar, and perhaps surprising, view: Those of us living in the materially developed countries, for all our industry and new technology, are in some ways *less* satisfied, *less* happy and to some degree suffer *more* than those living in less materially developed countries. One look at the demand for Zoloft, Prozac and other anti-depressants in the U.S. certainly supports this. How do we explain this? And more importantly, *what actions might we take*, should we choose to take active steps in bringing more happiness, less suffering, greater peace, a healthier balance and better results to our lives? Ultimately, that is what this book is all about—sharing with you a ***new place to look*** in our search for what we're calling happiness.

I have heard the following story used to illustrate this situation: Late at night, an inebriated man was seen on his hands and knees, under a lamppost, crawling about. Another guy approached him and asked him what he was doing, whereupon he replied *"Searching for my keys."* "Where did you lose them?" asked the passer-by. *"Oh, over there, out in the street."* "Well then, why are you looking for them here?" *"Because the light's better here!"*

The approach that I will share with you has been "out of the light" in this sense: Since I've been involved in this work I have not heard one single person report that he or she learned this—or something very like it using different terms—in a traditional primary school or college environment. What's within these pages is also not something that's readily available for us to pick up in our normal course of living, working and doing what we do. In my experience, this way of seeing things is definitely not part of the mainstream curriculum. That being said, however, I do believe that growing numbers of people (myself among them) have come to points in our lives where we're more willing to look a little deeper and question some previously unquestioned assumptions about ourselves. For whatever reasons, we're now more willing to question some previously taken-for-granted "facts" about who we are, how we got this way, and *our own roles* in bringing about the experiences and situations we seem to find ourselves in. This book is absolutely about just this sort of questioning and re-thinking.

I have come to believe that one of the main reasons that many of us have not been finding the experience of happiness is this: *we've been looking in the wrong places!* It's not that we haven't been looking hard enough; we've simply been going down avenues that, in the end, have not produced the sustainable change or the lasting results we're looking for.

In many ways, we've been looking _through_ language and taking it for granted as do what we do, living our lives. Here, we'll be looking _at_ language instead. And this, to put things simply, changes everything.

This is not a book of tips and techniques and it is not a how-to manual, although I promise—and I know this is a big promise—that you will absolutely be able to do things you are not currently able to do as a result of practicing what you learn here. And one more big promise I make to you: That what is within these pages can support you in more effectively and successfully using _ANY and ALL self-improvement, relationship-improvement and leadership-improvement_ approaches on the market! I say this because what I will share with you is a level "underneath" all of those, and by shifting our perspective here we suddenly make visible entirely new sets of possibilities for use within any and all frameworks. We suddenly make visible entirely new sets of options, new sets of choices, and we also gain a new understanding of _why_ one approach or another actually works.

As the book title implies, my focus is on _language_—specifically, _human language_—and my intent is to share with you the incredible possibilities for us that become available by taking a new look here. We won't spend any time on subjects and verbs, nouns and pronouns, grammar and sentence structure; instead, our journey will take us in an entirely different direction. But here's the kicker, and this is key: when we start taking a new look at language in this way, it quickly becomes apparent that what we're also doing is taking a new look at _ourselves_, a new look at _human beings._ And this, to me, is where things get exciting. Said another way, what's within these pages will absolutely enable you to be _more effective_ in virtually every aspect of your life... but if we limit our attention to _effectiveness_, we'll truly miss the larger point. We'll miss the whole shift in perspective, the more important _change in how we're defining and understanding ourselves to be_ that makes the effectiveness possible in the first place!

I am honored to be able to share with you what I have had the privilege of learning and teaching over these past years. For me, this place to look was so close, so obvious that I didn't see it at first. But once I saw it, something shifted and I could never go back to the way I saw things before. Perhaps it will be this way for you, also.

It's with great gratitude that I have undertaken this project. First, gratitude to my wife Betsy for introducing me to this learning years ago and gratitude that we get to do this together. And gratitude that many of our seminar participants were also interested enough in this learning to continue to ask the question, *"Where can I get a book about this stuff?"* Also, I am so grateful for the many wonderful people who have been my teachers, coaches and friends along this path, sharing with me ways of understanding that truly shifted my world.

My goal is to share a body of learning that, for me and many others, has proven to be profoundly powerful, positive and important in our personal and professional lives. Does this mean I never have a "bad day?" Does this mean I never get unhappy, or that it's somehow wrong to ever be unhappy? Does this mean I believe there's never a time to be angry or sad? Of course not. What it does mean is that I am far more conscious about my role in creating my experience and about tools available to me to design something different, should I so choose.

Would you be interested in learning more about your own role in creating your experience? Or about acquiring a proven set of tools for directly intervening upon and shifting out of "negative" moods? How about a stronger ability to establish and maintain healthy, mutually beneficial relationships? Could you benefit from a clear, concise road map—steps to take—in order to get things done more effectively and produce new results, at home and at work? Would a powerful new way of understanding and bringing forth effective leadership (any level) be valuable to you? Are you interested in strengthening your ability to move through setbacks, problems and disappointments? Or to more fully realize and take advantage of opportunities? Would a stronger ability to create balance in your life be valuable to you? How about being better equipped to deal successfully with change? Or to improve your ability to learn—throughout your entire lifetime?

*Are you interested in learning how to dramatically influence, in a number of positive ways, the "quality of your journey," wherever your journey takes you?*

If you are, you've found the right book. I promise that what I'm sharing with you, within these pages, can serve as a new foundation, a new "starting point," and a new set of tools for all this and more. *Read on!* It is my direct experience that this way of understanding has great value at the levels of personal well-being, relationship-building of all types, effective leadership, organizational success and community building. More and more, though, I have begun to see even bigger possibilities. It is now my wholehearted belief that these ideas and ways of seeing things may also represent one set of tools that can directly serve us as we—all of us— attempt to live together on this planet in the years ahead. It's a privilege to share this with you.

*Chalmers Brothers*
Naples, Florida
April, 2003

# A WORD ABOUT PARADIGMS

In this book I will share with you what I have found to be extremely powerful ways of looking at language, conversations, ourselves, our relationships and how we actually produce the results we produce for ourselves in our lives. The following chapters contain a series of interpretations that I am offering to you. I am not claiming that they are the _Right_ way or the _only_ way or _"The Truth"_ about these things. I think it's more accurate to say that taken collectively, they do represent a new paradigm (**pair**-a-dime). This term—paradigm—has entered the pop culture and has perhaps been overused to the point of not being so meaningful to many of us. I like to understand paradigms in a simple way. To me, a paradigm may be defined as: _A way of understanding, believing, and taking action that I operate out of, that allows me to produce certain results._

And over time, our paradigms can slide to the background of our thinking to the point where we don't see them as _a_ way of understanding, believing, and taking action anymore; rather, we begin to see them as _the_ way of understanding, believing, and taking action. We begin to take our particular paradigms for granted, as if they are the Truth and the "obvious" or "natural" order of things, and this greatly limits our possibilities. In fact, paradigms may also be defined as: _A way of understanding, believing, and taking action that I have operated out of for so long that I now think it's the Truth!_

Paradigms are incredibly important for all of us—at home and at work and everywhere—because of one overriding reason: **They serve as the mega-context, the background, the major assumptions about "how things are" that are behind and underneath _all_ of our actions, interactions and choices.** And out of our actions and interactions and choices, we produce the results we produce for ourselves in the world, in a wide variety of areas. Our paradigms—in the background, of course—greatly influence what actions we take and how we take them. They influence what we see when we open our eyes, the choices we make and how we make them, the things we do and how we do them, and the results we get and how we get them.

Here are some examples of paradigms. Notice how they can become "transparent" and taken for granted, serving then as the backdrop against which decisions are made and actions are taken. Notice also _how different_ *our decisions and actions can be*, when we operate out of one paradigm or another:

- The earth is the center of the universe.
- The earth is part of one solar system out of millions, which itself is part of one galaxy out of millions...
- The universe is composed of unchanging, permanent objects.
- The universe and everything in it are incredibly dynamic and ever-changing.
- Our universe is the only universe.
- The world is flat.
- Heavier than air objects are not "meant" to fly.
- Atoms are the smallest unit of matter.
- Matter is the ultimate basis for everything in the universe.
- Energy, or spirit, is the ultimate basis for everything in the universe.
- Watches must be based on mainsprings.
- Women are not as capable as men in (insert one of many domains here).
- Women and men are equals and are different from each other.
- People cannot really change who they are over the course of a lifetime.
- People can change radically over the course of a lifetime.
- It is acceptable and "natural" for some people to own other people.
- Humans, by nature, are basically bad.
- Humans, by nature, are basically good.
- Human beings are logical animals.
- Learning is something that takes place at the beginning of one's life.
- Learning is something that goes on throughout our lives, not just at the beginning part.
- Diversity of thought, traditions and practices is healthy and positive for organizations and societies.

We could go on and on, in science and manufacturing and social/societal norms and educational approaches and medicine, religion and spirituality. Paradigms exist everywhere and are usually harder for the people "within" them to see than for those outside that particular culture or time-frame. Below is a key observation that may be obvious, but is important for where we are going:

*Our paradigms are not permanent, forever and always.*

Have you noticed that they have a way of changing? The term "paradigm shift" was invented to describe this movement away from one paradigm and toward another, the shifting of awareness or learning or experience that causes a few people at first, then larger numbers of people later, to drop one way of seeing things and adopt another. We can also say that *our paradigms are evolving*; that is, they are *including and transcending* what came before. Including and transcending, incorporating some of what was previously included, modifying or dropping some of what was previously included, and going further. This process of including and transcending is at the heart of *all* learning and evolving, and it's occurring in virtually every aspect of our lives.

Let me now share with you the traditional paradigm that we'll be dealing with (*and shifting away from*) in this book. Below is the orientation that most of us are very familiar with and may even take for granted:

***Language is a tool for communication and for describing how things are. To fully understand language, one must be primarily involved with grammar, sentence structure, subjects, nouns, verbs, pronouns, participles and so on.***

What I am up to within these pages is to share with you an alternative view, a complementary view, a different set of underlying assumptions and implications about language. And in doing so, as mentioned before, we'll also be exploring a different way of understanding ourselves, a different paradigm for understanding human beings.

As I have come to understand them, paradigms are not "good or bad," "right or wrong," in and of themselves. They just *are*. Now, some are clearly more *effective* in allowing us to achieve certain kinds of results than others, some are clearly more factually *accurate* representations of the physical world as our science currently understands it... but this isn't how many of us hold our paradigms. No, many of us are immediately thrown to questions of *good vs. bad*, and *right vs. wrong*. Notice how quickly we seem to automatically serve up questions such as "Is that way of understanding right, or is it wrong? Is it good, or is it bad? Is it the Truth with a capital T, or is it False with a capital F?"

It's also been my experience that in a great many situations, we have *not* collectively agreed on what constitutes *right*-ness and *wrong*-ness, *truth*-ness and *false*-ness… but this doesn't stop us in the least from using the Right/Wrong orientation. We tend to throw the Right/Wrong grid on top of many situations rather automatically, including situations in which the Right/Wrong grid absolutely does not fit and absolutely does not help. What if we instead began to orient ourselves with questions that are more directly connected to *results*? That is, what if we asked the following sorts of questions instead:

- What possibilities for *action*, and therefore what possible *results*, come out of seeing things this way vs. that way?
- What does this way of thinking—this paradigm or that paradigm—help me in being able to *do*?
- What would happen if a great many people adopted this way of thinking, or that way of thinking? What would be the *relationship impact* and the *collective impact* on how we live and work together?

Instead of Right/Wrong, I think the *works/doesn't work* grid is a far more powerful framework for moving through this book. It's in that light that I'm sharing what I've learned with you. I'm not claiming that what's here is Right, and that other ways of looking at things are Wrong. I'm not claiming that I've got "understanding" and that people who have different ways of looking at these topics have "mis-understanding." I *am* claiming, however, that the concepts and distinctions within this book *will* allow you to design your own life, create healthier relationships, improve your ability to lead effectively, and support you in creating a healthier balance of peacefulness and productivity in your life. The invitation here is to *use what works for you*, within these pages, and leave the rest.

# SPECIAL ACKNOWLEDGEMENTS AND SPECIAL THANKS

Everything in this book can ultimately be attributed to my great fortune in meeting and learning from two wonderful groups of people:

- Education for Living (EFL) Seminars Southwest, Inc.–Lake Charles, LA. Thank you for introducing me to a whole new world! Thank you Laurie and Henry Riquelmy, Ellen and Mike Papania, Chuck Smith and Jeff Spring for your love and friendship and for initially bringing us to this body of learning and being persistent in enrolling us. Thanks also for wonderful coaching, mentoring, and topic papers that have helped me (and continue to help me) understand and put into practice this powerful way of looking at things.

- The Newfield Network–Boulder, CO. Thank you Julio Olalla and Rafael Echeverria, for offering a way of looking at language and the world that was truly eye-opening to me and provided the connection I was looking for to the business world. Thank you for the opportunity to participate in the long course Mastering the Art of Professional Coaching (MAPC), which was the spark for me to formally change my career and begin making a new offer to my clients, one that I believe goes more to the heart of their issues. And thank you for teaching me about diversity and the beauty of our differences, and how beneath these differences lie many larger ways in which we are all similar.

Also, special acknowledgements would not be complete without acknowledging the contribution of Mr. Fernando Flores. I have not personally met Mr. Flores, but I understand that he has been a powerfully influential teacher of the key individuals behind Education for Living and Newfield Network, as well as many others involved in this education. He is also most directly responsible for the original invention of many of the key distinctions that have been built upon in this body of learning. The contribution of Mr. Flores is huge, and the lives that have been positively affected by this body of learning number well into the tens of thousands, perhaps much higher. Mr. Flores' creation and approach have, in turn, drawn upon big contributions from three primary sources:

- Humberto Maturana, pioneering and world-renowned Chilean neurobiologist;

- Speech Act Theory, originally developed at Oxford University by the philosopher J. L. Austin; with later contributions from the philosopher John Searle at the University of California, Berkeley; and
- The work of German philosopher Martin Heidegger.

Finally, one may also trace the origins of this body of learning back to ancient Greece, all the way to a gentleman named Heraclitus. In many ways Socrates and Plato and their followers were in one camp, and Heraclitus and his followers were in another. Socrates and Plato "won," so to speak, in that their version of what a human being is and their version of "reality" became, and is still today, the foundation of the traditional Western world-view. Of course, much of this is totally in the background of what we do. It's such an automatic and transparent part of how we think and act that we don't see it. In many respects the learning in this book is more in line with Heraclitus and his way of thinking. Broadly speaking, this body of learning represents a real shift from the background "drift" that is the legacy of Socrates, Plato, and Aristotle. At a basic level, it's a different way of thinking about human beings, language, change, relationships, objectivity and ultimately, what we've come to call "the way things are."

❋   ❋   ❋

*Throughout this book I'll be using "we" quite a bit. This is to recognize that while I may be the one sharing these distinctions with you via these pages, a great many others have truly pioneered this work and developed these concepts. I continue to be part of this community of learners, and this book represents a continuation of my learning. My intent is to introduce this powerful approach to as many people as possible, and to do so in a way that's (hopefully!) practical, accessible, and fun.*

❋   ❋   ❋

# SPECIAL THANKS

Thank you so much, James Mayo, for your excellent editing and insights in all areas, and for your continued friendship and encouragement. Your poetry has inspired me and continues to do so. Heartfelt thanks also to Dave Pendery for your editing, reviews and contributions, way above and beyond the call of duty. You're a true friend and partner on this path. And a very big thank you to Randy Cochran, Al Forrester, Mike Papania, Mark Robertson, Laurie Riquelmy, Michael DeMere, Bob Malkowski, Bill Thomas and Terrie Lupberger for your valuable suggestions, constructive criticism and support during this project. I know the book is far better because of your contributions, and I'm very grateful that you shared them with me.

# HOW THE BOOK IS STRUCTURED

The flow of the book, at least in general, comes from workshops and seminars conducted by my partner, Mark Robertson, and me in providing services to our clients via our consulting and coaching practice. Over the past years we have shared the concepts and distinctions within this book with a great many people, usually in the form of seminars and workshops for client organizations. On many occasions, during breaks or after the seminar, participants have asked us, *"Where can I get a book that contains this information?"* After hearing this question a number of times over the years, I finally decided that I had answered with *"I don't know."* for the last time.

❋   ❋   ❋

***Chapter 1: You Can't Change What You Don't See***, lays the groundwork for the book. The starting point for *any* meaningful change is our capacity to observe and specifically, to observe ourselves. Then and only then do we get to be *at choice* about making any changes in our lives. Throughout the whole book, my emphasis will be to improve your ability to observe yourself and what you're up to in language.

***Chapter 2: Language—The Tool We Cannot Put Down***, introduces a new way of understanding the phenomenon of language. This non-traditional interpretation of language is the new foundation upon which everything else in the book rests. This interpretation, for me, changed everything.

***Chapter 3: What's <u>Learning</u> Got To Do With Happiness? And What's <u>Language</u> Got To Do With Learning?*** Here, new ways of understanding the process of learning are introduced, as well as the strong connections that exist among learning, well-being, and language. How we understand and orient ourselves toward (or away from) learning has everything to do with our ability to produce *any* new results in our lives, including the results we're calling happiness, balance, well-being, and effectiveness.

***Chapter 4: Listening, Hearing, Beliefs, and Results.*** Our language and our conversations include two primary (and obvious) aspects: listening and speaking. This chapter focuses on *the listening side* and on many of our internal conversations and beliefs. It introduces a new way of understanding the differences between listening and hearing, and the impact that this awareness has on the results we produce for ourselves.

**Chapter 5: My Favorite Model: Observer > Action > Results.** This chapter introduces a simple yet powerful model of how we human beings actually produce the results we produce. Originally developed and expanded by Robert Putnam, Chris Argyris and Rafael Echeverria (among others), this model builds on the claim that each of us is a unique observer of the world. From the way we observe things to be, we act. And from these actions, we produce results—*in a tremendously wide variety of areas.*

**Chapter 6: An Artificial Separation: Language—Emotions—Body.** Continuing with the notion that we are each unique observers, this chapter introduces a way of looking at *the kind of observer* that we each are. It takes a closer look at the relationships that exist among:

- our *language* (our internal and external conversations, our speaking and our listening)
- our *mood or emotional state* (including long-term mood and shorter-term emotional pattern), and
- our *physical body and our movement* (how we stand, sit, walk, gesture...as well as what's going on at the level of our cells, molecules, hormones and other systems).

We all know, from our experiences, that these connections exist. What may have been missing—and what this chapter is all about—is an understanding of *how* these connections impact our lives, and a set of tools that can support us in *actually taking new action.*

**Chapter 7: We Speak Ourselves Into The World.** If new action is required for new results, what _exactly_ are the new actions we will take? What _exactly_ are the language "moves" that we will make? The four sections within this chapter introduce the *specific language acts* that we use in our internal and external conversations. Here, the focus is not on grammar or sentence structure or nouns and verbs; rather, it's on the commitments and actions accomplished with each language act:

- Section 1: Assessments and Assertions

- Section 2: Declarations

- Section 3: Requests and Offers

- Section 4: Promises, Commitments, Agreements

***Chapter 8: Happiness, Language, and the Present Moment.*** Here, the focus is on ways in which your language impacts your ability to purposefully live "in the present," and the connections to your relationships and experience (or not) of balance, fulfillment and satisfaction in your life.

***Chapter 9: Have-Do-Be or Be-Do-Have?*** This chapter explores our traditional way of understanding having, doing and being... and the impact of our language on our experience. It also introduces truly tremendous possibilities that emerge as a result of reversing our traditional way of thinking by 180 degrees.

***Chapter 10: The Bigger Picture and Looking Ahead.*** Here, we bring the book to a close by placing everything we've been talking about within a larger context. From this broader perspective, we take a look ahead to new possibilities, as we—all of us—continue growing, learning and living together.

In ***Appendix A: References*** I provide the references I have used in creating this book.

In ***Appendix B: Inspiration*** I list other books which I have found to be powerful sources of inspiration, wisdom and new ways of thinking. These books, while not directly involved in the creation of this book, are very consistent with the overall themes here and involve contributions from incredible thinkers in very diverse fields of endeavor.

In ***Appendix C: Organizations and Resources*** I provide information regarding how to contact people and organizations that I consider to be excellent sources for ongoing learning, personal coaching, leadership development and workplace improvement. These are people I know personally and feel 100% confident in recommending to you.

**Footnotes:**

1. *The Declaration of Independence of the United States of America*; July 4, 1776.

2. *Diogenes Laertius: Lives of Eminent Philosophers*, by Diogenes et. al.;Harvard University Press; 1938.

3. *The Varieties of Religious Experience*–A Study in Human Nature, by William James; 1902.

4. *Ethics for the New Millennium*, by His Holiness the Dalai Lama, Riverhead Books/Penguin Putnam, Inc., 1999.

# *Chapter 1*

## YOU CAN'T CHANGE WHAT YOU DON'T SEE

*"The true journey of discovery does not consist of searching for new landscapes, but in having 'new eyes'."* [1]

Marcel Proust

*"The range of what we think and do is limited by what we fail to notice; and because we fail to notice that we fail to notice, there's little that we can do to change, until we notice how failing to notice changes our thoughts and deeds."*

R.D. Laing

My main purpose for writing this book is to share with you an incredibly powerful way of thinking and observing, one that can be a new foundation for *designing your life* at home and at work. Said another way, a primary objective of mine is to support you in bringing about new

<u>RESULTS</u> for yourself in a variety of different areas, including what we're calling peacefulness and productivity (happiness). To that end, my emphasis throughout the book will be on supporting you in becoming a *more competent, more powerful observer of yourself.*

The drawing above is meant to signify *you* taking a look at *you*, for this is where each of us must start. My whole orientation here will be toward **helping you begin to see yourself and the actions you're taking in a new way.** This focus, in turn, is based on the following key observation: **Many of us—if not most of us—are very poor observers of ourselves!**

Has this been your experience? The great majority of us do what we do—produce positive *and* negative results for ourselves—without really noticing what we're doing. This is not a problem, of course, if we're steadily producing positive results. It becomes an issue, however, if we're not. And many of us are somehow much better about noticing things about others, particularly those close to us, than we are about noticing those same sorts of things about ourselves.

It's quite difficult to change something in order to produce a different result if we don't even see what it is that we're doing now. It's only after we observe something, notice something, that we can be *conscious* about either changing it or leaving it the same.

*So the first step, the most important step, is to notice.* This book is very much about cultivating the "big eye" muscle within each reader. Said another way, my intent is to support you in being able to notice things about yourself that you may not have seen before, to strengthen your ability to see yourself a bit differently. This increased ability to see and notice ourselves brings with it one key advantage: we then get to *choose*, we get to be more *at choice*, we get to have a broader playing field containing *more options*, as we go about doing the things we do and producing the results we produce in our lives.

And one of the absolutely most important things for us to begin to observe... *is the very way we tend to observe.* We can call this "taking a look at how we look at things," and it's represented in the drawing below.

Of all the things that we are poor at observing, this may have the biggest impact on our lives, both at home and at work. In many ways, this ability is the starting point for *any* meaningful, purposeful change.

Maybe the question shouldn't be "Why do I see things like I see them?" Maybe instead the key question should be "Is the way that I see things working for me–is it producing the Results I say I want?" The invitation here is to move through this book always with an eye toward yourself. Not in an overly harsh or judgmental manner, but with honesty, acceptance and with the overall intent being to notice. That's it–just noticing what is so. Later on, should you choose to change something, that option is always available. But for now, the first step is exercising and strengthening the big eye.

A quick note: I have shared the body of learning that's represented in this book with many people over these past years, in organizational and personal settings. And in virtually every situation, people are able to very quickly see—with remarkable clarity—how valuable these distinctions and principles are... *for **other** people in their lives!* For example, employees make it very clear to me that their bosses are really the ones who could benefit greatly from this. Leaders and managers are incredibly quick at noticing how valuable it would be if their employees could only get some of this. Husbands have no problems identifying ways in which their wives could benefit from this sort of learning. Wives see immediately the value of this for their husbands. And so on, and so on... As you move through this book, the invitation is to keep your focus on how what you're learning may apply to *you,* as well as on the new possibilities and new options for taking action which become available to *you.* This will give you the best "starting point" for moving forward.

❊   ❊   ❊

As we move forward, let's make some fundamental claims that further support the emphasis on becoming better observers of ourselves, and that underlie everything else which is to come:

**First basic claim: You cannot change another human being.** Who has tried? (Who has teenagers? A spouse or significant other? Co-workers? Friends? Relatives?) How much success have you had? In our workshops we have had nobody report ever successfully changing someone else, but we sure spend lots of energy trying. In fact, our first response when confronted with almost any kind of negative situation is often to look "out there" for solutions or blame. For many of us, this response is so familiar that it's become somewhat automatic and therefore somewhat transparent to us.

I'm not saying we have no way of influencing others. I believe we certainly can and do. I am saying that at a fundamental level, *you* can't change *me.* Only *I* can change me. But again, *I* can't change what *I* don't notice. *You* can't change what *you* don't notice. The first step is to notice, *then* we get to choose whether or not we change. We've gotten really good at observing others—we have lots of practice here—and we are often not very good at observing the one person that we can truly change! And in particular, we are *not very good observers of what we're up to, of what we're doing, in language.* And this severely limits our choices and limits our possibilities. We'll build on this point continuously, as it's one of the central themes woven throughout the book.

**Second basic claim: We are not hermits. We are always and already connected to other human beings.** This is a given. We can either be connected to others in such a way that it produces productivity and peace, or be connected in such a way that it does *not*, but we cannot punt. We are fundamentally social beings.

We do what we do being connected to others, doing what we do with and through others. My success isn't solely based on my competence in area X or area Y. My success, my results in a wide variety of areas, are also connected to how I "dance," how I interact, how I coordinate action with others. *Everything we do, we do in some community composed of other human beings.*

**Third basic claim: If you always *do* what you always did, you always *get* what you always got.** Our emphasis moving forward will be on *learning*, in areas not usually covered in school or college. Because of this, we are automatically directly involved with *taking new actions*. If you or I want to produce *new results* at home or work (including better relationships, more effectiveness, better balance, less suffering and stress, more peace), we have to take new actions. There simply is no other way. Producing a *result* I haven't historically produced requires that I take some *action* that I haven't historically taken. Somehow we know this, yet we forget that we know it. I will also point to ways in which a great number of the actions that we take are language actions, language moves, language choices that we make in the world.

**Fourth basic claim: We are always *at choice.*** That is, we always have choices available to us, and we are constantly making choices as we deal with the issues of our lives. Have you noticed that every time in your life that things were screwed up... *you were there?* We are each the common denominator in our own stories; we are the ones who keep showing up again and again! We claim that we are where we are, all of us, because of the choices that we make. And we are always choosing, every moment.

I heard an expression the other day that sticks with me here: *We aren't born winners or losers—we're born choosers.*

To me, the real value in the interpretations contained in this book is that they allow us to first observe, and then be *at choice* in situations, when previously we may not have seen any available choices at all. This doesn't mean that previously there *were* no choices available. It means that *we* didn't see them, *we* weren't aware of them, and so *we* operated as if no choices existed. In any event, I say that *more* choices, more possibilities for action, are better than *fewer* choices, fewer possibilities for action.

We can think of many situations involving our *choices* and how they serve as our "starting point" for taking action. For example, consider what it would be like to have a *new set of powerful choices* as you seek to create balance, happiness or any other "desired result" in these (and many other) situations:

- resolving conflicts with our spouse or partner—while at the same time maintaining our dignity and keeping the relationship strong
- moving out of resentment (and into something better) in any personal or professional relationship
- reducing stress and anxiety
- handling times of change and transition—personal and professional
- innovating and creating new ways of doing things at work
- dealing with "difficult" people
- handling leadership and teamwork challenges
- handling employee challenges
- handling economic challenges
- designing new products or services
- raising children
- cleaning up past misunderstandings with our spouse or partner
- moving "forward" out of difficult relationships; reaching "closure" effectively
- being productive without high levels of stress.

So this book is also very much about *choices*, about seeing choices where we may not have seen choices before, being a better observer of the choices we have, and about taking responsibility for the choices we make.

**And finally, our fifth basic claim: We live in language; we do what we do in language. We're linguistic beings. All of us, no matter what.** Julio's fish metaphor is useful here. We would agree that a fish is born into water and lives in water. Everything it does, it does in water. Water all around, everywhere. Here's a key question: When would the fish first know that it was born in water and lives in water? At what point would the fish first know this? Answer: *When it's taken out.* All that flopping around may be a key indication that the fish now notices that something has definitely changed.

In the same way, we're born into language and live in language. Language all around, everywhere. And many of us do not see this; we're blind to it. This book is an opportunity for you to be pulled (only temporarily) out of language, to take a look *at* language and what we're doing *in* language. What I'm up to is sharing some distinctions in language, some ways of looking at language that can allow us to be more conscious designers of our language and a wide variety of our Results—*because they are strongly connected.*

For example, even though you're silently reading this book (or in a workshop setting, would be listening to a speaker) we can say that you're still "in language." What is meant by this? Do you have that *little voice* inside your head? The one that right now may be saying "What's he talking about?"—well, that's the one I'm talking about! That voice, that set of internal conversations, narratives and stories is there for all of us. And many of us are not very powerful observers of this—that is, we don't see the extent to which that voice is already greatly influencing how we interact, how we feel, and how we do a great many of the things that we do in our lives. And even if we do happen to see this, we may still find ourselves not seeing any good choices to take in order to really change things.

So in review of these basic claims: we're always and already connected to others (we can say that we're always "dancing" with others, metaphorically speaking) and we can't change anybody else. But what if you can become a different observer of yourself? A more powerful observer, a more competent observer? When this happens, you begin to see choices that were literally invisible to you before. And from here, you can begin to do things literally unprecedented, truly brand new. In this way, you initiate a new dance step in your relationship. And this new step on your part, *which is often a language step* not involving your legs at all, may be just the opening that the other needs to begin changing as well.

Had you not noticed and then taken that first step, you may wait a lifetime for others to change. Your first step may very well serve as the catalyst, the invitation to move in a new way. And from here, a new dance unfolds.

This is truly a different orientation than constantly looking "out there," blaming everything and everybody when we're not getting the results we say we want. But it all begins with noticing. First, we must observe, and we must observe ourselves. As always, back to the big eye.

**Footnotes:**

1.  *Remembrance of Things Past*, by Marcel Proust; Knopf Publishers; 1982.

## SUMMARY—MAIN POINTS AND NEW INTERPRETATIONS:

- Many of us are *very poor observers of ourselves*. In many ways, we do what we do without being aware of our actions and how they contribute to our experiences and results.

- In particular, many of us are poor observers of *what we're each doing* in language, *what we're up to* in language.

- The only person you can really change is... you. But before you can do this, you must notice. Observing yourself is the necessary starting point for *any* real change. We call this the big eye, and we will continually point to it as a key for any of us desiring to bring about real changes in our lives.

- We always have choices available to us. We're choosing at every moment, and many of these choices manifest themselves as language choices, language "moves" we make in the world.

## HOW-TO: POSSIBILITIES FOR
## TAKING NEW ACTION

1. Big Eye: *Begin to pay more attention to your little voice*, the internal conversations you have that seemingly run on auto-pilot much of the time. Do this *without judging yourself* or blaming yourself or congratulating yourself; rather, just *notice* the types of conversations you tend to have with yourself. *Do you notice any patterns*, any similarities in them? If so, what are they?

2. *What are you telling yourself* right now, about this chapter and what this book seems to be about?

# *Chapter 2*

## LANGUAGE—THE TOOL WE CANNOT PUT DOWN

---

*"Your word is the power that you have to create. Through the word you express your creative power. It is through the word that you manifest everything. Regardless of what language you speak, your intent manifests through the word. The word is not just a sound or a written symbol. The word is a force; it is the power you have to create the events in your life."* [1]

Don Miguel Ruiz
*The Four Agreements*

*"You were born with the creative power of the universe at the tip of your tongue."* [2]

Neale Donald Walsch
*Conversations With God*

---

Let's talk about language—not about the English language or the Spanish language or the Italian or Maori languages, but the broader topic of *human language itself*. In this chapter I will introduce to you a way of looking at language—and looking at *your* language—that in some ways may run counter to what you have grown up thinking and believing, while in other ways may seem obvious and self-evident. I will share with you a new (and quite old) interpretation, a new way of thinking, a new paradigm about language. And in doing so, I will hopefully introduce you to a new way of thinking about and understanding yourself and your possibilities for designing your own life. The invitation here is to "try on" this way of thinking and to speculate for yourself about what may be possible, in a wide variety of areas within your life. Let's start with these basic questions:

## *What is language? What is language for?*

Ask the above questions to 100 people, and what will 99 of them say? The vast majority of us normally respond with "it's a tool for communication" or "a way of labeling and naming things so we know what we're talking about" or something to that effect. These are such widely held interpretations of what language is, that many people don't even view them as interpretations. They see them as *facts*, as the *truth* about language. Many people say that it's a *fact* that language is a tool for communication, not an *interpretation*. I beg to differ.

Certainly we communicate and describe using language. But there's much more going on here, whether we're aware of it or not. If we want to insist that language is a tool for communication, we must at least acknowledge that it's a *tool we cannot put down.* This one isn't like all the other tools—it's the one we *need* for all the other ones. Try putting this one down... we are always "in" language, and it's impossible for us to not be in language.

**This book has, as its foundation, a new interpretation of language. From this point forward, everything else in these pages rests on this new understanding, this new way of looking at language... and on the actions and choices which become possible as a result of it. To me, this new interpretation changes everything.**

We claim that language is *not* simply a passive tool for describing how things are. Instead, we say that language does much, much more. Yes, we describe with our language. Yes, we communicate with our language. But with language we also <u>create</u>, we <u>generate</u>, we <u>do things</u>, we <u>take action</u>, we <u>put in motion</u> events and situations that would not have been put in motion had we not spoken. And this, as we'll see, is the key. Let's explore.

Here's a rather everyday example. If you and I meet and I ask you to have lunch with me tomorrow at noon, and if you agree, we have literally created a tomorrow at noon that, five seconds ago, was not going to happen. Tomorrow was going to happen like it was going to happen, and *poof*, out of nothing we invented a new tomorrow out of what we spoke today. We aren't describing, we're doing. We aren't transmitting information, we're creating. We're bringing forth an event that was not going to happen had we not spoken. We spoke "lunch tomorrow at noon" into being.

Take the simple example of saying "Yes" or saying "No." Think about all the times in your life when you have said Yes. Really think about these. Now consider this: What if in each of those times you had said No? Would your life be different? Most of us quickly come to the realization that our lives would indeed be radically different, in a variety of meaningful ways. Enormously different personally and professionally. By saying Yes, we move one way, into certain possibilities, actions, and results. By saying No, we move into different situations and possibilities, actions, and results. The simple act of declaring Yes or No is not an act of *describing* anything. It is an act of *opening* certain possibilities and *closing* others, of *entering* into some situations and *moving away* from others. We are *generating* and *creating* out of what we speak. And the great majority of us already know this, although sometimes it's so close we miss it. It's so obvious, we don't see it.

One of my favorite stories (a joke, actually) that shows how language generates and creates goes like this: Two baseball umpires were sitting

13

around talking, and one says, "Old Joe, he's a great umpire. There's balls and there's strikes, and he calls 'em like they are." The second umpire then says, "Yeah, Joe's a great umpire... there's balls and there's strikes, but he calls 'em like he *sees* 'em." Just then Joe walks up and says, "You're both wrong... there's balls and there's strikes, but they ain't *nothin'* till I call 'em!"

Can you see that he literally declares them into being? The act of calling them makes them what they are. And you and I can be sitting in the left field bleachers, screaming "ball four, ball four" and guess what? If the umpire says "strike three," the batter's out. The umpire has the authority to make certain declarations (to say certain things). And when he or she makes these declarations, the world is different than it was before.

❀   ❀   ❀

Let's continue to look at ways our language creates and generates. Returning to our Declaration of Independence for a moment, we say that it isn't primarily a descriptive document. It didn't describe as much as it created. Although it did serve to describe the grievances against the King, we can certainly say that the country was not "independent" at that time. What the Declaration of Independence did was *create* and *shift* the prevailing context, and *create* a new set of possibilities. Suddenly, something (the birth of an independent country) became very likely, and something else (continued colonial life) became very unlikely. What's also important to notice is that this new context—that was *declared* into being—had the impact of changing how future events would be interpreted. Without the declaration, certain colonial and British troop movements and actions would have been interpreted one way. With the declaration in place, however, these same future actions were interpreted very differently. Generating a new interpretation is taking a new action. And different actions, of course, lead us to different results.

Let's look at an everyday example. As a parent, let's say that you declare "No more TV after 9:00. School is starting back up, and I say that no more TV will be watched after 9:00. I'm the daddy, I get to say that." This you do on a Friday night, and on the following Monday little Johnny watches TV at 9:30. Let's look at this a bit. Little Johnny's actions (watching TV at 9:30) that didn't raise an eyebrow last Thursday show up as "wrong" on Monday. And the only thing that happened in the meantime

14

is... *somebody said something*. You, the parent, have some authority and made some declaration. Little Johnny's actions didn't change, but the way his actions are *interpreted* has absolutely changed. The way his actions are *perceived* has absolutely changed. The *meaning* of his actions has absolutely changed. This is one of the key actions available to us through language—to influence how future actions get interpreted, and to do so purposefully. This has to do with creating *context*, of course. The house is still the same house physically, but the house has changed. This used to be a house in which TV could be watched at all hours, and now it's a house in which TV may only be watched till 9:00. The context has shifted. And it shifted in language.

For *groups of people* (organizations, teams, clubs, families, countries, etc.) context is also created in language. For groups, context is brought forth or shifted by mission statements, statements of purpose, goals, or declared priorities. These create a context, a background, in which certain future actions get interpreted as "appropriate, good, right" while other future actions get interpreted as "inappropriate, bad, unacceptable." This is directly connected to *leadership*, of course, and is a powerful phenomenon to notice.

Now, the extent to which leaders (and all of us) act consistently or inconsistently with these declarations has another creative or generative effect. By acting consistently with our declarations we produce an identity for ourselves of "committed" or "consistent" or "high integrity," and by *not* acting consistently with our declarations we produce a public identity of "hypocrite." If we're in a position of leadership or authority, this also usually produces a climate or environment of cynicism and mistrust. One way or the other, we're creating. *And here's the key: we're doing so whether we notice it or not.*

❋ ❋ ❋

We create out of what we speak. Let's take a commonplace example, using a question for everyone who is married. If you're married or have ever been married, consider this question: *Is it different being married, than not being married?* My answer is Yes! It's quite different being married than not being married, in many, many ways—it's different legally, it's different socially, it's different emotionally, it's different financially... we could go on and on. I'm married, and I know. And this is important—how did we go from being not-married to being married? The answer is: *some-body said something.* That's it. In one moment the people *aren't* married, then they *are* married, and it's different. And the only thing that happened in the meantime is that somebody (the person performing the ceremony, the people involved) said something. They weren't describing anything—they were creating. They were doing. And they did it with language. They did it *in* language.

Let's continue with a related example. At most weddings a point comes at which the person performing the ceremony asks the people if anyone present feels that there is some reason why this man and this woman should not be married... to speak now, and if they don't say it now, to forever hold their peace. I claim that if you were to stand and loudly say *"I object!"* in that moment, you would absolutely be creating something! You would not be describing; you'd be creating a result. Possible results you may create in such a moment include: a crisis, a great shift in your relationship with the groom, a big change in your "public identity," a shift in the wedding plans... you get the picture. The key point here is that in these moments, we do a great deal more than "communicate" or "describe how things are."

Many of us have been in situations with another person when we argued, got a little hot, said some things to each other, and then had some time to reflect and quiet down. After a bit of reflection, how many of us have ever said (out loud or to ourselves) "I wish I hadn't said that"? Most, if not all, of us have had that experience at one time or another. Here's the question—why do we say that? Why do we say "I wish I hadn't said that"? We say that because we notice that we *produced* something, we *created* something, out of what we said. We didn't just describe. We <u>*did*</u> something. We created some result, and it wasn't the result we wanted.

We create, maintain, and shape virtually *all* of our relationships out of what we speak. Think about this: Consider all the relationships you have in your life, personal and professional. Of all of these, what is the percentage that are physical or sexual? For most of us, it's a tiny fraction. The great, vast majority of them are constituted, constructed, composed of the conversations we have. We can say it this way: these relationships are *conversational in nature.*

**Do you want to change your relationship with someone? Then change your conversations with that person.** Let's say Bob and I only talk about sports and the weather. That's it—every time we get together, it's "Nice day, huh Bob? Yes, a really good day. How 'bout those Braves? Heck of a game last night." Let's say that Randy and I talk about sports and the weather, but also talk about his concerns, my concerns, his plans and aspirations, my plans and aspirations, what's important to him, what's important to me... you get the picture. Then you ask me about Bob and Randy, and I say something like, "You know, Bob's a good guy but I just feel closer to Randy. We have a stronger, or better, or deeper relationship." Well, of course we do. We talk about different things.

Our relationships with people change over time, of course. We all have had instances where at one point in our lives we were close to someone, and for whatever reason seem to have "drifted apart" (even if we happen to live next door). The nature of the relationship has to do with the nature of the conversations, whether these be face to face, email, over the telephone, via written letters, or whatever. Just as relationships change, some relationships come to an end. In our country, it's often the case that when two married people end a relationship, lawyers enter into the picture and a whole new set of conversations gets introduced!

Show me someone you have no conversations with, and I'll show you someone you have no relationship with. Inventing new conversations with someone equals inventing a new relationship with that person. *What is the action you take when you want to <u>start</u> a relationship with someone?* For most of us, we take the actions of introducing ourselves, starting a conversation. *What is the action you take when you want to <u>end</u> a relationship with someone?* For most of us, the action we take to end a relationship is to stop having conversations with the person. And this is often so close we don't see it.

❋   ❋   ❋

Consider this example in either a personal or business setting: Have you ever said, "I don't know what to do about Bubba. He's done this, he's done that, I'm at my wits' end and just don't know what to do." What that means, in this way of thinking, is: you don't know what to <u>say</u> to Bubba, or how to say it. What is there to *do?* Unless you're going to spank Bubba, the *doing* is in the *saying.* Not knowing what to do, for many of us and in many situations, equals not knowing what to say or how to say it. *Doing* is a metaphor. The actual actions are often conversational actions, actions of talking and listening.

17

If you're in business and, for example, you want to *build* a team culture of trust and ambition, do you need bricks and mortar to do that building? No, of course not. To "build" is a metaphor. What would a camera see you doing as you're doing that building? It would see you talking and listening, engaging with people in interactions and conversations. If you're in a family and you want to build a family environment of trust and mutual respect, the same thing applies. What actions would you be taking as you're doing that? You'd be talking and listening. We get so caught up in the metaphors that we sometimes lose sight of the actual actions involved. And in a great many cases, the *actual actions* are talking and listening. Our language, our conversations *are what we're using* to generate, create, build, and do.

Consider leadership, management, coaching, parenting, selling, administering. What are most of the actions that you actually *do*, in doing these things? Think very concretely. What would a camera see you doing as you're motivating, leading, directing, facilitating, coordinating, supporting, enabling, nurturing, negotiating, teaching, building... all the things that we say we do? As Rafael Echeverria first introduced to me, many of us *get paid to have effective conversations*–conversations that produce one result, and *not* another. And this is so obvious we don't see it. A great many of us get up, get dressed, go to work, talk and listen, and go home. Tomorrow we get up, get dressed, go to work, talk and listen, and go home. And so it goes, day after day. Consider this: even a carpenter, wearing a hard hat and steel toe boots, who hammers nails and puts buildings together (among other things) for a living, even this person must talk and listen to be successful. Unless he or she is a hermit carpenter, he or she had better be involved in talking with and listening to the electrician, the roofer, the customer, and others in order to coordinate the construction of that building. Anyone who's ever had difficulties related to home construction or remodeling projects knows what happens when these conversations *don't* take place! Our results are absolutely connected to our conversations.

How much time do we spend in conversations for the purpose of "cleaning up" previous conversations that didn't produce the result we wanted? And conversely, are there any conversations that we simply are not having–what we can call *"missing conversations"*–but that if we *were* having, would produce better results? Looking at both the professional and personal sides of this, it's clear that our conversations dramatically impact (not just describe) our productivity, our relationships, our emotions and a wide variety of our results.

## Three New Claims About Language

The examples and observations above can be distilled into three basic, fundamental claims we're making about language and human beings. These claims are:

1. Human beings are linguistic beings. We "live in language." All of us, all the time.

2. Language is generative and creative (vs. passive and descriptive).

3. Language is action. To speak is to act.

Briefly, let's review each of these. We'll keep building on this "language foundation" as we move forward through the remainder of the book.

**Our first new language claim—we're linguistic beings, *we live in language.*** This has to do with the analogy of the fish being born into water, living in water, and not being aware of it. We are born into language, live in language, and are often not aware of it.

Another one of my favorite examples is a story of a lion. Let's pretend I'm a lion, on the savannah, getting ready to hunt for a zebra. Behind me on my left are other young males, wishing it was their turn in the spotlight, their turn to hunt. Behind me on my right are the females, checking me out. I see the zebra I want, it's a slow one in the back, I've got him picked out. I take a running start, get ready for the final pounce, and kaboom, I hit a hidden log and down I tumble, in a cloud of dust. Getting up, I'm thinking "I *knew* I shouldn't have had that antelope last night... it was so filling, and I knew I was scheduled to hunt today... look at them all laughing at me... I'll never be king, not with this on my record... and look at her, I can forget our date for Saturday night... this is about the worst day in my life...I'm humiliated... in fact, I may have to join another pride!"

Key question: does a lion do that? As far as we know, does a lion do that? I say no, a lion doesn't do that. What does a lion do? Usually, the lion will get up and chase after another zebra or whatever. But *we* do that—human beings do that.

Here it is—any event happens, I don't care what the event is. (We're confronted with events and circumstances every day). And as human beings, we very quickly:

19

1. *Make up a story about it*
2. *Hold our story to be The Truth*
3. *And forget that we made it up.*

Is this not so? Is this not your experience? And this story, this narrative, this explanation, this interpretation lives in language. We claim that this is a very widespread phenomenon—we are all doing it.

This is not a problem, in and of itself. But because we forget that we made it up, we begin living as if our story, our interpretation, our explanation, belongs to the event. And nothing could be farther from the truth. We say no, the story doesn't belong to the event—your story belongs to you, my story belongs to me. We aren't just *reading* them, we *wrote* them. And the event belongs to itself. To summarize, we say:

<u>**EVENT**</u> **IS NOT EQUAL TO** <u>**EXPLANATION!**</u>

This is a major observation, one that is crucial for truly redesigning ourselves. And again, the key question does not have to do with whether or not my story is "right" or "wrong"; rather, the more powerful question might be **"Is my story—my interpretation, my explanation—is it <u>working</u> for me? Is it allowing me to produce the results I say I want?"** Because if it's not, I can learn—with time and practice—to begin authoring new stories, more powerful interpretations, ones that serve me more than my old ones.

❋    ❋    ❋

Have you ever been in a situation where you and someone else had the same experience (were in the same event), but each developed very different stories, different beliefs, different interpretations of what occurred? This is what we're talking about here. And we claim that the story each of us creates matters a lot, because it tends to frame the situation and orient each of us one way or another towards possible actions, which of course lead to possible results.

Here are a few examples of events and explanations:

**Event: Two colleagues are talking as I enter the room. As soon as I enter, they stop talking briefly, both look at me, then continue talking.**

**Explanation 1:** They're talking about me. I should have known I couldn't trust Bob to keep my performance evaluation in confidence. I bet he's telling Jim and now I'll be passed over for that project assignment.

**Explanation 2:** They acknowledged my coming into the room. They may want me to join them.

**Explanation 3:** Looks like a private conversation they're having. I'll ask Bob about the ABC project once they take a break.

**Event: I did not get the promotion I was hoping for.**

**Explanation 1:** The boss (Tom) is playing favorites, nothing more. I was the most qualified, and he simply likes Barbara better. I guess I need to start looking for another job, one where they appreciate me.

**Explanation 2:** I knew I wouldn't get it, I probably was just wasting my time even applying. These things never go my way. I'm not cut out to move up the ladder.

**Explanation 3:** Maybe there are aspects of my performance that are perceived as negative that I'm not aware of. I wonder if Tom would be honest with me about why he didn't promote me.

**Explanation 4:** Barbara probably sabotaged my chances by talking bad about me with that new client. I know that client guy is a golfing buddy of Tom's. She probably stirred things up with him and now he's told Tom and I can forget about ever getting promoted around here.

**Explanation 5:** As far as I know, Barbara has had nothing but superior client interactions. Maybe there are some things I could learn from her by talking with her about her approach.

**Event: My wife says she'll be home at 6:30. She actually arrives home at 7:30.**

**Explanation 1:** Something unavoidable came up that prevented her from keeping her commitment.

**Explanation 2**: I can't trust her. She probably is unhappy in our relationship and is looking for ways to spend less time at home. I need to be extra vigilant to see if she's sneaking around on me.

**Explanation 3**: Something's wrong at work. She spends so much time there, something difficult must be going on. She may need support in dealing with it.

**Explanation 4**: I knew she wouldn't be here on time. I can't remember the last time she kept that kind of commitment. I'm getting sick of her blowing me off like that.

We could go on and on. And notice—each of these explanations serves as a starting point for our future actions, which then lead to certain interactions and results. The explanation—not the event—is what's important because it—not the event—serves to orient us toward certain actions/results and away from others. And we are each the authors of our own explanations. Some of us are simply more conscious of this phenomenon than others (the big eye). And to the extent that we are conscious about it—that we are aware of it—we can at least begin to speculate about the different actions/results which may occur as a result of creating different interpretations. This new awareness may also lead us to the realization that *we really don't know what we want.* In this way of thinking, whether or not we articulate and declare our desired results is absolutely connected to whether or not we ever reach them. The articulating and declaring, which occur in language, have the effect of creating a context in which the desired results are more likely to occur. We'll talk more about context, enrolling others, and declarations later.

❊   ❊   ❊

Another key observation related to events and explanations is this: **The moment I begin thinking that my explanation of what happened _is_ what happened, I stop listening.** And this has an impact on my relationships and my ability to coordinate action in a mutually respectful and beneficial way. In that moment, I become terminally certain in such a way that I close down possibilities for myself. I keep myself from seeing the new opportunities that new explanations could reveal. And often I don't see what I'm doing to my relationships, to the people closest to me. And closing down possibilities for certain types of relationships, without seeing what I'm doing, is definitely not a result I'm trying to produce.

✻  ✻  ✻

So we live in language, we're immersed in language, all of us, all the time. The basic questions are:

- ***Do you even see yourself as making up a story in the first place?***
- ***Are you even aware that you are interpreting, creating explanations and building internal narratives for yourself—and that you've been doing so your whole life?***

*Because if you're not aware that you've always been creating your own explanation or story, the option of authoring a more powerful story (a more powerful explanation) will simply never occur to you—it'll just never come up. It'll be off your radar screen, so you'll never even see it as a possibility.*

We are creatures of habit, not just physically but linguistically as well. We pick up stories from our parents and from when and how we grow up and live, and we live out of these stories every day. We get so familiar with our own story and our own habitual ways of seeing things and interpreting... that after awhile, we may not even be aware that we are interpreting at all. We may begin to believe that we see things "as they really are." And with respect, I say that nothing could be further from the truth.

To increase this awareness in as many people as possible—back to the big eye drawing—is absolutely *one of my primary aims* in creating this book. It is one of the primary invitations here, that you become an active observer of your own stories, and of what you're up to in language. A quick way to frame this may be to ask this question of ourselves: ***Am I telling my story, or is my story telling me?***

Julio Olalla said something about this in a workshop I attended, and the way he said it struck me in a powerful way. It has to do with this same issue, the issue of who is designing, who is leading, who is really living my life. He said: ***You are not the conversations you have become.*** And I have never forgotten that.

✻  ✻  ✻

**Our second new language claim—Language is *generative* and *creative* (vs. passive and descriptive).** We've already talked about much of this, but to summarize we claim that language generates:

- Relationships
- Moods (for individuals and for groups)
- Public Identity
- Context (and especially important is context related to our own learning, or non-learning as the case may be)

As we've previously mentioned, most of our *relationships* are not physical or sexual—they're conversational. They're truly constituted out of the conversations we have and how we have them. Change them, and you change the relationships. Stop them, and you stop the relationship.

In addition to relationships, we say that language has a great deal to do with generating *moods and emotions.* For example, if lots of people within an organization or family have what we can call "bitching and back-biting" conversations, does this have anything to do with the *mood* of that organization or family? I say yes, and to such an extent that I can't separate the conversations from the mood. Maybe it's not so much that the mood is *allowing* those conversations to happen; instead, maybe those conversations are *producing* a moodspace of cynicism and resentment. What if when a person initiates this type of conversation, lots of people started responding in a new way: "I decline your invitation to participate in this conversation. I can't do anything about your situation anyway. I think Bubba's an adult, why don't you bring it directly to him?" I claim that if enough people began inventing and practicing these sorts of conversations, the mood of the organization or family would shift. A new mood would be designed. What we're doing is *reversing the causal element*—and making it much easier to purposefully deal with this thing called mood.

And individually, we make the same claim. Our personal, internal conversations are absolutely connected to our individual moods and emotions. For example, have you ever known someone who complained to you about a past event or situation, over and over, and after awhile the main advice that seemed to be wanting to leap from your lips was: *"Get over it!"* Many of us have had this experience, and it's also certainly possible that we've each been on the other end of this scenario a time or two. It's clear that our mood in such a situation is one of resentment or anger or frustration, certainly not what most of us would purposefully create for ourselves. What's not so clear is the connection between *getting over it* and language.

*To "get over" something (as well as to "move on"), we don't need strong legs!* To *get over it* and to *move on* are metaphors, of course. The actual actions required for me to *get over* something are language actions: I must *stop* having certain internal and external conversations, and *start* having others. Our conversations serve to influence, design and shift our mood, every bit as much as our mood serves to influence our conversations.

We've claimed we're always at choice. We exercise that choice by taking new actions, some of which definitely include new language actions, new conversations with ourselves and with others. Because *new actions* are involved here, the whole field of *learning* now becomes very important for us. We'll return to this shortly.

We also say that language generates and creates our *public identity.* Let's explore. Is it possible that the way *you* see you isn't the way that *others* see you? Is it possible that the way *I* see me isn't the way that *you* see me? Yes, of course it's possible... it's more than possible, it's likely. The way that others see us is what we're calling our *public identity.* The key observation to make here is that each of us also generates our public identity largely out of our language.

As social beings—non-hermits—we are already connected to others in virtually every aspect of our lives. And we therefore already have a public identity—how we "show up" for the community of listeners around us. This is how others "see us," who we "are" to them. Others may know nothing of our hidden dreams and unspoken expectations. All they know is what they observe, what they see of our actions, which include our speaking and listening, our conversational "dance" with others. (Hermits, by the way, have no public identity. By definition, that's what makes them hermits.)

This is not to say that language is the *only* way we create or shift our public identity. We can also do so through means not connected to language. For example, come to work nude one day, and you will absolutely generate a new public identity for yourself! Come to church really intoxicated a time or two, and your public identity will definitely shift. Or you could wear clothes or a hairstyle that are obviously way outside the norm for your area, as well as do certain physical activities. But a broader, more common generator of our public identity is how we *talk* and how we *listen*, how we *dance in language,* how we *make and keep commitments,* how we *coordinate action* with others.

Public identity can also be examined through the use of what's called the Jo-Hari Window [3], a pioneering tool used often in the field of psychology. While I am not coming from a background in psychology, we can use this tool in a simple way to explore further this notion of public identity and results.

|  | What I see or know about me | What I don't see or don't know about me |
|---|---|---|
| What others see or know about me | Obvious | Blindnesses<br>Public Identity |
| What others don't see or don't know about me | Secrets | Unconscious |

The combination of what I see or know about me and what others see or know about me—I'm a male, I'm wearing a brown shirt, I'm 5'11". These are in the upper left quadrant, and are what we call *Obvious.* Not much new learning here. We won't spend much time here.

In the lower left we come to what I see or know about me that others don't see or don't know about me... we call these my *Secrets.* These will also not be our focus.

What about the area in which I don't see or don't know about me, and you don't see or don't know about me? Here, nobody knows. We can call this the "*Unconscious,*" after Freud, and we'll definitely not be spending much time here.

However, the intersection of what I don't see about me but others do see about me is quite interesting. This is what we call the place of our *Blindnesses.* Here, others see what I am somehow blind to. And a great many of us are often blind to at least part of our *Public Identity*, to at least part of how we show up for others.

For example, is it possible that I consider myself an excellent manager, that I perceive myself as a good listener, one who genuinely cares about my subordinates and works hard to remove barriers to their success... and at the same time, all of my subordinates view me as moody, unapproachable, and not open to their suggestions? Is this possible? We say yes, it's very possible and happens all the time. Here, I am blind to how I show up. I am producing a public identity—composed of the collective assessments of those around me—and I'm not aware of it. Others see this, but I don't. Because I'm blind to it, I am not able to purposefully change my actions, change my results, and create a new identity. My results are clearly at stake here, in a number of ways: my career, my productivity, my chances for advancement into upper management... and all the while I remain gloriously unaware.

It's possible that even if I did know something about my public identity in this situation, that I wouldn't change my behaviors. I may be committed to something else, something that my subordinates don't know about and I'm not at liberty to share... I don't know. But in any event, remaining blind to it greatly limits my choices. Remaining blind to it means I never consider it as a possible area for me to work on.

*Who is responsible* for your public identity? *Who is responsible* for taking care of it, improving it, repairing it? In this view, you are. Would you like to know more about your public identity? Would you like to have a more accurate or adequate understanding of how you show up in the world? Can you see possibilities that may open up if you had such information? If so, please keep reading. We need to invent some conversations we haven't historically had. We need to give people permission to be truthful with us (which is different than giving other people permission to tell us The Truth about ourselves). We need to have some tools that will help us listen to such information in such a way that we maintain our dignity and enhance our capacity for self-design. We will be moving into all these areas, and more.

We've also claimed that language creates *context*. Context in this sense is not physical, but it's real. Whether it's a parent declaring that no TV will be watched after 9:00, or an organization's statement of purpose, or an individual's new private commitments to eat healthier foods, all of these have the effect of creating context. And this context is the *back-*

*ground against which we interpret* actions that have not yet occurred. Context is immensely important in many arenas. Consider the following:

- Context has everything to do with *meaning*, and meaning is central to our lives. We human beings apparently are creatures that *must* make sense of things, in an ongoing way and in virtually every aspect of our lives. And *how* we make meaning of events and circumstances is directly connected to the context in which we place the events. Of course, we aren't physically "placing" anything anywhere—all this occurs in language.

- From one context, a given event means X. From another context, the same event means Y. And from meaning X we take one *action* and produce one *result*, while from meaning Y we take another action and produce another result. Context is directly connected with results—for individuals, marriages, personal relationships, business relationships, organizations, nations, even perhaps on a human scale, worldwide.

- For individuals, private declarations about who we are and who we aren't create our *personal context*, our personal identity out of which we take action in the world. We are each the author of our own declarations, our own identity. One invitation in this book is to purposefully become a stronger observer of your own "personal context," as well as to possibly make new and more powerful declarations for yourself.

- Within *organizations*, clear and consistent context enables clarity and consistency in decision-making and results. Context has a great deal to do with whether or not an organization can bring about effective empowerment and make it work. And the ability to more actively and productively involve people at all levels, including those closest to where the action is, appears to be part of the mix required for sustainable business success today.

- For organizations and individuals, context has to do with *orienting* ourselves toward certain results (and away from others). Declarations of mission, vision, desired goals or results can be said to "set the stage" for actually achieving the goals; what we sometimes fail to notice is that the declarations come *before* the result. These declarations are profoundly generative and creative, not passive and descriptive.

- Context affects the *mass media* of our culture, especially television and its use of short "sound-bites." Often, the main complaint about this is precisely that the context is missing, thereby leading to interpretations which would not have been arrived at had a fuller context been provided.

- *Leadership and context* are closely connected. We can speak of personal leadership as well as organizational leadership here. Leaders create context through declarations of vision, of purpose, and of priority. On the organizational side, this is directly connected to what we call "corporate culture." It is from this declared context that actions are taken and future alternatives and situations are evaluated.

- Context is directly connected with *learning*, for individuals and for organizations. We are speaking here about our capacity, over the course of a lifetime, to continue learning, adapting, and changing. We claim that purposeful learning is an absolutely required capacity for those of us committed to designing our own lives. This goes beyond, obviously, the learning that occurs while we're involved in formal education of some sort or another.

- Whether or not we actually learn –as individuals and as groups–has a great deal to do with our ability to create *a context that supports learning!* And this we do in language.

The next chapter deals with learning in greater depth, particularly the *connection between learning and language.* Learning to learn may very well be one of the most important life-skills of all, for all of us. Change is everywhere, and therefore our ability to continually learn is directly connected with our happiness, well-being, peace, and success.

✻   ✻   ✻

**And our third new language claim—Language is *action*, to speak is to *act*.** If I make a request, and you say Yes, we've got a promise. If I make an offer, and you say Yes, same thing. And with this promise, tomorrow is different. Today is different. We have just put in motion events and actions that would not have been put in place had we not spoken, had we not make that agreement.

Language conveys not only information, but commitment. And commitments, promises, agreements–these are the fundamental ways that we achieve non-hermithood. These are the fundamental ways that we achieve coordination with others, that we accomplish *anything* collectively. Think about it. Promises are *everywhere*. In business we call them contracts. The way that everything works in the social domain is through this fundamental language act called a promise. Our entire system of finance is based on promises, from stocks to options to dollar bills. What does it say on the bottom of a credit card slip? Usually it's something like "I *agree* to pay...". Every event, from conferences to ball games to meetings to doctor visits to work in organizations and factories, is connected to making and keeping commitments, at a multitude of levels.

Language is far more than a way of communicating, far more than a way of describing how things are. A powerful way of looking at language, introduced by Fernando Flores and taught to me by Julio Olalla and Rafael Echeverria, is that for human beings, language has to do with *Coordination of Action.*

Broadly speaking, we can consider a great deal of the actions we take in the world—whether at work or with our families or with friends or volunteer work or whatever—as actions involved in *Coordinating Action* with each other. This seemingly obvious statement is at the heart of the power of this new interpretation, because the way we coordinate action with each other is in language. The ways in which we coordinate action with other non-hermits have a great deal to do with our emotional life, as well as with our effectiveness in a wide variety of areas. So let's take a quick look at the whole arena we're calling "coordinating action." Because unless we're hermits, we're going to be dealing with this for the rest of our lives.

Some animals, for instance, obviously coordinate action with one another. Wolves hunt together, ants work together to carry the big beetle back to the anthill, animals have sex... many other examples can be found. In each case, the animals are engaging jointly in some activity. So humans aren't the only creatures that "coordinate action" with each other. But one big area which appears to be different is _how_ we human beings coordinate action.

As far as our science can tell, ants are not gathering the night before and discussing who gets the head of the beetle and who gets the tail, or when the exploration party should meet to begin searching for other dead insects, or how many ants need to go, and so on. As far as our science can tell, ants coordinate action through their biology, through the use of phermones or other "instinctive" means. Said another way, ants don't appear to _plan_ to carry the beetle—they just carry the beetle. Human beings can plan to carry the beetle. In other words, we not only coordinate action with one another—we _can coordinate the coordination of action!_ And this is the action of language. This _is_ language.

What we call "action" is tightly connected to language and to making/managing commitments. What we call "action" is directly related to specific "language acts" which enable us to coordinate action and do things with others. We claim that there are a finite number of these specific acts (each will be covered in an upcoming chapter), and that by understanding and practicing them, dramatic new results are possible.

The key interpretation we offer is that for humans, for us, _our language is how we coordinate the coordination of action_. We can not only meet at the library for a joint project—we can schedule it, commit to it, and plan to meet at the library tomorrow at 7:00 am for this. This commitment, in turn, frees us up to enter into other commitments with other people, at work and home, as we do what we do. Our language is how we do this, vs. using phermones or hormones or sense of smell or other biological "instinctive" means. Without this capacity for purposeful coordination of action, we'd only be able to accomplish whatever we could singly accomplish. We would obviously be _much_ more limited in our possibilities and capabilities; in fact, everything would be different.

The recursive nature of our language allows us to also engage in _reflective action_. We can turn our language on itself. By this we mean that with our language, we can talk about our talking. We can think about our thinking. And the results of this reflective action often lead to new public conversations, new private conversations, new commitments, new coordination of action, new results. In fact, that's one of the very aims of this book—to offer new interpretations and distinctions in language, which lead to a new process of reflection, for the purpose of bringing forth new choices, new options, new actions and new results for you. And it all happens in language.

✳   ✳   ✳

The following authors also point to a powerful, creative, generative understanding of language in their books on leadership, social change, and organizations. What I'm attempting in this book is to make explicit what is often implicit... but we're all pointing to the same thing.

> *"The ultimate impact of the leader depends most significantly on the particular story that he or she relates or embodies, and the receptions to that story on the part of audiences... the most basic story has to do with issues of identity." ...My analysis of leadership comes to focus, therefore, on the stories conveyed by representative leaders."* [4]
>
> Howard Gardner
> *Leading Minds*

The stories Mr. Gardner speaks of live in language. The receptions to the stories have to do with interpretations, with listening, with building an internal story about the story, all of which occur in language. I've also heard it put this way: A big shift has occurred in how we think about effectiveness in leadership. This shift may be seen as one from *command and control* to *inspire and enroll.* And as a leader, what you're enrolling me in is your story.

> *"Organizations are linguistic structures built out of words and maintained by conversations. Even problems that aren't strictly communicational—failures of mechanical systems for example— can be explored in terms of things said and not said, questions asked and not asked, conversations never begun or left uncompleted, alternate explanations not discussed."* [5]
>
> Walter Truett Anderson
> *Reality Isn't What It Used To Be*

More and more, it becomes clear to me that any effective approach to "improve performance" within an organization simply must deal with the conversational nature of organizational work. Underneath every physical process are what can be called "commitment processes," which include how the people who make up the organization make commitments to each other and—in an ongoing fashion—manage those commitments.

> *"Every organized human activity—from the making of pots to the placing of man on the moon—gives rise to two fundamental and opposing requirements:*

- *the division of labor into various tasks to be performed, and*
- *the coordination of these tasks to accomplish the activity.*

*The structure of an organization can be defined simply as the sum total of the ways in which it divides its labor into distinct tasks and then achieves coordination among them."* [6]

Henry Mintzberg
*The Structure of Organizations*

Mr. Mintzberg is pointing to one of our basic claims: we are not hermits. Our results are not based only on our individual technical or functional skill sets. For the great majority of us, it's also all about how we "dance" with each other—how we *coordinate action* with each other—in language, of course. This is glaringly obvious in organizations, though it's also present for us in relationships of all sizes and shapes.

## Footnotes:

1. *The Four Agreements: A Practical Guide to Personal Freedom*; by Don Miguel Ruiz; Amber-Allen Publishing; 1997.

2. *Conversations with God: An Uncommon Dialogue; Books 1, 2, and 3*; by Neale Donald Walsch; G.P. Putnam's Sons Publishing; 1996.

3. *Of Human Interaction*; by Joseph Luft and Harry Ingham; Palo Alto, CA; National Press; 1969.

4. *Leading Minds: An Anatomy of Leadership*; by Howard Gardner; Basic Books / Harper Collins; 1995.

5. *Reality Isn't What It Used To Be*; by Walter Truett Anderson; Harper & Row Publishers; 1990.

6. *The Nature of Managerial Work*, by Henry Mintzberg; Harper Collins; 1973.

# SUMMARY—MAIN POINTS AND NEW INTERPRETATIONS:

This chapter introduced new ways of understanding language, conversations, and effective human communication. This chapter is all about a new interpretation of language, a new way of understanding language, and corresponding new possibilities that are brought forth. To summarize:

| Old Interpretation | New Interpretation |
|---|---|
| Language is a tool for communicating and for describing how things are. | Language is highly *creative and generative.* For individuals and for organizations, we do much more than describe with our language; we create relationships, moods, public identity, context, and commitment. We make things happen and "move" in the world. |
| Sometimes we're talking and sometimes we're listening; otherwise, there's not much going on that involves language. | We're always "in language." Except for rare times—in deep meditation, for example—we live in an ongoing soup of language. Our "little voice" rarely is silent. It is with us at virtually every turn, whether we're engaging with other people or not. And it has a great deal to do with our peacefulness, productivity, and results. |
| We perceive events pretty much as they are. | What we perceive has a great deal to do with the *story*, or *explanation*, we build around whatever event has occurred. This explanation lives in language, as an internal conversation, and it (not the event itself) serves as the basis for moving forward, taking action in the world. |

Language is only of interest to linguists, grammar teachers, and other "academics."

Language is crucial for our *well-being*, and all of us are already "in" language. Learning something about it can be extremely helpful for *all* of us.

Communication is the transmission of information.

Effective communication is all about successfully *coordinating action* with others; for individuals as well as organizations.

Action is primarily physical activity.

A great deal of what we *do* is actually accomplished through what we *say*. Action is always based on commitments, which are generated by a finite set of *speech acts*. These speech acts are discussed in Chapter 7, and are the specific actions we take as we do what we do, in virtually every aspect of our lives.

# HOW-TO: POSSIBILITIES FOR TAKING NEW ACTION

1. Big Eye: *What are you telling yourself* about this new way of looking at language, this new interpretation and the possibilities it claims to open?

2. Identify a *relationship or situation that you say you'd like to improve* (personal or workplace). Write it down. This is your SAMPLE SITUATION, and from this point forward it will serve as your "real life" test case for applying what you choose to apply from the book.

3. What is the *particular new Result* that you say you want in your SAMPLE SITUATION? Write this down. For example, are you looking for:

    - Better cooperation and less blaming
    - Fewer arguments that end badly
    - More productivity
    - More peace of mind for you
    - Fewer misunderstandings and screw-ups that need to be fixed later
    - A more enjoyable, mutually respectful relationship
    - Or something else?

4. Big Eye: Identify one way in which <u>*your*</u> external conversations and internal conversations have contributed to things being like they are in your SAMPLE SITUATION. Be as specific as you can be. In other words, *What have you said out loud*, and how have you said it? What result did this lead to? *What have you said to yourself,* and how have you said it? How did this influence your thoughts and future actions?

5. Identify any recurring "negative" conversations you have with yourself. That is, internal conversations that you seem to have on a regular basis, that you say are *not helpful* in moving you toward where you want to go. Let's call these NEGATIVE INTERNAL CONVERSATIONS. We'll also refer to these in future summaries.

6. What kind of public identity *would you like to have?* Write this down, especially if you think it's different than the public identity you

*currently have.* What might you need to *learn* in order to take new actions that produce this new public identity?

7. What kind of public identity *have you actually created for yourself?* In other words, how are you now "showing up" for others around you (at home, at work, socially, etc.)? Do you know? If not, *identify one possible way* for you to find out.

# Chapter 3

## What's _Learning_ Got To Do With Happiness?

## And What's _Language_ Got To Do With Learning?

---

_"In times of change, those who are prepared to learn will inherit the land, while those who think they already know will find themselves wonderfully equipped to face a world that no longer exists."_ [1]

Eric Hoffer

_"If you always do what you always did, you always get what you always got."_

Anonymous

---

Let's start here: Can we agree that we live in a time of relentless, ongoing _change_? Is this such an obvious statement that it's become a cliché? For most of us in our society today, it's very apparent that change is upon us, and it's not showing any signs of slowing down in the near future. In fact, the pace of change seems to be accelerating.

So we say that change is pervasive. Everywhere. All the time. Even as we speak of new or different Results, or happiness where now there is resentment or resignation, or more productive and peaceful ways of

39

working and being together where now we report something different...
to even speak in this way is pointing to some desired *change*. So *any* conversation about creating new results occurs within a context, a background of ongoing change. How we relate to change, how we orient ourselves toward change, and the actions we tend to take as these changes
occur have everything to do with producing new *results*. Because of this,
we need to take a look at *the phenomenon of change*.

Our grandparents also had change—a model T is different than a
horse and buggy—so we absolutely aren't the only generation that's dealt
with this. We are claiming, however, that our *orientation toward change*
has a dramatic and powerful impact on the results we produce as individuals, families and organizations.

*So given this, what can we say about learning?* How valuable is
learning, given this background of relentless change? How important is
learning—for individuals, for organizations, for all of us? Said another
way, *What are the likely consequences for people who live within an
environment of relentless change... and who do not learn?* When asked
this question, many of us would probably respond with a list that includes
these probable consequences:

- "...getting left behind"
- "...stagnating"
- "...difficult to succeed"
- "...not growing—not innovating"
- "...can't keep up"
- "...get made obsolete or irrelevant" (organizations)
- "...can't be flexible"

You can probably think of others to add to this list, for both individual
and organizational examples.

Imagine what would happen if all the employees at a given company
stopped learning. Perhaps they *chose* to stop learning, or simply became
closed to learning *without being aware of it...* but the end result is the
same—no learning. What would happen to these employees? To their
careers? To their ability to participate successfully on any workplace
teams, to achieve whatever goals they've set? What would happen to their
relationships? To their happiness?

Now, let's look at the impact at the company level. What would happen to the company's relationships with its customers? With suppliers?

With any alliance or co-op partners? What would happen to the company's capacity to innovate? What would happen to the company's identity in the marketplace/world? To its anticipated futures? To its results?

Let's take a look at all of these results, for individuals who don't learn and for organizations who don't learn. It's not really going out on a limb to claim that these results are *bad and undesired results*! These are not results most of us would want to be creating for ourselves. They do not take us where we want to go.

So, for all of us, learning becomes hugely important. Learning is directly related to power, to capacity for action, to our ability (or not) to produce results in our lives. We are talking about the *process of learning*, the *phenomenon of learning itself*, and we're not limiting ourselves to the classroom. Let's take a look—maybe a new look—at learning itself. Whether we're talking about learning algebra or learning rug repair, learning how to be a more effective leader or parent, or learning how to build more satisfying relationships, or learning how to take better care of ourselves—regardless of the subject matter involved, *let's explore learning itself*. It's a fundamental part of the context or background in which we live.

❋ ❋ ❋

Many organizations today speak of "core competencies;" that is, of a set of skills or actions or attributes that absolutely must exist in order for the organization to succeed. Many of us have come to this observation: maybe, for today and tomorrow, the "mother of all core competencies" for individuals and for organizations, is *learning how to learn!*

Learning is tied to language in some obvious and not-so-obvious ways. In addition, learning has a great deal to do with our bodies, not just with our heads, as well as with our moods and emotions. This chapter offers a *powerful way to look at the process of learning*, especially in a way that is relevant for adult learning, for learning in areas not confined to formal education.

*It's my hope that this chapter on learning serves to "set the stage" for you, as you move into the rest of the book. It's my intent that this be a solid starting point, a solid context for those who will actually bring some of the other distinctions in this book into practical, everyday use. (In other words, it's my intent that this chapter support your learning!)*

## Changing Our Model of Learning

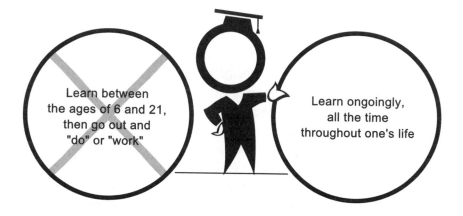

One way that we've shifted is in how we think about <u>*when*</u> learning occurs. Most of us are probably familiar with the circle on the left. This is a very traditional view, going back many years. This view says that in the early part of one's life, the learning takes place. This learning is adequate for whatever may be coming later in life. Once we're through learning, we then go out and "do" or "work" or "raise a family" or "live." At this point, we apply the learning–which we acquired earlier–in doing our jobs and living our lives.

Growing numbers of people have already embraced the right hand circle, the part of the model that offers that purposeful learning should occur ongoingly, all the time, throughout one's life. The line between our *doing* and our *learning* is now very blurry. In order to continue doing what we need to do, we must continue to learn. In fact, the expression *life-long learner* has appeared on the landscape, applying equally to us as individuals as well as to our organizations. Many of us fully understand that our desired results, in many domains, depend on our ability to continue to learn, to adapt, to re-invent, as we do what we do.

❊ ❊ ❊

**Learning is not primarily "of the head" but occurs more "in the body"**

Let's explore a bit. For example, how many of us now, or at some point in our lives, know or knew how to ride a bike? Virtually everybody. So how did we learn to ride a bike? Did anybody read the book *How To Ride A Bike*? No! We learned by doing it, by shifting our weight from one side to the other, from leaning and turning and pedaling, from training wheels and help and a friendly push. We learned to ride the bike by riding the bike.

I don't disregard that a type of learning occurs when we read something, and that in many ways the reading may be the first step. But look at us, in real life. How many of us would say we're better parents, better swimmers, better speakers, better leaders, better teachers, better carpenters, better architects, better campers, better doers of what we do than we were 10 or 20 or 30 years ago? And how did we get this way, how did we get better? We learned. And we learned by actually parenting, speaking, swimming, camping, teaching, leading, by putting our **bodies** into it, by doing. And we call this practice.

To me, one of the best, and certainly one of the most simple definitions of learning is this. ***Learning = Time + Practice.*** We get better, we learn by practicing, by doing. What happens to your marble game if you play enough marbles? You get better. It's not magic, it's cause and effect. It's practice.

Learning *about* X or Y by reading may be the first step and it may be very important. But let's be clear—without time and practice, learning does not occur. Give me enough time and enough practice, and I can do most any job. Now it may take me a lot of time and a lot of practice... similarly, with time and practice, you can do the same.

The amount of practice and time which are often involved bring one other element to light: the element we call *rigor*. Rigor may be defined here as "practicing even when you don't really feel like practicing!" In many situations, we can see very clearly that ***Learning = Time + Practice + Rigor.***

A couple of other ways of looking at this come to mind here. First, a saying attributed to Vince Lombardi, the legendary coach of the Green Bay Packers:

***Practice doesn't make perfect... perfect practice makes perfect.***

And another one which I learned from my friends at Newfield:

**Practice makes perfect... so be careful what you practice!**

These point to the notion that whatever we do over time, we get really good at. We get very competent, very effective at. Now, these may or may not be actions which produce the results we say we want, but by golly, we get really good at them anyway.

❋ ❋ ❋

## Learning About is _Not_ the Same as Learning To Do

Learning *about* and learning *to do* are both real phenomena. Both happen in the real world. But these are two very different phenomena, two very different things. Different results get produced when I learn *about* something than if I learn *to do* something. I take different *actions* *(physical actions as well as language actions)* in order to learn *about* something than I take if I'm interested in learning *to do* something. This clearly moves us toward a view of learning that has to do with action, and away from the primary metaphor for learning being that of a lonely scholar, poring over a lamp, late at night, with books piled up everywhere.

Many Eastern traditions have long embraced a model of learning that many of us are just now coming to understand. In this way of thinking, learning may be said to happen in steps or levels, as shown below:

1. Intellectual understanding. Learning "about" something.
2. Practice. Gaining experience. Doing.
3. Embodiment. Actualizing the learning. Being.

We in the industrialized West tend to equate learning with Step 1, emphasizing this in many ways, and somehow forgetting the practice, the experience, the embodiment parts. Many of our schools tend to reinforce this, as do many of our organizations. In addition, the way learning is often portrayed by the mass media tends to also reinforce this. We'll talk about barriers to learning shortly—what many of the different barriers seem to have in common is that, in the end, they keep us from practicing.

❋ ❋ ❋

**Learning Has To Do With Taking Action**

And we know this already. The way that we use the word *learning* in our everyday speech already points to this notion of action, of doing, of results. For example, what would you have to observe in the real world before this statement would ever come out of your mouth: *"Bubba learned auto mechanics."* What would you have to observe before you would ever say that? Most of us would say that we'd have to observe Bubba fixing a car, and that no matter how many books we saw Bubba read, we'd never say that he learned auto mechanics without his actually doing the work. We may say "Bubba read 12 books" but not "Bubba learned auto mechanics." Now, of course, you may go pick up your car from Bubba and find that he did <u>not</u> learn auto mechanics!

Consider other examples from our everyday lives: "John learned how to handle tough customers" or "Sue is managing that situation better" or "Bubba didn't learn that X doesn't work." In these and many other cases, we already know that *learning and action are connected*. We have some notion already that learning has to do with an assessment that a person can take some *action*, produce some *result*, at time period B that they could not take or produce at time period A. When we see that, we say that learning has occurred. When we don't see it, we say that it hasn't.

❋ ❋ ❋

*Learning = Doing the thing (whatever is to be learned), while not being able to do the thing.* That is, learning to ride a bike = riding a bike while not being able to ride a bike. Learning to be a better manager = managing while you're not yet a "better manager". Learning to be a better parent = parenting while you're not yet a "better parent".

The key, for us, is the interpretation that learning must include the body, that indeed learning occurs—in a tangible, physical way—in the body. New findings in the area of neurobiology tell us that every time we take a new action, do a new thing, that new neural passageways are being activated and new (microscopic level) structures are being formed. Our brains and bodies are apparently incredibly plastic, able to be reshaped and malleable to our environment and actions. We are *literally* becoming somebody new, out of the actions we take in the world. We are producing a new structure, out of which new actions are then more able and more likely to spring.

The Chilean biologist Humberto Maturana has led pioneering new work into the *nature of living systems*, into which human beings obviously fit. A key conclusion he's drawn is that living things are *closed systems* and that we are *structurally determined*; that is, what's possible for living things has to do with the structure we possess. How we respond to what our environment serves up for us has everything to do with us... and not so much to do with the environment. The environment is simply a trigger. A second major conclusion is that human beings' structure is not fixed and permanent, that new actions (including new conversations) on our part have an impact on our physical structure.

If we change our structure, we create the possibility for taking new action. And if we don't change our structure, we may find new action to be impossible. In this sense, we can say that learning is *literally* embodied.

✾ ✾ ✾

## One Interesting Connection Between "Learning" and "Knowing"

When you say "I don't know X" or "I don't know Y"... in what sense *do* you know something? In other words, when you say "I don't know trigonometry," what *do* you know? How can these statements about not knowing also contain key elements of knowing?

Many readers will have seen this before, although perhaps not in the particular way I'm attempting to frame it. For us, it's important enough to review. When I say "I don't know rocket science," what I'm really saying is this:

I <u>know</u> that I don't know rocket science.

That is, I am aware of something out there called rocket science, and I'm also aware that I don't know enough about it to teach it or to be a rocket engineer or whatever. I acknowledge the existence of the domain called rocket science, while at the same time acknowledge that I'm not competent to take certain actions and produce certain results in that domain.

So if it's possible to *know* that we don't know (let's call this "ignorance"), is it also possible to *not know* that we don't know? Yes, of course. Let's call this a type of "blindness." We claim that all of us operate in some degree of blindness, all the time. There are many, many things that we don't know that we don't know. For me, this entire body of learning that

I'm sharing with you was such a thing—back in 1988, I didn't know that I didn't know this.

Socrates discussed this phenomenon a long time ago, in the context of wisdom. His claim was that he was wiser than another man, even if he and the other man both didn't know X. The distinction he made was that the other man assumed that he knew X when he really didn't (he was "blind") while Socrates assumed that he did not know from the outset.

What are the consequences, then, on learning? If I don't know that I don't know algebra, how many questions will I ever ask you about algebra? Zero! Algebra just never comes up for me, does it? It's off my radar screen. I don't even acknowledge the existence of the domain itself. So far, we've said that :

- Ignorance = "I don't know" (but I know that I don't know).
- Blindness = "I don't know that I don't know".

We claim that when we say, "I don't know," we're not *describing* anything as much as we're *producing* something. What do you and I produce when we say, either to ourselves our out loud, "I don't know"? **This is key:**

**When we say "I don't know," we *produce* an opening for learning where one did not previously exist.**

Out of nothing, we declare into being a space for learning, a <u>context</u> in which something (learning) is suddenly very likely and available. This points again to the central theme of this book—the capacity of our language to generate, to create, as well as to describe.

Taking this one step further—it's also possible to <u>be aware</u> of the phenomenon called blindness, or to <u>be unaware</u> of the phenomenon of blindness:

- Being aware of blindness = *I know* that I don't know that I don't know.
- Being unaware of blindness = *I don't know* that I don't know that I don't know.

Without (hopefully!) getting too tangled up here, let's now make a few claims:

- *Ignorance* (declaring "I don't know") is a key first step in learning—regardless of the particular subject matter involved.

- Ignorance is not the *opposite* of learning, but is the threshold of learning. It is the necessary "jumping off point" from which learning can begin. If I can't get to "I don't know," I'm going to have a difficult time learning—no matter what the subject matter.

- *Being unaware of our blindnesses* is a big barrier to our learning. This shows up, often, as denying the new as impossible. We say things like "it can't be that way," and close ourselves to new possibilities. And in a time of ongoing change, this is not trivial.

- Learning is critical for all of us, given the world of change that we live in. Not from a purely academic standpoint, but because of its impact *on our ability to ongoingly adapt, modify, be flexible, improve—* which have everything to do with the results we produce in our lives. These results occur in our personal lives as well as in the domain of work.

- Learning occurs "in the body." Learning = time, practice, and rigor.

- Learning is strongly connected to language. We "speak into being" for ourselves a context that either supports our learning or makes our learning very unlikely (*regardless* of the external situation or events).

❊ ❊ ❊

One final point here: How many of us feel spoken or unspoken pressure to "know"? Our experience is that many of us have the interpretation that it's definitely not okay to not know. We don't want to show up, at work or at home, as not knowing. What happens to us, in workplace or personal settings, when we say "I don't know"? And further, what is our reaction to others when they say "I don't know"?

For organizations and families, this is critical. How we treat people who say "I don't know" has everything to do with creating a context (or atmosphere or environment) that either supports or suppresses learning. If I get my hand slapped for acknowledging I don't know something, I'm certainly not going to be eager in the future to acknowledge an area of not knowing. Earlier, we observed that lots of bad consequences seem to occur when change happens and learning does not. And if "I don't know" is the first step in learning, and given that change is upon us and learning is critical, this is important to notice.

For individuals, this is also important as we seek to produce happiness and well-being and other desired results in our lives. *When we're faced with recurrent breakdowns, with situations that seem to occur over and over again and that we aren't navigating through effectively, what's now available is to declare ignorance and <u>open ourselves up to learning</u>.* We can call this *declaring oneself to be a beginner in a certain domain of learning.* This is the starting point for <u>*any*</u> journey of change and improvement.

❋ ❋ ❋

**Friends and Enemies of Learning**

Given the importance of learning, especially in a time of ongoing change, let's discuss ways in which our learning can be supported, as well as ways in which our learning is discouraged or not supported. In other words, *what helps us learn?* And what seems to *keep us from learning,* seems to keep us from taking the necessary actions that equal learning?

<u>**Enemies of Learning**</u>
- Inability to admit "I don't know"
- When you don't know that you don't know, but you act as if you do
- Being unaware that we live in blindness (arrogance)
- "I should already know"
- "I have to be clear about everything, all the time"
- Forgetting the domain of emotions and its impact on learning
- Distrust
- Confusing "knowing" with having opinions or information
- Addiction to novelty
- Addiction to answers
- Not granting permission to be taught
- Making everything overly significant
- Making everything trivial
- Living in permanent assessments or judgments
- Living in the belief "I cannot learn, given who I am"
- Forgetting the body as a domain of learning

49

## Friends of Learning
- Willingness to declare "I don't know"
- Listening
- Openness
- Respect and admiration
- Willingness to question your questions
- A mood of perplexity and inquiry

This summary, originally developed by Julio Olalla and shared with me by friends at Education for Living and Newfield, contains what we describe as primary supporters (friends) and non-supporters (barriers or enemies) of learning. Notice that many of the *barriers to learning are not physical barriers*. That is, the barriers to our learning appear to have a great deal to do with that little voice inside (language), as opposed to something physical. Let's take a closer look at several of these, starting first with barriers to our learning.

### Inability to admit "I don't know"

Rest assured, if you are not able to say "I don't know" from time to time in learning situations, not much learning will take place. By declaring "I already know" we are producing (not describing) a context in which learning is simply highly unlikely. For example, how many of us have ever tried to teach someone else something, when the prospective learner thought they already knew it?! What's your experience as a teacher in those situations? The single most popular answer to that question is "frustrated." And how much learning took place for the other person? Not much. Big barrier to learning. Not a physical barrier, but a powerful barrier nonetheless.

We see this as being connected to a moodspace of *arrogance*, with the view that nobody around us could possibly have anything that could be valuable or useful, that it's virtually impossible that others know things that we don't. Moods and emotions have an obvious impact on our ability to learn. In fact, becoming a better observer of our own moods and of their accompanying internal conversations is a key place to start for those interested in improving their capacity to learn.

"I don't know" can be seen as a declaration of awareness that you're currently unable to perform effectively in a particular domain, based on some standard. That's it—it's not a character flaw. What's missing is your

50

ability to take certain actions and produce certain results. And so out of this declaration, you move purposefully and more openly into learning. Without this declaration, the whole context is quite different. Without this declaration, in the end, you're not going to learn very much—regardless of the subject matter.

### When you don't know that you don't know, but you act as if you do

Clearly, this is a big barrier to learning. It is precisely because we don't know that we don't know that learning is difficult here. We don't acknowledge the blind spot. We are blissfully unaware of the whole range of possibilities that knowing and learning could bring. And so because of this, we have the notion that there's nothing out there to move toward, nothing out there to go for... and we have absolutely no ambition for learning.

### Being unaware that we live in blindness

This unawareness also points to a type of arrogance. Here, we don't acknowledge the fact that each of us, each human being, by virtue of how and when we were raised and the life experiences we've had to date, brings to the table perspectives and traditions and capabilities that are uniquely our own. And of course, there's no way that we could *possibly* know about all of the others and their unique aspects. We've lived our whole lives up to this point totally unaware even of the *existence* of many of them!

In some ways the perspectives and capabilities of others differ greatly from our own, and in other ways the differences are more subtle. Our arrogance shows up when we're not able to acknowledge that it's possible and quite likely that new distinctions, new ways of seeing, new concepts and capabilities actually do exist and have existed for a long time. It's just that given our particular history and the particular observer that we have become, we're not aware of them.

### "I should already know."

This is common for many of us, especially as we move "upward" through an organization or as we gain experience or age. As we perform and are promoted into jobs or situations with more or different types of responsibilities, we often hear this inside. And if we do this enough, we call it *"should-ing on yourself"*! We can spend so much energy telling ourselves that we should already know it, when it may be more valuable to simply accept that in this moment we do not know, declare ourselves a beginner, and move into learning.

**"I have to be clear about everything, all the time."**

Or "All my questions must be answered." Do you tend to be a procrastinator in any areas? If so, this may sound familiar to you. This belief, that unless every single one of my questions is answered fully, I can't take the first steps... is a barrier to learning because it's a barrier to taking action. For example, with 10 items on my to-do list, I move very quickly into the 7 for which I already have all the answers. But the 3 items that have some uncertainty, some open-endedness about the outcome or how to go about it... these seem to get bumped to tomorrow's list, then the next day, and so on. Have you ever noticed, though, that sometimes the answers come once we begin moving, once we've started taking some action? This is a fairly common phenomenon, that of the answers "coming to us" once we begin moving. But if we never move till we're 100% certain of everything, we may *never* move. And we may never learn. And here come all the bad consequences of not learning in a time of change. And in a time of such change, not being 100% certain of some things may be the rule, rather than the exception.

**Forgetting the domain of emotions and its impact on learning**

Emotions are strongly and directly connected to learning. By not taking them into account, we leave out a key and inter-connected element of the whole picture. Emotional spaces of anger and resentment, for example, simply do not provide a context in which learning is at all likely to occur. They provide a context in which punishing and getting even are quite likely, however, given any particular trigger. Make sense? Imagine situations in which you have found yourself angry or resentful. Were you open to learning then? Was learning even available to you at all in those times? We all have had the experience of emotions influencing *what* we do and *how* we do it, in many ways.

It's possible for each of us to become much stronger observers of our own moods and emotions, and to then become much more active in influencing and designing them. The first step is to acknowledge that we each have moods, we live in them all the time, and they are continually impacting our ability to learn and to be open to new possibilities for adapting and changing. We will move into moods and emotions more a bit later.

### Distrust

Distrust is an enemy of learning, for a number of reasons. Trust and distrust can be seen as moods/emotional spaces, as well as assessments (judgments made in language) about someone or something. Let's explore briefly this issue of trust before moving on with other barriers to learning.

Without trust it's very difficult to imagine a learner finding and keeping a competent teacher or coach. Such a relationship requires trust in order to be successful. Trust is also required in many cases for the learner to begin trying new actions, even if he/she doesn't fully understand why the new actions are required. And if the new actions are not taken (no practice), then no new results get produced. The movie *Karate Kid* comes to mind here... the part about "wax on, wax off". The old master had the new student wax his car over and over; the student was frustrated and did not immediately follow the instructions. What the student didn't know was that the repetitive motion of putting wax on and taking wax off was exactly the motion needed to build "muscle memory" which would be extremely useful to him in his further development. Ultimately, trust was required in order for him to take the new action, build the new competencies. Trust was required in order for him to learn.

As moods or emotional spaces, trust and distrust are the contexts, the backgrounds out of which actions (or non-actions) spring. This background is the framework against which all possibilities are considered and decisions made.

Distrust impacts relationships at all levels, and in our view a great deal of learning occurs socially, with and through others. By limiting or damaging relationships—which is a predictable byproduct of distrust over time—we limit our ability to be with people and we limit our opportunities to learn from and with them.

Let's now look at the language side of trust. *I trust you* and *I don't trust you* are *declarations* that we make, based on three *assessments* or judgments that we come to. (We'll cover assessments and declarations in more depth in Chapter 7). These three types of judgments are:

- Our assessment of sincerity
- Our assessment of competency
- Our assessment of reliability or credibility

If we have negative assessments in any one of these, we then declare that we "don't trust" someone. When we have distrust and we look a little closer, we can usually find that *at least one of these is missing*. Either I assess that you're not sincere when you say you'll do something, or I assess you're not competent to do what you say you'll do, or I assess that you've broken so many commitments in the past that I can't risk another one this time.

I can trust Dr. Jones to fix my gall bladder, but not my brakes. Here, the issue is competency. Or I can not trust in a situation in which I think the person is sincere and competent to do what they say they'll do, but I've got evidence that in each of the last 3 times we did things together, promises weren't kept and things fell through the cracks. Here, the issue is reliability. And out of these different assessments, we can have different conversations, we can dance in a different way.

Trust always involves risk, because no matter how well I try to assess, the other person may take new action which is different and unexpected. The person I extend trust to may let me down. My assessment of sincerity may prove to be off-target. Risk is involved. The *Trust Matrix* shown below provides a summary of where we end up, given two variables:

- *How competent we are* at making grounded assessments in 3 areas: sincerity, competency, and reliability; and

- *How willing we are* to take the risks inherent in trusting.

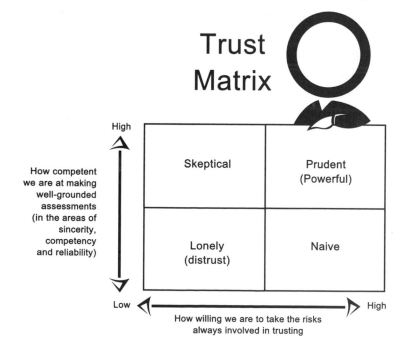

54

*But not being able to distinguish between "prudence" and "distrust" is absolutely an enemy of learning.* Prudence has to do with making grounded assessments (connecting my opinions to facts and having some conscious standards against which to judge, coupled with a willingness to risk in certain situations) while distrust is an unwillingness to risk, unwillingness to coordinate, almost "no matter what." In the end, with enough distrust comes loneliness and involuntary hermithood. In south Louisiana, we say that the lower left quadrant is the loneliest bayou there is—we call it being *"By yo' self!"*

Not trusting, even when there may be evidence that some trust is warranted, is the upper left quadrant—what we've labeled *skepticism.* Skepticism done well can be healthy and helpful; skepticism done poorly looks and feels more like cynicism and usually doesn't help our relationships or our results.

Extending trust when there are solid grounds to do so, when some evidence for trusting can be pointed to, is trusting with my eyes open and is considered to be *prudent.* This is a very powerful orientation, one that lends itself greatly to learning, building relationships and interacting, coordinating with others in a positive way.

However, extending trust without solid grounds, or extending trust when there may even be evidence to suggest that *not* trusting may be wiser is the same as being taken advantage of. On our chart, this is what we call *naïve* or *gullible.* It can also be seen as the "shadow side" of optimism. Not a great place from which to learn.

A key problem with distrust is that we often build walls of it, without even being aware that we're doing so! For instance, we generalize when someone betrays us and then from that day forward, we not only don't trust Mr. Jones, who happens to be a plumber... we now don't trust <u>any</u> plumbers! Or we simply work in organizations or grow up in families with pervasive backgrounds of distrust, and we gradually adopt that mood. Or we confuse promises broken (in which trust certainly becomes an issue) with unspoken expectations unmet (in which trust has nothing to do with anything). Or we have the notion that because I don't trust Ann to be my financial advisor, then I can't trust her in any situation. The invitation is to flex the big eye muscle, to become a stronger observer in this area, so that you can create a "window of trust" big enough to allow you to begin learning and making the changes you desire.

## Confusing "knowing" with having opinions or information

Imagine yourself on an airplane, and the stewardess comes on over the intercom: "Ladies and gentlemen, you'll be pleased to know that our captain today isn't actually a licensed pilot ... (pause) But he <u>does</u> have a lot of opinions about flying!" In this situation, we can readily see the difference between knowing how to fly and having opinions about flying. Knowing how to fly = capacity for performing certain actions, while "recreational opinions" are an entirely different thing.

## Addiction to novelty

Here we see the inability to stick with anything long enough to see it through. Big barrier to learning. It's a constant shifting and changing direction, and it shows up as college students changing majors 9 times during the first 2 years on campus. It shows up as organizations chasing every management or leadership "fad of the month" and implementing in such a way that if dramatic results aren't seen quickly (and usually without any real change on the part of management), the effort is abandoned in lieu of yet another. It appears as individuals changing careers or hobbies or projects very frequently, as well as in a number of other ways. Learning = time and practice, and in these situations not enough time and practice are allowed.

## Addiction to answers

Have you ever known someone who, no matter what the question, always has an answer? The mailman Cliff Clavin of the sitcom *Cheers* comes to mind here. On the show, Cliff appeared to be utterly incapable of saying "I don't know." For Cliff and for the rest of us in real life, this obsession with providing answers is connected to difficulty in learning.

Here's a thought. We have, in our society, whole systems for the purpose of qualifying *answers*. These systems are integrated throughout our entire educational process. The name we give to this process of qualifying answers is *grading*. What if, on the other hand, we had a system of qualifying the best *questions*? What if we had teachers and leaders who convened sessions in which questions would be listened to and those deemed "best" would be recognized and acted upon? Would this lead to a new opening for learning, to a context in which learning would be likely? I say it would. But we'll never move in that direction as long as we think learning and knowing have to do primarily with "having the answers."

### Not granting permission to be taught

Not granting permission may be directly connected to distrust. It's unlikely that you'll give me permission to teach you if you don't trust me. The teacher-learner relationship is declared into being only if the learner gives permission for the teacher to teach. It's also possible that not granting permission has more to do with arrogance, with a moodspace and belief that I already know it anyway, so what can this teacher possibly teach me? Regardless, learning is not very likely to occur at all.

### Making everything overly significant

This is holding every single part of my past and my history with a great deal of drama and heaviness and significance. It's as if nobody could have possibly had the things happen to them that have happened to me, and I relate and live these stories with great drama and assign tremendous weight and heaviness and meaning to them. The way we hold our experiences (which of course we do in language, not with our hands) has a great deal to do with whether or not we're able to produce the emotional space needed for designing something new. We would say that some lightness here is very helpful—being able to laugh at ourselves is a big friend of learning. At the same time, it's important to be able to get serious for the purpose of generating the commitment needed to move forward. But seriousness is not the same as significance.

### Making everything trivial

The opposite of significance is triviality, being unwilling to ever let the conversation get serious enough to get to the real issues. It shows up when we crack a joke just at the time when something important is about to be revealed, or when we constantly divert or deflect everything using humor.

### Living in permanent assessments or judgments

Here, the barrier to learning shows up as an inability to ever update my assessments (opinions) about myself, others, and everything else. This is usually consistent with the notion that they aren't opinions anyway—they're the Truth! Another way of describing this is not knowing the difference between "having" opinions and "being" my opinion. It's as if ten years ago I generated an opinion about X, and from that day forward am not willing to look at any new data or listen to opinions different from my own. Again, in many of these cases we don't even see our opinions as opinions at all, and therefore render ourselves powerless to change them. Big barrier to learning, especially in a time of change.

### Living in the belief "I cannot learn, given who I am"

Here's an example to illustrate this one. Imagine a doctor delivering a new baby, and the doctor exclaims "Oh, this is a geometry baby... this baby, later on, will have the ability to learn geometry and be an engineer... that's great and wonderful... the future looks great for this baby." Now imagine the doctor delivering another baby and saying "Oh, unfortunately, this is a non-geometry baby... this baby, no matter what, will never be able to learn geometry... there's a built-in organ, right behind the spleen, called the geometry inhibitor, and this baby's got it... this baby is fundamentally, inherently incapable of ever learning geometry... too bad."

I don't discount the fact that we each bring our own biological pre-dispositions into the world. But in a great mumber of cases, these are not what get in the way of our learning. On the other hand, if I have <u>belief</u> that "I can never learn geometry," it shows up in real life as a profound *pre-disposition to take no new action* in the domain of geometry! The belief sets a context in which new actions on my part will be highly unlikely. Because learning = time and practice, we can predict then that I will produce *no new results* in the domain of geometry. This, of course, then allows me to look back and say "See? I told you I could never learn geometry." Well of course not—I didn't <u>*do*</u> anything!

Which came first, the belief or the result? We say the belief came first, and this belief "lives" in language. It's a story, an interpretation, and it impacts our mood. It's a profound barrier to learning because it serves as a pre-disposition to take NO action. No action, no results. Not magic, all cause and effect.

Another example here is how many adults tend to relate to computers and technology. When confronted with a situation in which learning to do something new on a computer is required, let's imagine we hear the following: "I could never learn that. You young people do all the computer stuff, I'm too old for that." or "You can't teach an old dog new tricks." or "A leopard can't change his spots—I'm low-tech all the way, and that's the way it is." Let's notice something important here: these interpretations take us away from the *one thing that is needed* in order to learn to do anything—that of actually practicing, of actually doing something, of actually taking some new actions. In order to learn how to use computers you have to, at some point or another, "mash the button!" Conversely, because many young people just jump right in and start pushing buttons and tweaking levers (taking some action... practicing), they seem to learn rather quickly.

This phenomenon is, of course, not limited to math or computers. It has to do with virtually every aspect of our lives. We are constantly encountering situations in which we need to do things we haven't done before, in order to produce some new results. Our beliefs are incredibly powerful filters through which we see the world. They absolutely impact our orientation toward some possible actions and away from others. And (back to our big eye drawing), many of us are not very aware of this. We don't see that this is occurring.

These types of beliefs seem to stay hidden from view, and as long as they do, we can do nothing about them. Until we can see them, until we take a look at them, *they've* got us, *we* don't have them. In my role as a personal coach, much of what I do is connected to supporting people in this way. Being able to see and articulate what have historically been hidden or unseen beliefs is almost always a powerful starting point for designing something different.

### Forgetting the body as a domain of learning

We say that learning occurs in the body more than in the head. Recall one definition of learning, that *Learning = time + practice*. Not practicing is the same as not putting your body into it. No practice, no new results. We focus so much on "head learning" and memorizing that we forget that learning has to do with capacity for new action, which requires that we "do" the thing that's to be learned.

❋ ❋ ❋

*Do you notice any of these in your own life? You may find value in listing the barriers to learning which seem to show up for you, those which seem to get in your way. In moving through the rest of the book, you can then make connections back to these as you're considering how to best actually move forward with new action.*

❋ ❋ ❋

Let's take a look now at some **friends of learning**. We say that these can greatly support us in our learning, regardless of the type of learning we're involved in.

### Willingness to declare "I don't know"

This is perhaps the most obvious friend of learning—our capacity to declare "I don't know." This is an act of consciously declaring into being a context in which learning is likely. As we said earlier, this declaration of ignorance is not the opposite of learning but the threshold of learning. It's the *necessary first step* for learning to occur. As adults, many of us find this difficult. It was very difficult for me early in my consulting career. After being a consultant for a large consulting firm for awhile, I began to think that I pretty much had to know everything anybody ever asked me. Now, since I clearly *didn't* know everything, this produced quite a bit of suffering for me! I also believe most of us have a pretty good "radar" for detecting people who claim to always know everything, to always have an answer for everything. With a few more years under my belt, it's now much more obvious that we build stronger and more authentic relationships—at work and in our personal lives—out of our ability to genuinely acknowledge areas of current not-knowing. We also make it much more likely that we'll actually learn. And as a side benefit, it's also a heck of a lot more peaceful this way.

Now, when we say "I don't know and I'll find out by next Saturday," this is a different game. Now we've introduced commitment, and I need to take care of my promises or my public identity will surely suffer. *But in the <u>initial moment</u> of not knowing, when I first become aware of it, am I able to say "I don't know"? This is the key.* And many of us simply haven't declared ourselves beginners here, we haven't practiced this, we haven't yet developed the competency to declare "I don't know" in these situations.

One of my favorite expressions here is: ***Success is a learning disability***. What is meant by this? How can success be anything but great? We all know people that, by virtue of their success, are utterly closed to learning. They reach a point where they never allow themselves to say "I don't know." They assume they already know whatever it is they need to know. They are supremely confident that what they did in the past that got them where they are in the present will be all they need to take them to where they want to go in the future. Maybe. Maybe not, especially in a time of ongoing change.

### Listening

Imagine a person who has declared that they want to learn something, while at the same time showing no interest or ability to listen to anybody around them. It's very difficult to imagine such a person learning, isn't it? In a wide variety of situations, *whether* we listen and *the ways that we listen* are strongly connected to our ability to learn. We will cover listening more thoroughly in the next chapter, but we can say here that listening is far more than passively receiving objective information; rather, listening is active and generative and can serve to strongly *orient* or *pre-dispose* us toward learning... or not.

### Openness

We say we learn more when we're "open to learning" than if we're "closed to learning." These are obviously metaphors; our heads are not physically open or physically closed. (Although later we will point to the impact and importance of how we carry ourselves physically, how we move our bodies as we do what we do). Here, the open and closed refer to our internal conversations, our listening, our mental flexibility, our ability to "get off it" and be receptive to the possibility that another's perspective may provide us with the opportunity to learn something new. In this way of thinking, finding out more about something isn't automatically equated to agreeing with it. For the *actions* of exploring, of moving into more questions and speculating about possibilities, openness is needed.

### Respect and admiration

Do you learn more from someone you respect or admire than from someone you don't? Most of us say yes, we do. Is it possible, then, to increase the number of people that we "respect"? We say it is, that this attitude or mood or state of mind can be designed on purpose, for the sake of our own learning. We'll explore this more later.

### Willingness to question your questions

This is one of my favorites. Have you ever noticed that *every single question you ever ask*, no matter what the question, is *already resting on top of something that you are assuming or presupposing?* We claim this is so—that no matter what, our questions are not "objective" or "valid" in and of themselves; they are always built on top of something we have already presupposed. A powerful way of exploring this, which I first heard from Julio Olalla, is: "What is the orbit of the sun as it revolves around the earth?" What am I presupposing? Here, I am presupposing that the sun does indeed revolve around the earth, and for quite a few years, many people chased that question! The presupposition was wrong! Another question: "What's wrong with Bubba?" What am I presupposing here? That something is indeed wrong with Bubba. Sometimes the presupposition is meaningless and rather trivial, and sometimes it's not. Sometimes the presupposition is everything.

A big friend of learning is our ability to question our questions, to not take for granted the foundation on which our questions sit, but instead examine those presuppositions on purpose, explicitly and overtly. What is it about me, the observer I am, that has me produce these questions? Why do you, in the same situation as I am, produce different questions? This is interesting. Now we're in a space which is very conducive for learning. It's not physical, but it's real.

### Moods of perplexity and inquiry

We've touched on moods already... would you agree that people have moods? Most people quickly say yes, we all do. Would you say that organizations and families and relationships also have moods? Most people say yes, they all do. States, countries, time periods have moods... we can go on and on. We claim that moods have everything to do with learning, or lack thereof. A mood of optimism, for example, is a far different pre-disposition, a far different "orientation" towards learning and taking action in the world than is a mood of cynicism. We can say that all moods are not created equal, in that different moods produce very real differences in how we orient ourselves toward action (or not). This, in turn, absolutely impacts the actions we actually take (or don't take) and thus the results we achieve (or don't achieve). And the key—we often don't even notice that this is happening.

For example, your mood as you're reading this book impacts the way you interpret and orient yourself toward the material, how well you're able to step back and observe yourself and acknowledge situations in which your actions or inactions impacted certain outcomes and results, and so on. Your moodspace directly impacts the degree to which learning may occur. And my mood as I'm writing and organizing has a great deal to do with my ability to continue persevering and moving forward, as well as with the way I build chapters and how I take in feedback and use constructive criticism in my attempt to create a readable and useful book, and so on.

We say that our moods absolutely impact our ability to do virtually everything that we do, and we'll go into them a bit more later. Certainly, to even talk about happiness at all requires that we enter into this topic. For now, let's look at a few particular moods and their impact on learning.

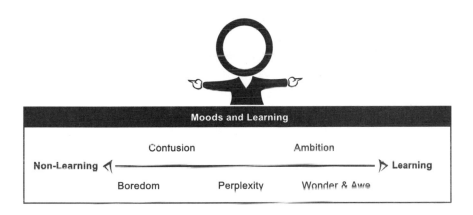

Let's take a look—what are the "background conversations" for someone in **Boredom**? These may sound familiar: "There's nothing new for me to learn here. There is no possibility that something here will be of interest or value to me. Whatever this is, I don't care." It's absolutely no coincidence that bored people do not learn very much. The internal dialogue simply is not conducive to learning at all.

**Confusion** comes with internal conversations similar to: "I don't know what's going on here, and I don't like it. I don't like that I don't understand. It's not okay with me. It shouldn't be this way." In this moodspace, a lot of the energy seems to be around how "wrong" it is that I don't understand. And in this moodspace, learning is not very likely.

*Please notice that I'm not saying "Never be bored or confused" or that it's somehow "wrong" to be bored or confused. Virtually all of us have spent some time in boredom and confusion, at one point or another. The key observation here is that people who spend a lot of time in these moods do not learn very much.* The end result of being in these moods a lot is that learning is not supported very much, learning doesn't occur very much. And without learning to take new actions, we don't produce new results. Again, this is no problem if we're steadily producing only the results that we want.

Moving now into moods that support learning, we define **Perplexity** or *being perplexed* as not knowing everything about the given subject or situation, but *being okay with not knowing*. It represents a shift "up" from Confusion. We still know we don't know, but here, we're okay with it. We're not beating ourselves up because we don't know. We simply accept that at this moment, we don't know, and this is the starting point for what's next. We're perplexed, and with this softer stance comes an opening for learning.

Can you feel the difference between this and Confusion? This orientation, this moodspace, this internal dialogue, brings with it some openness, some acceptance, and a much greater possibility that learning will occur. Many of us have experienced firsthand the shift from Confusion to Perplexity, though we may not have called it that or used the same words we're using here. Have you ever been confused or frustrated about something new that you weren't "getting," and reached a point where you just said to yourself "OK, I know I'll get it, let's just relax and see what happens. It'll be all right." You stopped beating yourself up for not knowing, or you stopped blaming someone or something or your background for not preparing you better, or you stopped holding it as so significant that you don't know, or whatever. The shift seems to be one of acceptance, of OK-ness, that it's okay that I don't know. And with this shift in mood—which is absolutely connected to a shift in internal conversation—comes a shift in possibilities for learning.

Moving further up the scale we see **Wonder**. Here, the internal dialogue may be more like "I don't know what's going on here, and isn't that neat! I don't fully understand, and what excellent opportunities this represents!" Similarly, we say that **Awe** is a moodspace that brings with it this same embrace of possibilities and not knowing, sprinkled with profound joy and big doses of gratitude for just being able to be here.

Two key questions: Given these moodspaces as a framework, where would you say most little kids, most small children, live? What are the predominant, "natural" moods of kids 2, 3, and 4 years old? Most of us would say that little kids live in Wonder and Awe most of the time. Next question: Do little kids learn a lot or a little? Most of us have experiences that lead us to say that little kids are sponges, they learn a lot. And it is absolutely no coincidence.

❊ ❊ ❊

## Levels of Learning and Competence

Let's continue exploring learning by taking a look at the levels we move through in this process. We offer that our orientation toward learning, what we say learning is and what it isn't, how we understand learning and approach learning can land us in one of two major camps: _Suffering_ (or ineffectiveness, unhappiness) or _Effectiveness_ (or success, growth, happiness). This framework, called _Scales of Excellence_, was initially shared with me by my friends at Education for Living. It is a simple yet powerful way of framing our growth and learning, and also for bringing us a measure of peace along the journey.

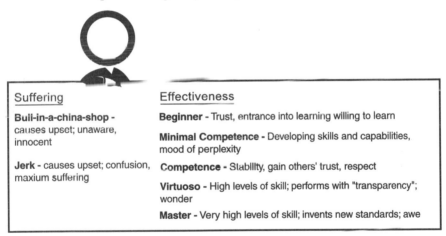

| Suffering | Effectiveness |
|---|---|
| **Bull-in-a-china-shop -** causes upset; unaware, innocent | **Beginner -** Trust, entrance into learning willing to learn |
| | **Minimal Competence -** Developing skills and capabilities, mood of perplexity |
| **Jerk -** causes upset; confusion, maxium suffering | **Competence -** Stability, gain others' trust, respect |
| | **Virtuoso -** High levels of skill; performs with "transparency"; wonder |
| | **Master -** Very high levels of skill; invents new standards; awe |

Let's first take a look at the side of _in_effectiveness, of _un_happiness, of _non_-learning, of "suffering."

## "Bull-in-a-china-shop"

A Merrill Lynch commercial of a few years back showed this huge longhorn bull, wandering around in a beautiful and well-inventoried china and crystal shop, going aisle to aisle, trotting up and down the store... and not breaking a single thing. We know that in real life, the bull would cause major upset, breaking beautiful, valuable items left and right. And the bull's not doing this on purpose, he's not being mean, he's not really aware of it–he's just being a bull.

65

Have you ever known a person who, from time to time, seems to operate like the bull? They just don't seem to see what they're doing. This can happen to any of us. For example, is it possible that we could gather a bunch of our friends and colleagues together, fly to a foreign country, and within 10 minutes be offending people all around? Is this possible? Of course. And we find that we really don't have to go as far as another country. We can do this with folks from a different state, or a different region within the same state. In middle Tennessee, where I used to live, lots of people originally from Michigan and other parts of the upper Midwest have settled, mostly within the past 15 years or so. Saturn and Nissan have major plants there, and other automotive-related businesses have followed. Well, guess what? What's viewed as a common courtesy in the south (saying "ma'am" to women in many situations) is sometimes viewed as insulting and sarcastic by those growing up with different traditions. We could find an endless number of examples here, using many different scenarios. Regardless of the specifics, this is the bull in action—causing undesired results and upset, while being innocent and unaware, sleeping gloriously at night.

Said another way, the bull doesn't know he doesn't know—he's operating in some way in blindness, and producing results from this blindness.

### "Jerk"

Let's now contrast showing up as a Bull with having the public identity of a Jerk—someone who is causing upset, but in this case he/she knows the standards and chooses to violate them anyway.

For example, let's say I'm at a new job, first day, and I'm told there's a 9:00 staff meeting this and every Monday morning. I attend, but arrive a few minutes late because of some paperwork I was finishing up. At about 9:20 my cell phone goes off and I excuse myself, trying to be polite and discreet as I back away from the table to take the call. When I get back I figure I'll get to know my colleagues, so I tap the guy next to me and introduce myself (rather quietly, because the meeting is still going on). I may even try to "lighten things up" by telling a joke or two to my neighbor on the left. As the meeting moves into a discussion of some division that seems to have nothing to do with me, I decide I may as well break into that ham and egg biscuit I brought.

Let's also say that, unbeknownst to me, this staff meeting has some definite rules, do's and don'ts. The main rules which simply must be adhered to are:

- Everyone show up on time—do <u>not</u> be late to this meeting. Actually, a minute or two before 9:00 is preferred.
- Only bring a notepad, calendar and pencil/pen into the meeting. No other materials are to be brought in.
- Coffee is ok; no food is allowed.
- No cell phones, pagers, or other electronic devices.
- Pay attention to whatever is being discussed.
- And nobody talks until the boss recognizes you.

These were the rules, widely known by everyone—but me. Here, I show up as a bull in a china shop. I'm causing upset all around me, being totally unaware, and am somehow innocent in the whole process.

Let's now say that a colleague pulls me aside and lets me know clearly about the ground rules for this meeting and how important they are... and next Monday morning I still arrive late, though not as late as the first meeting. I have a little side conversation with the guy next to me, then answer a quick cell phone call, as I'm finishing the last few bites of my breakfast biscuit. If I do this a time or two, I get to show up as a "jerk." I create for myself the public identity of "jerk." ***I begin to achieve full Jerkhood in the world!*** Here, I've been made aware of the standards and that I'm producing negative results, and I choose to continue taking the actions anyway. After a few weeks, when someone asks "Who is Chalmers?" the answer that seems to leap from everyone's lips is "Oh, he's a jerk!" And moving forward I keep wondering why good things aren't happening in my life, why I don't get the promotions I deserve, and so on.

It's important here to be clear that we're not making a claim on who the "real Chalmers" is, or what my "core being" is. We <u>*are*</u> simply pointing out that in this case, my public identity is that of a jerk. That's how I show up at work. That's who I "am" to them. And let's be clear—the world interacts with my public identity, not with who *I* think I am. The world interacts with your public identity, not with who *you* think you are. It's precisely because of this that being aware of our public identity is so valuable.

## Levels of Effectiveness

Let's say you want to move away from the "suffering" side—no learning, no new results, no success or satisfaction—and begin a journey of learning, of increasing your ability in a certain area. How do you begin? For starters, step one is a language step. It is for you to declare, either publicly or internally: *"I don't know."* This declaration is the catalyst for learning, producing an opening where none existed before. With this declaration you move over to the Effectiveness side of the chart.

## Beginner

This is the first level of ability, the first level of competency. We all know what beginners are like, in any area. They are not very proficient at doing whatever they're doing, and they require close supervision and assistance. They trust and are willing to learn from the teacher.

A beginner is fully aware that he/she is not competent in certain areas (hence you will hear beginners speak "I don't know"). It is precisely this awareness of not knowing that moves us into "beginnerhood" in the first place. Learning begins when we "declare ourselves a beginner," and we can all do this, at anytime. It makes a big difference. Here's an example.

About 5 years ago, I was enrolled to take a 6-week course from Education For Living. As I mentioned earlier, this is the company that was my first—very powerful and very positive—introduction to this body of learning. My wife and I attended our first workshop back in Louisiana in 1989, and it was a very eye-opening event for me, to say the least. It put me on a path that ultimately led to a major career change, major personal changes, as well as this book. Even so, when the course was offered my wife and I both discussed participating, knowing that we'd certainly learn a lot and benefit from it, and dreading the time commitment we knew it would entail. I then had the thought that "maybe I shouldn't really be participating as a learner/student in this workshop at all... maybe I already know this stuff... maybe I should be a staff member." After all (I was thinking to myself), I've been involved in this learning in a very steady way for a few years now and have attended lots of other courses and have been facilitating and leading workshops for large numbers of people. So I called Laurie, one of the co-owners of the company and a great friend and coach, and she offered this: *Allow yourself to be a beginner*. And it was a perfect suggestion. A weight seemed to lift from me, as I contemplated being in the room but not having to be the "expert," but just being a learner and recognizing that I was certainly a beginner at this class—I'd never taken it before and of course there were many things to learn. I did that and I learned a ton—the course was wonderful, and was of great value to me. I also recognized how my own arrogance could close possibilities for learning. The first step in changing something—changing anything—is to notice.

Interestingly, it's only by accepting–not denying–such periods of arrogance that I can begin to move out of them and create something different. By opposing or denying them, I take myself away from the very actions that are needed to design something different. This is somehow the opposite of what many of us have come to think. We claim that acceptance of something–*which occurs as a declaration made in language*–is often the first step toward changing it, and this shows up at a multitude of levels.

How many of us have been in situations when we didn't know something, but didn't feel safe enough to admit it? How much learning takes place during that time? Usually it's not much. Most of us, in those situations, have internal conversations similar to "Please, I hope no one asks me a question" or "Oh, my gosh, what am I going to do if...". Not very peaceful. Not very productive. And in organizational settings, how we treat other people who say "I don't know" is also critical. For all of us, gaining competency in making and practicing this declaration is central to our ability to learn.

## Minimally Competent

Here the person has learned to do some, but not all of the new actions, and still requires a fair amount of supervision. Progress has been made, but the degree of proficiency is not yet where others fully trust this person on his/her own, in this area.

## Competent

Here, trust is achieved. The person can perform X or Y without direct supervision and can handle many types of unexpected "breakdowns" or "problems" or "issues" successfully.

## Virtuoso

Above competency is the level we call virtuoso. Here, high competency is achieved. People at this level do what they do as if it's "transparent" to them. They appear to not be explicitly focusing on it, and they've done it so long, perhaps, or do it so well that it seems to "flow." They handle many types of significant breakdowns or problems with what appears to be fluid ease. NASCAR drivers, for example, are virtuosos at driving stock cars. Many aspects of driving appear transparent to them; they don't, for example, consciously consider every shift or brake or turn. With lots of practice, they've learned–their bodies have learned, so to speak, and now many of these actions occur without conscious consideration. This frees them up for "higher level" things, like race strategy and specific tactics, or others. Virtuosos appear in virtually every domain, of course—not just race car driving.

## Master

Above the virtuoso we find what we call the Master. People at this level are already virtuosos in a given field or domain, and they go a step further. They actually invent new standards, invent new practices, new technologies, new processes, new ways of doing things… that others in the field then begin to adopt and use. Dick Fosbury (Fosbury Flop—the first to go over the high jump bar on his back, rather than the front side), and Michael Jordan (represents professional basketball played at its peak) are considered to be masters in their given domains. There are others, in virtually every industry or field of endeavor, personal and professional.

Our observation is that we can't skip levels. We may not stay in each level for the same period of time, but we simply must move in the direction of less competency to more competency as we learn. And it's critically important to initially get on this side of the page—to get in the "effectiveness" column in the first place.

Let's take a look at some scenarios and questions, considering these levels of learning:

- Do we give ourselves permission to be beginners? In all areas of our lives? In some areas? Which ones?

- Why is it difficult for us to declare ourselves beginners? Why don't we do it more than we do? What story—what interpretation—have we made up about that? Would another story be more helpful?

- Do we give our employees (and especially our newer employees) permission to be beginners? And do we give others close to us, including family members and significant others, permission to be beginners?

- My wife and I have three children, ages 12, 10 and 7. I think I'm a pretty good parent. Do you honestly think that my approaches and skills in parenting young children will be just exactly what I'll need when, for example, they're all teenagers? No indeed not! This is what great numbers of folks in our workshops have said. What results would you predict for me if I cannot or do not declare myself a beginner in the domain of parenting teenagers? What would be the consequences of this? Everybody I spoke with told me that I could pretty much depend on heartache, problems, *un*happiness, absolutely not the Results I'm trying to create.

- Who gets to set your standards for competency within the domains of your life (for example, body/nutrition, career/work, money/finance, family/parenting, relationships, social/civic, learning/education, spirituality)? Do you set your own? If so, how? Publicly or privately? If you don't set your own, who does?

- How clear are we about how competent we *desire to be* (our standards) in these domains? Is it our goal to be a master in some or all of them? If so, how committed are we to do the learning that's necessary to achieve that level of competency? Is it our goal to be competent or minimally competent in some other domains? Are we okay being beginners in some domains? Which ones? Our experience is that a great many of us are not clear at all; we don't even acknowledge the existence of some of these domains, and so we certainly haven't consciously set a standard of desired competence or performance within them.

- How clear are we about how competent we *currently are* in these domains? Are we beginners or competent? Virtuoso? Master? Who gets to assess our competency? Have we given anyone else permission to give us feedback about how we "show up" for them?

- Do you share your standards with anyone else (significant other, or friend, for example)? Do you enroll others (via conversations) to support you in these areas?

- Are you able to declare yourself a beginner in any of these domains? Are you willing to acknowledge that there is some action you don't yet know how to take and some result you haven't yet been able to produce (since you haven't yet taken an action that will produce this result)? Are you willing to be a learner? Are you willing to give someone permission to teach you or to coach you?

For example, setting your standards in the domain of <u>Body</u> may include these reflections and decisions (declarations): What do I say my body should look like? What does "healthy" mean to me? What is my standard for nutrition? Exercise? Sleep? Posture? Weight? Pulse rate? Cholesterol? What measurements will I use here? Do I want to be a virtuoso or master in the domain of body, like an Olympic athlete or master-level martial arts student? Or will I be peaceful with being minimally competent or competent in this domain? *And this is the key—at what level will I declare "I'm satisfied" for now, and thereby find some peace, some acceptance... some happiness?*

Standard-setting in the domain of <u>Education</u> may include these: What level of formal education do I declare to be "necessary"? What learning am I engaged in ongoingly? Do I attend workshops usually? Should I? What types? Do I read certain types of books as a purposeful practice? Again, the same key: What is the level at which I will declare "I'm satisfied, I'm okay with this"?

Standard-setting in the domain of <u>Career</u> may include these sorts of issues: What does success look like for me? Am I achieving it, and how do I know? What is the contribution I am making or want to make? What is an acceptable balance between my work responsibilities, my compensation and my vacation/family time? Am I achieving this? Am I learning and advancing at acceptable rates? What does my future growth track look like? Can I influence it in a way that's acceptable to me?

Many of us have not consciously set standards in these areas. We just do what we do, sometimes seeming to be happy with where we are and sometimes not. If we do have conscious standards, it's likely that we may be, to some degree, blind to the influence of the popular media and our own particular kind of society. Madison Avenue is quite competent in "creating demand" and "shaping preferences." In fact, this is a primary function being performed by the advertising and marketing industries. A quick look at everything from beer commercials to clothing ads tells us that there are a great number of people willing to set your standards for you—and mine for me—if we so allow. But the first step here is to notice, to notice what's going on. Then we can choose something different.

Let's continue—if I don't have a set standard in these areas, and I couple this with an internal conversation of "I'm not good enough or smart enough or assertive enough or whatever enough," we can say *Welcome to Suffering*. Think about it. The good stuff never comes because we have no standard in this area, so we never acknowledge any progress or movement or declare satisfaction, and we continually suffer in our "not-enoughness." It's almost as if we say "I don't know what I'm trying to achieve here, I just know I haven't done it yet." We have no standard so we don't know what action or result will allow us to declare satisfaction or achieve some degree of peacefulness. We just "know" that we haven't reached it. Welcome to suffering, welcome to <u>un</u>happiness.

Is it possible that just because we don't perform up to our standards in one area, that we "collapse domains" and consider ourselves to be poor (or ineffective or bad or worthless) in ALL domains? Have you ever known someone who seemed to do this? Have you ever done this? Many of us have. We say that having some rigor here—keeping domains separate and distinct from each other—can allow us room to improve and create in certain areas, while declaring satisfaction (being "happy") in others.

❈ ❈ ❈

Here is another way to look at levels of learning, shared with me by one of our workshop participants. These four broad categories are very consistent with how we understand learning, competency, and results. They are also consistent with how we understand the power of language to serve as a catalyst for this learning:

- Unconscious incompetent—*we don't even know that we don't know*. We are unaware of even the existence of the possibilities represented by the new learning.

- Conscious incompetent—*we know that we don't know*. We are aware of the new possibilities, and are also aware (and declare) that we aren't competent to perform to certain standards in the new domain.

- Conscious competent—*we know that we know*. We have moved into some level of competency, others begin to trust us in this domain, and we are able to perform effectively and deal with certain types of problems on our own.

- Unconscious competent—*we don't know that we know*. We just do it. We perform at a very high level, and our bodies seem to have internalized or embodied the learning. We move in transparency, at some level of auto-pilot, and are able to handle even the most difficult situations without breaking stride.

❈ ❈ ❈

Let me now close this chapter on learning by introducing you to "distinctions." My focus here will be on how the particular distinctions each of us possess are directly connected to our ability to observe certain things and take certain actions. Then we'll proceed forward as I share with you some new distinctions.

### The Notion (and the Power) of Distinctions

This understanding of *distinctions* was shared with me by Julio Olalla, Rafael Echeverria, and Mike Papania. To me, it represents a very powerful way of understanding how what we see when we open our eyes has much more to do with what's "in here" than with what's "out there." And what we see matters, because it's from this observation that we take action, and from those actions that we produce the results we produce. Here we can also see, very clearly, another powerful connection between learning and language. Let's explore.

As a starting point, we can view distinctions as *concepts* or *ideas* or *terms,* although distinctions are not seen as mere definitions of things or labels for things. The power of distinctions can be summarized as follows:

- Distinctions in any domain allow us to **SEE** what others do not see—and what we ourselves did not see before we had the distinctions.

- Upon seeing what others do not see in that domain, we can then **DO** what others cannot do in that domain.

- Distinctions in any given domain = **capacity for effective action** in that domain.

- **No** distinctions = **no** capacity for effective action.

- **New** distinctions = **new** capacity for action.

- New action is required for **new results**.

Distinctions in any given domain (like forestry, auto mechanics or leadership) allow us to take actions and produce results in that domain that those without the distinctions cannot. With new distinctions comes the capacity for each of us to take truly unprecedented—brand new—action. Let's take a look at some examples.

## In the domain of FORESTRY:

### Distinctions
Pine, oak, maple, callicarpus, calluna, fatsia japonica, various propagation methods, humus, lichen, cinch bug, mealy worm, 2-bladed secateurs

### Actions made possible
- Effective conical pruning of 2-year old fatsia japonica

- Successful propagation of unfertilized calluna through zones 5-7

- Appropriate eradication of first spring mealy worm hatch, without damaging any callicarpus

## In the domain of PLUMBING:

### Distinctions
Ballcock, proset flange, flapper, quarter turn angle stops, fernco, no-hub bands, risers, expansion tanks, PRV valve

### Actions made possible
- Regulate water pressure to individual apartment or condo units

- Replace worn proset flange to stop leakage

- Properly adjust ballcock to allow appropriate water level

- Properly connect PVC pipe together

## In the domain of AUTO MECHANICS:

### Distinctions
Electronic transfer case, fuse relay center, torque lock, BTSI, fuel solenoid, injectors, fuse block busbar

### Actions made possible
- Effectively dampen noise from torque lock

- Successfully re-load fuse block busbar

- Stabilize electronic transfer case

- Check fuel solenoid and refurbish, if necessary

**In the domain of LANGUAGE:**

### Distinctions

Assessment, assertion, declaration, request, offer, promise, mood, listening, hearing, public identity, observer, learning, beginner, conversations for results

### Actions made possible

- Purposefully design and create a family or workplace mood or "culture" of shared understanding, shared commitment and ambition

- Create relationships that work; keep relationships "clean"

- Resolve problems in such a way that relationships, mood and future interactions are enhanced

- Take care of your public identity; proactively design how you "show up" in the world

- Reach greater clarity about what influences "poor results" that you may be achieving, as well as what actions to take to improve

- Listen to feedback about your actions without "taking it personally"; create accountability with dignity

- Purposefully and systematically build trust

- Make clear and effective requests

- Take advantage of diverse perspectives while still making decisions and moving forward

- Reduce stress and sense of "overwhelm"

- More effectively coach others

- ***Achieve a more balanced combination of peacefulness and productivity.***

Can you begin to see where this is going? By learning and acquiring new distinctions, in these and many other areas, we see what we didn't see before and can do what we couldn't do before! This points to one of the primary claims we make about language: we literally make visible what was previously unseen. An expression I learned from Julio Olalla and Rafael Echeverria sums up the way distinctions impact our capacity to take effective action: **"You cannot intervene in a world that you do not see."**

❋ ❋ ❋

Let's continue with these examples, starting with the domain of forestry. Imagine a room full of people, one of whom is a professional forester. Now imagine that this room full of people is looking out through a plate glass window onto a huge forest, right there in front of everybody. Our claim is this: what the forester sees isn't what you and I see, and the difference has nothing to do with his or her eyes. I see big trees and little trees; the forester may see a second growth maple undercanopy, with semi-mature fatsia japonica, including possible cinch bug infestation at the red oak outer periphery, coupled with a mature mid-layer of deciduous and fern-based cover.

This is very important–because the forester *sees* what I don't see, in the domain of trees, the forester can *do* what I can't do, in the domain of trees. The forester can conically prune the unhealthy 2-year old red maples... while I can chop down some trees! Here we can say that the forester has distinctions in the domain of trees. These distinctions allow the forester to take actions in the domain of trees that the rest of us can't take, and that the rest of us *may not even see as choices to begin with*. This doesn't make the forester better or smarter or anything else. It does make the forester more powerful–having more capacity for effective action, more capacity for producing desired *results*–in this domain. And that's what it's all about.

❋ ❋ ❋

For another example in another domain, let's take auto mechanics. Do you see what a professional auto mechanic sees, as you're both peering under the hood? You both have eyes, but you absolutely do not see the same thing (unless, of course, you happen to be a mechanic yourself.) A mechanic may see spark plugs, the fuse relay center, the fuel solenoid, a fuse block busbar, electronic fuel injection, rotor heads, different types of gaskets, oil pans... while I see a motor. And because the mechanic sees what I don't see, in the domain of auto mechanics, he or she can do what I can't do in this domain. A mechanic can change the spark plugs, or modify the electronic fuel injection settings, while I can pull some wires. The mechanic and I have very different capacities for effective action in this domain, because we have very different sets of distinctions we're operating out of.

Let's say you were at a restaurant and saw a sophisticated-looking woman who happened to be a wine connoisseur, swirling a glass of wine, pinky raised up just so. This person has distinctions in the domain of wine that I absolutely do not have. Such a person could order a '69 Napa Valley dry-to-medium dry Merlot, and could do so on purpose—while I could order red, white, or beer. Not only that, I don't even see the particular '69 Napa Valley wine as a choice to begin with!

We could look at farming, and how farmers see what we don't see when they walk in the fields. And because they see what we don't see, they can do what we can't do. Look at pilots and their instrument panels. Computer technicians and the insides of computers. Coaches in every sport and the movements and actions of those they coach. Western-trained doctors and pictures of ultrasounds or x-rays. Eastern-trained doctors and flows of energy. Engineers and their tools and formulas. Fishermen and their equipment and different types of fish, boats, motors, and bait. Meteorologists and clouds. Administrators and their offices, procedures and workspaces. Parents and their children. We could go on and on. And in every case, differences in what is observed have to do with differences in the *distinctions held by the observers* (vs. differences in our eyes or in our biology). *And these distinctions live in language.*

Pick a domain, and we can explore the impact of distinctions. If you were to teach me how to do your job, you would be teaching me distinctions. Virtually any area of learning has to do with the teacher offering the distinctions to the learner and the learner acquiring the distinctions.

**<u>No</u> *distinctions in a domain = no capacity for purposeful action in that domain.***

**<u>New</u> *distinctions in a domain = new capacity for purposeful action in that domain.***

❊ ❊ ❊

**If you teach me new distinctions in the domain of forestry, I promise you that my next walk in the woods is different.** The trees haven't changed, but what I observe when I look out there has absolutely changed. *My "world" has changed. My possibilities have changed.* This is the power of distinctions, and how they impact our capacity for action within given domains.

Being specific, what is it that would prevent me from being able to effectively prune, in conical fashion, the 2-year old fatsia japonica? How do we explain my inability to successfully propagate, using the Johnson method, any unfertilized calluna through zones 5-7? Why would I not be able to successfully re-load the fuse block busbar? Why can't I take the action of stabilizing the electronic transfer case? In layman's terms, we would say that I can't do the above actions because I don't have the necessary knowledge. We don't disagree—but being more specific, the knowledge I lack is made up of distinctions. The knowledge *is* the distinctions, and the distinctions *are* the knowledge.

We say the reason I can't take the above actions is precisely that I don't have the necessary distinctions. I don't have the distinction "fatsia japonica"—so when I look out at the world, I don't see any fatsia japonica to prune! I don't see the fuse block busbar, or the electronic transfer case, either. This doesn't mean those things don't exist—just that they aren't visible, aren't available, *to me.*

And we can clearly see that since those *things* don't exist for me, aren't present for me, then those *actions,* therefore, are not available to me. They're off my radar screen, not even in my "universe set" of possible actions to take in the first place. The first step toward taking these actions—obviously—is to acquire the distinctions. Then and only then can I begin to set standards of competency for myself and enter into learning.

❊ ❊ ❊

**We claim that we see with our eyes, but we observe with (and through) our distinctions.** People with different distinctions live in different worlds. You and I definitely do not see the same things as we walk down the street. We both have eyes, we may share a very similar biology, but what we *observe,* what we *notice* when we look out at the world has a great deal to do with our distinctions. And these distinctions live in language.

*Innovation* has everything to do with distinctions. In a time of ongoing change, many of us would agree that innovation is important—for individuals and for organizations. To innovate = to invent new distinctions that allow us to take action to address recurring breakdowns or situations that we couldn't address before. And once we settle in, using the new distinctions for a time, guess what? New recurring breakdowns or situations present themselves, new distinctions are invented, innovation occurs, and the process begins all over again.

So far we've been speaking about linguistic distinctions, distinctions that are created and live in language. Distinctions are also learned by our bodies, with time and practice. For example, Mike Papania shares his experience fishing, and the different feeling produced in the body by hooking a redfish vs. a speckled trout. As someone who has caught both reds and specks, I can agree—and most people who have done any fishing at all will report similar findings. In most cases, we can tell within a matter of seconds; our bodies have learned these distinctions.

Learning to drive a standard shift car also provides a good example of how our bodies learn distinctions such as "grinding the gears" and "popping the clutch" and the way to let the clutch out while simultaneously accelerating in order to have smooth (and whiplash-free) shifting. We begin to develop a feel for the right amount of pressure and the right speed and the right timing between clutch and gas pedal. Our bodies begin to learn.

Mike also shared with me an example about duck hunting, in which he and his son (an avid hunter) were in a duck blind in south Louisiana. Mike, being more of a fisherman, had less experience duck hunting than his son. At some point, his son whispered and pointed *"Look at the ducks—over there! Stay down,"* and Mike responded "Where?" His son replied as he pointed *"Right over there...see?"* whereupon Mike said "No...where?" *"Right there!"* "Where? I still don't see 'em..." Until at some point the ducks became visible to Mike as small specks traveling just over the horizon..."Aha—yes, I see them." From that point forward Mike had a much easier time seeing ducks. His body had learned the distinction "flying ducks" and with time and practice, he was much more able to pick up the birds against the dawn skyline.

The same is true in countless situations in countless areas, whether we're talking about people fishing or driving a standard shift car or living in earthquake-prone areas or playing music or dancing or performing surgery or playing baseball. Distinctions are learned and they *live* in our bodies. And with time and practice, we get very competent at recognizing the distinctions and using them in ways that become transparent to us. Remember our ways of looking at levels of competence—how with much time and much practice we move into "unconscious competence?" This is what we're talking about here. We have embodied the distinctions to such a degree that they become transparent to us. This is precisely why some people who are extremely competent in certain areas may have difficulty teaching beginners. They have embodied the distinctions so deeply, they have become so transparent to the person that they themselves can't really articulate "how" they do what they do. They just seem to do it.

❀ ❀ ❀

What I'm up to for the remainder of this book is to offer distinctions in a domain that's bigger than forestry, bigger than auto mechanics, bigger than plumbing and bigger than wine. This book is about offering distinctions in the domain of *language*. And of course, my claim is this:

**These distinctions in language—coupled with our generative and creative interpretation of language itself—are the basis for designing and creating new results in virtually all aspects of our lives.**

Like the fish in water, we say we're always "in language." It pervades our every domain, every action and interaction. And new distinctions allow us to see what we didn't see before. Then, we get to choose. Then, we get to design.

When I see people engaging in action (talking, listening, doing things together, being certain ways) I see what many people don't see. In this manner, I can do what many people can't do, in the domain of personal coaching. And I also say that the people who have been my teachers in this field are more competent than I am in the practice of coaching. They are more competent precisely because they see what I don't see, and can therefore do what I can't do. They observe the world, and interact with the world, through some distinctions I don't yet have.

Remember: **New distinctions in a domain = new capacity for action in that domain.** So as we've said, if you teach me new distinctions in the domain of _forestry_, I promise you that my next walk in the _woods_ is different. I'll see what I didn't see before, including new possibilities. And from these new possibilities, I can then do what I couldn't do before—or at the very least, I can now do these things consciously, purposefully.

And so if you teach me new distinctions in the domain of _language_, I promise you that my next walk in the _world_ is different. I'll see what I didn't see before, including ways in which my language serves to orient me and frame situations, open and close possibilities, create and sustain and change relationships of all types, generate commitment to get things done, influence my mood and emotional space, and greatly shape my public identity—who I "am" in the world. I'll also see the extent to which I am the author of all of this, and become aware of new possibilities—new choices—for learning, adapting, and designing my life. And these possibilities are directly connected to our happiness, our well-being, and to the many different kinds of results we produce in our lives.

❊ ❊ ❊

Native American novelist Leslie Marmon Silko points to a perhaps more universal recognition of this power, the creative power of language and distinctions to bring forth new worlds and new possibilities, when she says in her book _Ceremony_: _"Thought-Woman, the spider, named things and as she named them they appeared."_ [2] Well, we are going to "name things" here, and in the process new possibilities will appear! That's what the rest of this book is about.

**Footnotes:**

1. _The Academic American Encyclopedia_ - Hoffer, Eric; New York: Grolier Electronic Publishing, Inc., 1993.

2. _Ceremony_, by Leslie Marmon Silko; Penguin USA; 1988.

## SUMMARY—MAIN POINTS AND
## NEW INTERPRETATIONS

Learning is simply *required* for those of us seeking to produce new results—<u>ANY</u> new results—in our lives. *Being able to learn continually*, throughout our lives, seems to be directly connected to our well-being and to our effectiveness, in a wide variety of situations.

Learning is connected to our *language* in key ways:
- Being able to say (either to ourselves or out loud) *"I don't know"* is a primary step in creating, in generating an opening for our own learning. It creates a new context, one in which learning is far more likely than it was before.
- A great many *barriers to learning are not physical barriers.* They are barriers in the form of interpretations and beliefs (language) that paralyze us and take us away from practicing.
- Learning involves *acquiring new distinctions* in whatever domain is involved. These distinctions live in language.

Learning is connected to our *bodies* in key ways:
- Learning = time and practice.
- Learning occurs in the body.
- Learning "to do" requires that we put our bodies into it. Learning "about" does not.

Learning is connected to our *moods/emotions* in key ways:
- All moods do not support learning equally well.
- Moods of perplexity, acceptance, and ambition are far more supportive of learning than are moods of boredom, resentment, and confusion.

## HOW-TO: POSSIBILITIES FOR
## TAKING NEW ACTION

1. Big Eye: *What are you telling yourself about learning and about your ability to change?* What are you telling yourself about your ability to gain competency in certain new areas, your ability to adapt, your ability to produce new and better results for yourself?

2. Refer back to your SAMPLE SITUATION identified earlier. In that case, *what do you think you need to learn, or learn how to do,* in order to improve the relationship or situation? Write down your responses.

3. *Declare yourself a beginner in one area* identified for your SAMPLE SITUATION above. This might take the form of an internal or external conversation such as: *"I am a beginner at X. There are many things I don't know here, and I am willing to learn. I am committed to improve my ability to take effective action here and produce the results I want to produce."*

For example, you might declare yourself a beginner and a learner at:

- Creating relationships based on more mutual trust and more mutual respect
- Handling differences of opinion or disagreements without a big argument and damage to the relationship
- Having conversations in which people really understand each other
- Standing up for what you believe to be the best course of action
- Listening more openly to other perspectives
- Changing "negative" behavior that you've been doing for a long time
- Creating a more powerful public identity than you have now
- Creating a workplace or family or relationship "mood" of trust and ambition
- Requesting that others change certain aspects of their behavior— while at the same time keeping the relationship strong and healthy
- Moving past previous "negative" events or situations
- Creating a more powerful and positive self-image
- Bringing more peace to your life
- Effectively handling certain workplace issues with employees

- Building a more cohesive team
- Etc.

4. If at all possible, *enroll somebody else* in what you're up to. Agree on ways in which the other person will support you in your practicing and your learning.

5. Which of the BARRIERS TO LEARNING seem to most apply to you? *Review the list and write your responses.* (Hint: A great many of these apply to a great many of us!) Keep these and refer to them later, as you move through the following chapters.

6. *Share* what you're learning and noticing with someone close to you. Listen to their observations and perspectives.

# *Chapter 4*

## LISTENING, HEARING, BELIEFS, AND RESULTS

---

*"What we got here... is a failure... to communicate."* [1]

Boss Man
*Cool Hand Luke*

---

When we speak of language and conversations, we're obviously involved with how we communicate, do things with and relate to one another—our speaking and listening. Before moving into some distinctions connected to the speaking side, let's explore listening and hearing. Let's take a look at some distinctions related to *listening* that can help us see what we don't now see, so we can begin to do what we can't now do. Remember—try to continually flex the "big eye" muscle, taking a look at yourself and what goes on for you in these situations.

First, a few examples. Have you ever given 10 people instructions, only to have 7 do it one way and 3 do it another? What's going on here? Or have you and a colleague ever been in the same meeting, heard the boss make some announcement or handle some issue, and after the meeting have very different views on what just happened? How about a family member, remembering what mom or dad said about some situation? Have you ever been in a situation in which you'd say you've been misunderstood? Have you ever had the experience of having misunderstood someone else? What's going on? How do we explain this? Or have you ever been in a roomful of people attending a seminar or class of some sort, and after the session have conversations about the seminar and it seems as if you were at different events?

In the above situations (and countless others), was somebody listening and somebody else not listening? Was somebody getting it "right" and somebody else getting it "wrong"? Was somebody "understanding" and somebody else "misunderstanding"? Or is there another way, perhaps a more powerful way, to look at this phenomenon?

Toward that end, I offer the following key distinction:

**LISTENING and HEARING are two entirely different things!**

We know this already, but let's explore a bit more and maybe in a different way. Listening and hearing are both real, they both exist, but *they aren't the same thing*.

- Listening and hearing are two very different phenomena. The names or labels we use here are not important. We could call them tacos and burritos, but let's be clear: one of these is a *biological* phenomenon, and the other is a *linguistic* phenomenon.

- We choose to say that hearing is biological—it has to do with a bone vibrating by an eardrum, and when this happens we have the biological experience of hearing. Hearing, defined this way, involves physics and biology, with sound waves and how our bodies are. People who are hearing impaired in some way have a different biology than those who are not hearing impaired.

- We then say that listening is linguistic, it lives in language. Listening is active interpretation, active internal storytelling to myself. Listening is definitely <u>not</u> passively receiving objective information, but instead has everything to do with building a story, building a narrative, creating an interpretation about what was said or done. Listening is where *meaning* gets generated, and meaning matters.

- It's not what is said that's so important in many situations—it's what gets *listened*. It's what *interpretation gets produced*. Think about it. In the situations above, what the boss or parent or friend actually uttered isn't as significant as the interpretations that were built by the community of listeners. And the way that each of us builds interpretations has more to do with us, than with the words that were spoken by the other person.

❈ ❈ ❈

Let's continue with listening. Have you ever had the experience of forgetting people's names? How about forgetting someone's name 10 seconds after you first met them? Many of us have. What's going on? There are many ways to look at this, from "not paying attention" to "didn't really care" to "thinking about something else." I don't disagree, but would offer it in a different way. Often, we are *listening to the wrong conversation!* We're so busy listening to our own internal conversation that we don't even hear their name at all. We're lost in "What will she think about my hair?" or "I wonder how the Braves'll do tonight" or "I'm getting pretty hungry" or "That's Sheila, from down the street, she's the one who's been doing X or Y" or "I hope I don't look stupid" or whatever.

In this way of thinking, anytime 2 people are in a conversation, there are actually 3 conversations going on. One is the public conversation—the external conversation that a tape recorder could faithfully record and play back for us later, capturing our spoken words. The other two conversations are, of course, the private ones—the ones that each person is simultaneously having with him/herself. We can say that the external conversation is what we're *hearing*, while the internal conversations say more about what we're *listening*.

Another observation about listening: Notice that listening with the *intent to respond* is different than listening with the *intent to understand.* How many of us, while we're listening to someone else, are also constructing and readying our response? I'm listening to you, for example, and when you're about halfway through I'm saying to myself "As soon as you shut up I can say what I want to say... once you be quiet I'll be able to make this very good point... come on, come on, hurry it up...". And it's very possible that I totally miss what you have to say, and that what I want to say isn't even relevant by the time I speak. The first step to begin listening with the intent to understand is to notice—notice the automatic-ness with which we begin to create stories, and then quiet the voice. With practice, this can absolutely be done. Without practice, it cannot.

Another way of listening is what we call *listening to make wrong*. Here, the listener is poised, ready and waiting for the chance to pounce on the speaker and make the speaker wrong about item A or item B or whatever. The whole orientation of the listener is toward spotting and leaping on opportunities to make the speaker wrong. Obviously, this manner of listening greatly influences how the listener interprets what is said. It also has the listener totally miss a great deal of what's said, as so much of the internal conversation is busy elsewhere. As many of us have experienced, a person who listens to make wrong, over time, usually produces a negative public identity for him or herself. (Hermits, of course, have no such problem.)

Often, what may also prevent us from listening more deeply with the intent of further understanding is a belief. This belief is: To seek more information about something = to agree with it. It takes strength to listen with openness to ideas that are different from the ones we currently hold, to create a space for the other person to feel free enough to share with us. Again, practice is everything. Maybe upon further listening I still don't agree with you, but I can certainly be more well-informed in my disagreement.

❋ ❋ ❋

This is critical to observe for those of us interested in designing our own lives. To repeat—the way that each of us listens, interprets, builds our internal story, has a great deal more to do with _us_—with the observer that _we_ are—than it does with the words that were spoken or the events that have occurred. This is precisely why you and I can *hear* the same thing or *see* the same event, but absolutely *listen* something different. And what we listen matters greatly. It's this listening that tends to "frame" the situation (not physically, of course... it happens in language) and orient us toward some actions and away from others, thereby producing some results and not others.

We human beings appear to be creatures that *must* make sense of things—have you noticed this in yourself and others around you? It occurs in every situation, at home and at work and everywhere in between. We do not simply experience events and circumstances and that's the end of it. No, for us, that's just the beginning. From some event as our starting point, we then actively go about making sense of it, we then actively make meaning and add significance and construct interpretations and stories. And have you ever known someone who tended to make up un-powerful interpretations? For example, some event happens to John and the story that he builds around it has the effect of paralyzing him, of limiting his choices, of *not* moving him toward effective actions. Has this ever happened to you? My experience is that this occurs for all of us, at one time or another. This has everything to do with our own particular listening, our own particular way of interpreting. Fernando Flores has summarized the power of listening in this manner: **"The key is to stop producing interpretations that have no power."**

❊ ❊ ❊

Let's now move to the speaking side, and into models of *effective communication.* Many of us grew up on a model of communication that was originally developed in the field of engineering and is very applicable for TV, radio, and computer/digital communication. This model is represented below:

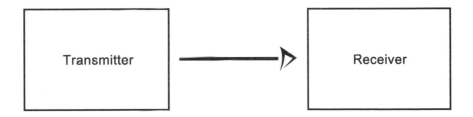

In this traditional model, the transmitter sends a signal directly to the receiver, which passively receives the signal (hopefully) exactly as it was sent. We can say that effective communication has occurred if the receiver can duplicate, replicate, the signal. For example, a radio or TV set or computer may be viewed as a receiver. Effective communication occurs when the receiver receives the signal exactly as it was sent, without any "noise" or distortion or loss of data.

We have a big problem with this model, especially as we seem to be using more and more machine metaphors to try and understand human phenomena. For one thing, this model says nothing about *meaning*! How can we possibly talk about effective human communication without bringing the issue of meaning into the equation? The TV set and radio care not about meaning; they only care about replication of the signal. We human beings, however, care a great deal about meaning. Meaning is somehow at the heart of what we're talking about here.

We have speakers and listeners, not transmitters and receivers. In this way of thinking, we don't have direct brain-to-brain data linkups with each other. The claim is that the direct line of communication shown in the engineering or data transmission model is simply not possible for us. We do not and cannot communicate via such a linkup. So if human beings are not communicating in this direct fashion, what are we doing? How are we communicating at all? We say that at the heart of all human communication is *interpretation*, as shown in the model below.

# Interpretation

Speaker                                    Listener

We are interpreting from the get-go, in every situation, all the time. No matter what, we're interpreting. So what is it that has me interpret (listen) differently than you? What is it that has a room full of people listen something different from each other, even though the speaker said one thing, one time? What is going on such that we hear the exact same thing, but listen something very different?

We say that at least three things have direct and powerful influences on how we listen, and that for each of us these are:

- Our life experiences (but more accurately, the *beliefs* we draw from these experiences)
- Our mood/emotional state
- Our body

First, our life experiences. Most of us have an intuitive understanding that our life experiences absolutely influence how we "see things" (which by now, we understand to mean how we listen, how we interpret, which occurs in language, not via our eyes). Everything from our age, race, sex, bus driver, travel, no travel, school, major, significant incidents or events we were involved in, sports, you name it. All of these impact how we tend to listen, how we tend to interpret situations. But here is a key question: Is it possible for two people to have the exact same *experience*, but draw from it two very different *beliefs*?

We say the answer is yes, and it happens all the time. And it's not so much the *experience* itself that influences how I interpret or listen later on. It's the *belief* I draw as a result of that experience. And this belief lives in language, it's a story I created which, from this point forward, tends to influence or shape how I interpret and orient myself toward some actions (and away from others).

A story comes to mind about this very thing. A TV program from several years ago showcased a woman from a town in New York who was experiencing significant depression and was withdrawing from her family, friends, and community. She enjoyed fishing, and so as a last resort they decided to organize a big fishing trip to the Florida Keys for her. They chartered a boat and off they went. Lo and behold, she hooks a very large barracuda. A barracuda is a large, fast-swimming torpedo-shaped fish that has a mouthful of extremely sharp teeth. Somehow, as she was fighting the fish, she was straining against the rod and the fish just shot out of the water like an arrow, heading straight towards her. The fish slammed into her leg, and the sharp teeth cut a very deep, very serious gash on her thigh. An emergency situation ensued, with Coast Guard helicopters airlifting her out for emergency, life-saving surgery. When she recovered and was able to talk to her family, she said that her recovery instilled a belief in her that there was still something more to live for, something left for her to do with her life. Two years later, in a follow-up, she was fully active and engaged in her life, family, church, and community. She was "back." Her level of happiness, her well-being, the quality of her journey had obviously shifted.

Now, is it possible that she could have adopted a different belief as a result of that accident and her hospital stay? I say yes, it's very possible. Other possible beliefs may include: "One more bad thing to happen to me, I guess I'm snakebit" or "I told you we shouldn't have taken this trip, nothing good would happen." Now, this is not to minimize the seriousness of clinical depression or to say that depression can be overcome by a fishing accident. But it is important to notice that it wasn't so much this lady's *experience* that influenced how she interpreted things later on; rather, it was the *belief* she created (in language) as a result of her experience. We are each the authors of our own beliefs, and they absolutely influence how we listen, how we interpret words and actions that haven't happened yet. *(And this is somehow not taught to us at an early age!)* From our interpretations, we act. And from our actions, we produce results.

And let's be clear—we aren't just talking about religion or church or spirituality. We have beliefs about everything. Men, women, money, tall people, short people, skinny people, fat people, long-haired people, short-haired people, African Americans, Caucasians, Asians, Native Americans, unions, management, Fords, Chevys, imported cars, Canadians, neighborhoods, oak trees... we even have beliefs about beliefs. And we're not saying that it's somehow wrong to have beliefs, or that certain beliefs are always wrong while others are always right. We *are* saying that the huge numbers of beliefs we have, in the myriad areas in which we have them, absolutely impact our listening, absolutely influence how we interpret situations.

We *are* saying that our beliefs open and close possibilities, and that we often don't see this. We tend to look *through* our beliefs, and often do not look *at* our beliefs! Beliefs may be viewed as part of the lenses of a pair of glasses through which we see the world. We say that sometimes, it's worthwhile to take the glasses off and look at the lenses themselves.

The more powerful question may be "Are your beliefs serving you, moving you toward the results you say you want?" as opposed to "Are your beliefs the right beliefs or the wrong beliefs?" For example, if I have a belief that I can never learn algebra or that I will never learn how to manage the department well, these beliefs strongly influence how I interpret situations involving algebra or issues in the department. And these interpretations, in turn, strongly influence the actions I take or don't take, which create the results I produce or don't produce. Specifically, beliefs that include "I can never..." almost always lead us to *in*-action, to *no* action, in the particular areas involved. No action, of course, means I never learn.

Consider this example: A gentleman named Stan was in a personal coaching session with Pat. In the course of conversation, Stan declared that what he really wanted was a committed relationship with a woman. That was his desired result. He had been divorced awhile, was in his late 40's, was tired of the single/dating scene, and was now ready for a committed, monogamous relationship with a woman. Pat understood and said *"That's great, let's take a look...what are some of your beliefs about women?"* The very first thing out of Stan's mouth was "Well, you can't trust 'em"... upon which Pat stated *"I think this may be a good place for us to start!"*

Can you see that Stan's belief that "you can't trust women" will not lead to the result he says he wants, that of a committed, partnering relationship with a woman? Regardless of whatever experiences he's had in the *past*, this belief is what's in the *present* and is what will influence how he interprets and listens in the *future*. He may start a new a relationship with a woman, she will be 2 minutes late from some errand, he'll notice it and say "See, I told you I can't trust you" and the relationship dance will start down a road that probably won't lead to the result he says he wants.

Once we adopt a belief, we can find it difficult to alter it, update it, or let it go. Many of us have had this experience—I know I have. And many of us don't see that this is happening, because we don't see them as beliefs in the first place—we see them as "the way things are." I've heard this story about a man who has very strongly-held beliefs about "women drivers." Anybody who knows him is aware that he thinks that as a group, women should not be allowed on the road because of their inattention to what they're doing, lack of knowledge about rules of the road and highway etiquette, and other problems with safety, proper speed, and general competence. He's driving down the road one day and gets behind a vehicle moving very slowly and hesitatingly thru a downtown area. Immediately he's fuming and thinking "those x&*%#!! women drivers, can't they ever get it right... wouldja look at that, no bleeping idea what she's doing..." The car finally pulls over and the man passes by, looking over to see who was driving. To his great surprise, he sees a man, not a woman, behind the wheel.

Let's imagine now that each of us is this person. Do many of us, upon this realization, think to ourselves *"Hey, here's some evidence to the contrary of my beliefs. Here's a great opportunity for me to be lots more open and possibly update my beliefs about women, etc"?* No! Instead we say *"Hey, that guy drives like a woman!"*

For relationships, important conversations that are often missing are those about beliefs. What are our beliefs about discipline? About money? About sex? About having children? About child-raising? About what constitutes a healthy relationship? About the role of men and women? About spirituality and religion? Having these conversations is different than not having them. You will produce different results and different relationships by having these conversations than you will by not having them. We create out of what we speak.

Where do many of our beliefs come from? Where did we get them? (And do we ever update them?) For many of us, our beliefs were given to us by our parents or whoever was involved in our childhood. That was certainly the case for me. I have beliefs about Chrysler products that were definitely influenced by my father and our experience with cars growing up. Same with the type of gas to buy. Certainly our cultural, religious, or spiritual beliefs have a great deal to do with when and where and how we were raised. Now, we may certainly adopt new beliefs as we grow and learn and change, but the ones we change *from* usually have their roots in our childhood and the society in which we were raised.

I adopted many beliefs from my parents, from my father perhaps more than from my mother. And I suppose that my father adopted many beliefs from his parents, possibly his father. But at some point in his life, my dad said "these are *my* beliefs." A few years ago I remember thinking "when do *I* get to do that?" That is, when do *I* get to declare which beliefs are *mine*, regardless of those of my father or anyone else? My experience is that different people do this at different times during their lives. I know young people who have definitely adopted their own beliefs by age 25, and I know older people who still have not done so. I know people who, once they come up with beliefs, seem to be able to update them when confronted with new information, while others do not. Interesting. It's an important question—are your beliefs working for you? Are they allowing you to achieve the results you say you want? And do you see them as *your* beliefs in the first place?

In Peter Senge's *The Fifth Discipline Fieldbook* [2] Rick Ross outlines what is called The Ladder of Inference. In many ways, what he is offering serves to reinforce what we've been discussing here—and it all happens in language:

*"We live in a world of self-generating beliefs which remain largely untested. We adopt those beliefs because they are based on conclusions, which are inferred from what we observe, plus our past experience. Our ability to achieve the results we truly desire is eroded by our feelings that:*

- *Our beliefs are <u>the</u> truth.*
- *The truth is obvious.*
- *Our beliefs are based on real data.*
- *The data we select are the real data.."*

He goes on to say that very quickly, we climb up what Chris Argyris calls a "ladder of inference" (remember going from Event to Explanation?). According to the author, this is a very common mental pathway of *"increasing abstraction, often leading to misguided beliefs."* This ladder is summarized below, in order of when the steps occur:

1. *Observable data and experiences occur; some "event" occurs*
2. *I select "data" from what I observe; some details and actions; (I miss other details and actions)*
3. *I add meanings (cultural and personal)*
4. *I make assumptions based on the meanings I added*
5. *I draw conclusions*
6. *I adopt beliefs about the world*
7. *I take actions based on my beliefs.*

And, of course, we produce *results*—including the nature and quality of relationships, our own well-being, efficiency, effectiveness, happiness—based on the actions we take.

❋ ❋ ❋

The following authors also point to the power of beliefs, and the connection that our beliefs have with our bodies, our moods and emotions, and *ultimately on the results we produce in our lives:*

*"The power of belief shapes your actions, your experiences, and your results. Believing involves the whole body. Your beliefs are not found only in your thoughts, they are found everywhere, even in the subtle shapes of your posture and in the dynamics of your movements. Your habitual ways of reacting to people, events, and feelings tell the story of your beliefs. If you are to make the changes you desire, you must harness the power of belief.*

*As you believe, so you behave. As you behave, so you become. As you become, so becomes the world." [3]*

Stuart Heller, PhD
*Retooling On The Run*

*"All that we are is the result of what we have thought."*

The Buddha

*"You are the product of your own thought. What you believe yourself to be, you are". [4]*

Claude M. Bristol
*The Magic of Believing*

*"If thou canst believe, all things are possible to him that believeth."*

The Bible—Mark 9:23

*"Believe that you have it, and you have it."*

Old Latin Proverb

Notice how instead of automatically asking the question "Are my beliefs *working* for me or not?" that many of us are quickly thrown to a different question, usually something to the order of "Is my belief *right* or is it *wrong*"?

All of us grow up in what are called *background conversations*. These are societal conversations, or beliefs, that you and I did not invent personally. They were here when we got here, and we just picked them up. And in our work, we have observed one particularly powerful background conversation, especially for Americans. This background conversation, this belief, is:

### *I'm Right*

Notice this about yourself? About others? My kids, at very young ages, were talking about the right way to do Lego and the right way to play the made-up game and the right way to ride the wagon. Incredible. And I know I didn't explicitly teach them that. They just picked it up from being alive in early 21st century USA.

My partner Mark tells a personal story to help illustrate this. He and I both used to work for the same international consulting firm. The firm had a strong commitment to ongoing learning and education/training, with a full campus training facility outside of Chicago. Thousands of people from across the world spent many hours training at this facility, and courses ranged across the board. He and a friend were at the social center (the bar) and ended up in conversation with a young lady from South Africa. It was about the same time as Apartheid was ending and lots of changes were occurring there, and the conversation had to do with whether or not we were receiving true news reports and what it was really like to be there, and so on. She then told them she had been in America a few weeks, visiting several states and sightseeing around our country. Seeing that she'd been in the U.S. long enough to see a few things, having visited different areas and spent time with different folks, Mark asked her what she thought about America and Americans. Her immediate response was "You Americans are so arrogant!" Mark and his friend were surprised and taken aback. "What do you mean?" they responded. "You think you live in the best country in the whole world," she stated. Mark and his friend looked at each other, looked back at her, and in unison replied *"We do!"* What this exchange illustrates, I think, is how the I'm Right conversation is often very present for Americans, and we don't see it. It's not so visible to us, but it becomes very visible to someone who does not come from this culture, this background conversation.

We tend to listen so as to make our beliefs right, and this definitely includes our beliefs about ourselves. We love being right, and it shows up everywhere. What prevented the male driver from seeing data that was different than his beliefs about female drivers was his commitment to being right. What prevented the gentleman from creating the healthy relationship with a woman that he said he wanted was his commitment to being right. What often prevents many of us from exploring new possibilities or being open to new avenues or taking new action... is *our commitment to being right.*

❋ ❋ ❋

Let's clarify a bit here. There are many ways to do many things, and still produce positive results. There are many ways to take action in many situations and still produce good outcomes, all the while still staying within ethical or legal or procedural guidelines. Being *right*, in this context, is not the same as being *correct*. If you're typing my blood for a transfusion,

100

please be correct. If you're fixing my brakes, please be correct. But that's different than being *righteous*, being convinced that my way of doing something or my way of looking at something is cosmically, Objectively Right, and anyone who does it or sees it differently is just plain Wrong. What's the right way to get married? The right way to get buried? The right way to manage a conflict? The right way to deal with new opportunities? The right way to raise kids? We could go on for awhile here. Is it possible that what's right for me and my life is wrong for you and your life?

This topic, that of being committed to being right and how it shows up in our lives, reminds me of a powerful question that was shared with me by my friends in EFL, and I'll share it with you now. This question is: ***Who would be wrong if your life worked?*** This question is not one in which an immediate answer is sought; rather, the real value may be in reflecting upon this over time, to hold this as an ongoing question that we live with for awhile. The answers may surprise you. In any event, the answers may provide an excellent starting point for letting go of some conversations that haven't worked for awhile, inventing more powerful conversations to live in, and perhaps gaining the commitment (and enrolling the support) needed to have some new conversations in the world.

❄ ❄ ❄

This new communications model emphasizes that we are always interpreting, no matter what, and that our life experiences (beliefs), mood/emotional state and body influence how we interpret. We'll return to these connections again in the next two chapters. Using this model, it becomes easy to spot another type of blindness we all share. **We say that this type of blindness is inevitable, for individuals and for organizations. It's not right or wrong, it just is.** Nobody does, or can, see things "as they are," at least in our traditional way of understanding how things are. Rather, each of us is biologically limited by how our bodies are—we don't have access to the native environment. We're also predisposed to listen or interpret or perceive in certain ways, based on our predominant moodspace, as well as our distinctions and social and historical background and beliefs. We're all interpreting, automatically and transparently to ourselves. To me, this way of understanding how we human beings communicate is more powerful than the "transmitter–receiver" model in several key ways, including:

- We can now build relationships with others by starting from a place of respecting their viewpoints as equally valid (not necessarily equally powerful in terms of opening or closing possibilities for action; not necessarily equally desirable, from my point of view) but valid in the sense that the other's interpretation is coming from their experiences, beliefs, moodspaces just as mine are. *None of us has privileged access to the Truth. We are all interpreting.* Quite possibly, many of us are limiting the types of relationships we're available for out of an understanding of human communication that makes it very easy to quickly make those who are different than we are "wrong." And in a world that's getting smaller every day, this new orientation can better serve us in creating and sustaining more ethical relationships among individuals, communities, organizations, and even nations.

- This model allows us to deepen our learning by having dialogue about "how you went from observation to belief in such a different way than I went from observation to belief." Because this model assumes that nobody sees things "as they objectively are," this sort of dialogue is much more probable, much more likely to occur. And because this action is much more likely, the results which come from such dialogue are much more likely. These results include a better foundation for long-term success, deeper degrees of shared understanding among each other, enriched relationships, more adequate understanding of the situation at hand, and more choices for effective action.

- This model, in fact, allows us to even have the distinction between *discussion* and *dialogue* in the first place. Discussion may be defined as a type of conversation that has as its desired outcome agreement on a certain course of action. Many of us are very practiced at this. *Dialogue*, however, is defined as a different type of conversation, one in which the desired outcome is explicitly declared to be a deepening of our shared understanding. That's it—not agreement necessarily, but a deeper level of understanding than we had when we started. By declaring this type of conversation up front, we can enter into it much more productively. This context—one of having the whole purpose to be a deepening of the level of shared understanding—is very powerful and, as a great many people will attest, can allow truly miraculous things to happen.

- This model allows each of us to take more active responsibility for the interpretations we produce—for the way we listen. (I can flex the big eye muscle, taking a look at myself—the only person I can change anyway.) If the way I'm interpreting isn't leading to the actions and results I say I want, I can take a look in a more powerful way at what's "underneath." That is, I can take a look at my beliefs, stories and explanations *on purpose.* I can take a look at my predominant moodspace and emotional patterns *on purpose,* and I can take a look at my body *on purpose.* I can enter into new learning, I can update my beliefs, and I can have conversations with others to enroll them in supporting me in this way.

❅ ❅ ❅

We claim that we are each unique listeners, each unique Observers. And back to the big eye drawing—this has to do with becoming a more competent *observer of the observer* that we are. This has to do with taking a look at how we look at things. If there are infinite ways to "see things," and if each of us is seeing things in a personal, unique way, what is the *particular way* in which we're doing that? And *is the way that I'm seeing things working for me?* This is a powerful question, one that can serve as the basis for truly redesigning our lives.

We have many common expressions in our language that point to this. One of my favorites is: **When you're a hammer, everything looks like a nail.** What does this expression really mean? To us, this means that we each tend to "see things" (interpret in language) based on how we are. What we observe has more to do with our own way of being than it does with what's "out there." We'll move more directly into this very topic in the next chapter but there are many examples we can point to now: A physicist and a chemist do not see the same things, even when they are both looking at the same slide on the microscope. A professional forester and a woodcarver do not see the same things, even when both are looking at the same forest. A western-trained physician and an eastern-trained physician do not see the same things, even when they are both looking at the same patient. We could go on and on. What they see— what we see—has a great deal to do with who's doing the looking and the beliefs, distinctions, and moodspace from which the observer is observing.

Back to our background conversation: If I think the way I listen, the way I interpret, the way I "see things" is Right, and yours happens to be different, what does that make you? It makes you Wrong. And how many of us find ourselves gravitating toward people who constantly make us wrong?

*"Oh, I just love being with Bubba because I get to be made wrong all the time. Yes, I love being with him and I love how it feels to be made wrong a lot. It makes me want to spend so much time with him. Oh, how excellent it feels to be made wrong at every turn!"*

How ridiculous. But notice how quickly we tend to make others wrong, how we come from this background conversation of I'm Right; and if I'm Right, and you happen to have a different view, then you must be wrong. What else could you be?

Mike Papania has also shared with me a powerful connection between *I'm Right*, listening, and distinctions. *We often make people wrong who don't have the same distinctions we do.* For example, a husband asks his wife "Honey, go in the garage and get me that Phillips screwdriver, will ya'?" She doesn't know tools, goes in, searches the best she can, and comes back with a hex-nut driver. "Were you not listening?" he says. "How many times do I have to say it?" Or she asks him "Honey, will you get me that taupe shawl-collar cocktail dress from my closet? It's right by my Capri pants." He's utterly lost and comes back with goodness-knows-what, and it's "That's what's wrong with our relationship...you never listen!" This is very powerful to begin to observe, our tendency to make others wrong simply because they do not have the same distinctions we do. It impacts our relationships at all levels, personal and professional, with adults and with children. It impacts our happiness, the quality of our jour- ney in many ways.

Most of us will not voluntarily be with, work with, associate with peo- ple who constantly make us wrong. At some point we take our toys and find another sandbox. We wonder why our spouse or kids walk right by and don't want to sit on the couch next to us, or why our colleagues never invite us to join them for lunch. Maybe they're tired of being made wrong.

❋ ❋ ❋

Back to the *I'm Right* background conversation; we did a workshop in Canada and when we got to this point, and put *I'm Right* on the board, the room erupted. Many said "Yes, you Americans are so right about everything!" They really saw this, very clearly. But they said that for them, it wasn't such a common background conversation, it didn't resonate with them so much as Canadians. We were intrigued and asked them if there was a Canadian equivalent. One of the participants said "Maybe it's *'How can we both be right and not have a confrontation'*" and immediately heads nodded in agreement.

I can honestly say that *"How can we both be right and not have a confrontation"* does not resonate with me. It is absolutely not my experience. But *"I'm Right,"* I'm familiar with! And my kids are familiar with it, as are very large numbers of people I've worked with over the past 15 years. These have a lot to do with what we call culture, obviously, and we can see that different cultures produce and are produced out of different background conversations.

While we claim the *I'm Right* conversation is very prevalent in America today, there are certainly historical examples of its impact. What must Hitler must have been telling himself to allow him to kill millions of men, women, and children? What must slave traders have been telling themselves as they treated other human beings as they did? What must early American settlers and soldiers have been telling themselves as they killed Native American men, women and children on the frontier? What are people telling themselves, today, in many areas of the globe, as they point weapons and go to battle with each other?

This is a *very* powerful background conversation. How we orient ourselves with regard to it has *major* impacts on our relationships, our results, and our well-being—at the individual, family, organizational, and even national levels. To me, the ability for us—all of us—to successfully and ethically move into the future is connected to our ability to move past an "either/or" understanding here, and somehow create a space in which

105

"both/and" thinking at least has a chance. To me, the distinctions offered within these pages can be useful tools in supporting precisely such a shift.

❊ ❊ ❊

At the personal level, and especially with close relationships, we see a related background conversation show up. This background conversation is:

### I'd Rather Be Right Than Be Happy

Our experience is that many of us will definitely give up our happiness for the sake of being right, and it shows up—it reveals itself—in our language. "Honey, how many times have I gotta tell you, the toilet paper comes over the top, not under the bottom" or "the right way to load the dishwasher" or "the right way to clean the floor" or "Look, I've told you, my remotes have to be on this table, stacked in order of size, or the whole setup is ruined" or whatever. Or we have to have the last word in a conversation, and when we really look at it, it's for the sake of being right. Or "I hear what you say, but the reality of the situation is..." Get ready, because someone is about to be right.

An expression I learned from Jeff Spring is: ***You can be right, or you can be in relationship, but not both.*** And this has been my experience, both personally and as a coach and seminar leader. A practice I've learned and continue to practice (sometimes well and sometimes not so well) is to ask myself a question before I respond in situations, especially if I'm emotionally triggered. My internal question is: ***For the sake of what am I about to say what I'm about to say?*** And often, I find it's for the sake of being right. Now I get to choose. How committed am I to being right? What am I willing to give up in order to be right? I will absolutely produce different results in my life, depending on how I orient myself in these situations.

Being right, *done well*, produces achievement, commitment to high standards, discipline. Being right, *done poorly*, produces a public identity of arrogance and "make wrong." Being right, done poorly, makes people want to go away. Being right, done poorly, damages relationships and produces <u>un</u>happiness. And many of us are not very good observers of this phenomenon, of this background conversation that impacts our listening, our relationships and our results.

106

This drawing represents, in the Eastern tradition, what is known as yin and yang; that is, the complementary-ness and cyclical movement that pervades much of our world.

It is also useful in our conversation here. We have said that being right, done well, produces achievement, commitment to high standards, and discipline (one side of the drawing). Being right, done poorly, is arrogance and other "negative" outcomes (other side of the drawing). But to try and totally get rid of the energy behind what's making me arrogant is not the answer, because this same energy is behind what makes me assertive and has me hold myself and others to certain standards.

Another example: Humble-ness, done well, produces inclusiveness, willingness to listen and openness to others' ideas and contributions. Humble-ness, done poorly, has me live my life a walking doormat. Make sense? Same kind of energy, either done well or done poorly. You can probably think of others here, as well. In a great many cases, we have two sides of the same coin. For many of us, then, the answer will not be totally ridding ourselves of all the energy that has us do what we do. It will be to modify, to make a shift, to re-direct in such a way as to produce better results for ourselves. And often, truthful feedback, coaching and support from someone we trust are powerful ingredients in such a change.

✻ ✻ ✻

A few closing points related to listening and to our communications model: First, have you noticed that we don't *try* to interpret the way we interpret—we just do. For example, I'm not consciously *trying* to see the world like a forty-something-year old white guy, born in south Louisiana, attended school here, got married there, had this job and this life experience, lived in Tennessee and now has 3 kids and lives in Florida. Another person isn't *trying* to listen (interpret) like a 36-year old African American female who was born here, had that life experience, traveled there and now lives in New York. All of us aren't consciously attempting to interpret in any particular way—it's happening, transparently to us. We don't see that we're interpreting—we have the experience of just seeing it like it is. And so it is with all of us. We're all doing it, and the vast majority of us aren't aware of what's going on. And this has everything to do with the nature of relationships we're available for and actually enter into, our ability to design healthy relationships over the long term, and our ability to design happiness, acceptance and peace into our lives.

Consider this: would say that you listen differently (interpret differently) when you're in a mood of anger, than when you're in a mood of joy or playfulness? Do you interpret things the same way in these two very different moods? I know I don't. (Remember the notion that *Event* is not equal to *Explanation*). The same event can occur, and my interpretation of it is radically different when I'm angry than if I'm joyful. And I offer that yours is, too. And back to the big eye drawing—*many of us are not very powerful observers of our own moods*. We don't see them. My wife can say "Chalmers, why are you in that mood?" and I say "What mood?" She sees it, I don't. And it impacts how I interpret, how I listen, how I build my internal story about what's happening. Again, this is not bad in and of itself. Let's just begin to be more competent in observing it. How many times have you been in a situation and heard someone say "I'm not being pessimistic, I'm being realistic?" Their mood is absolutely influencing how they interpret, how they see things, while at the same time they're claiming to have perfect Objectivity, to see things "as they are," and nothing could be further from the truth. We offer that our ability to design new results in our lives has a great deal to do with our capacity to be more powerful observers in this area.

In addition to our beliefs (language) and our moods/emotions, our communications model says that our listening is also strongly impacted by our *physical body*. How you sit, for example, is not disconnected from the way you listen during a classroom or seminar experience, and in all aspects of your life. Sitting upright and fairly erect is consistent with one way of listening, while sliding way down in your seat and leaning way back is consistent with another way of listening. Slumping forward and resting your forehead on your knees is consistent with, congruent with, yet another way of listening. Not right or wrong, but certainly different. Same with how we stand, how we walk, how we hold our head, back, arms and shoulders. Remember, we listen not only to words but also to events. If you've ever led a conversation in a group setting, or have ever been in front of a group giving a presentation, could you tell who's listening and who's not? We claim that many of us already have at least rough distinctions in this area, that we understand at some level that "body language" is important. We agree, and would perhaps go a bit further in the importance we place on this domain. We'll build on this point further in the next section, but for now we claim that the domain of the body—how we physically hold ourselves and move through space—is not innocent. It's connected and it plays a big role in how we listen, how we interpret, how we see things, and how we live our lives.

❊ ❊ ❊

This may be an obvious statement, but it must be said: ***The way you and I see things is just that—the way we see them.*** The way *we see* things has nothing to do with the way things *are*. Remember, we are always interpreting. We claim that nobody has pure Objectivity. Nobody knows what's *truly* going on. All I know, and all I *can* know, is what's going on *for me*. All you know, and all you *can* know, is what's going on *for you*. We don't have access to the way things are, independent of us. We don't have access to the native environment. Our biology only lets us see a certain spectrum of light waves, hear a certain set of sound waves. Does that mean nothing else is happening? Of course not. Just because we can't hear the high frequency sounds that dogs can, or the low frequency sounds that elephants can, doesn't mean those events aren't happening. It simply means that we interpret the world through a human biological system, which is different from the biological systems of other creatures. In addition to interpreting based on our biology, we also interpret linguistically, as we've been discussing here. You and I have similar biology, but it's entirely possible that we interpret (listen) an event or story in radically different ways. And it's quite unlikely that over time, any two people will interpret everything exactly the same way.

How many of us would say that we tend to develop habitual ways of listening? That we tend to, over time, listen or interpret in fairly predictable ways, ways that are consistent with our way of being? We say this is so, that this occurs with all of us. And so we repeat: ***Practice makes perfect, so be careful what you practice.*** However we listen, whichever way we tend to interpret or see things, we're going to get really good at it! Over time, we each become virtuosos at our own way of listening. It's like anything else, with enough practice we develop great competence. There is, of course, no problem with this if we're producing the results we say we want. In this case, we would say that our particular way of listening is working for us. That's great. But if we want to produce different results, this is an area that deserves a look. Remember our third basic claim:

> ***If you always do what you always did,***
> ***you always get what you always got.***

Can you see how this distinction of listening can make a difference? For the vast majority of us, the inter-actions with other people, the relationships, and the impact on public identity come into play in a powerful way. For those of us who *coordinate action* with other human beings in virtually every sphere of our lives, this distinction matters a lot. For those of us whose results, whose happiness, have a great deal to do with the nature of our personal and professional relationships with others, it matters a great deal.

At a very basic level, our ability to listen has a great deal to do with *our capacity to accept that others are different than we are*. Humberto Maturana states that our ability to accept the other as a *legitimate* other is strongly connected to ways in which we listen.[5] We can all point to situations in our own lives that support his observation: Whenever we claim to have privileged access to the Truth and whenever we assume that our particular way of being is the best or Right or True way of being, our listening is affected. And out of this, so are our relationships and our results.

**Footnotes:**

1. *Cool Hand Luke*; motion picture; Warner Studios; 1967.

2. *The Fifth Discipline Fieldbook: Strategies and Tools for Building a Learning Organization*; by Peter Senge, Richard Ross, Bryan Smith, Charlotte Roberts, and Art Kleiner; Doubleday/Bantam Doubleday Dell; 1994.

3. *Retooling On The Run: Real Change for Leaders With No Time*, by Stuart Heller, PhD; Frog, Ltd.; 1995.

4. *The Magic of Believing*, by Claude M. Bristol; Prentice-Hall, Inc., 1948.

5. *The Tree of Knowledge*, by Humberto Maturana, Francisco J. Varela and Robert Paolucci; Shambhala Publications; 1987.

## SUMMARY—MAIN POINTS AND
## NEW INTERPRETATIONS

- Listening and hearing are *two very different phenomena*. We say that while <u>hearing</u> is biological, having to do with a bone vibrating by an eardrum, <u>listening</u> has to do with interpretation, with actively building an internal story about whatever's being discussed or observed. Listening is *active and creative*, not passive and descriptive.

- *Many of us are not very powerful observers of the way that we listen.* We interpret "transparently" to ourselves; that is, we don't see ourselves as interpreting at all. From our individual perspectives, it seems as if we're "getting it like it is." And for all of us, nothing could be farther from the truth. We tend to *listen in such a way* to make ourselves, our stories, and our moods "right."

- A traditional model of communication uses Transmitters and Receivers, with 100% of the Message or Information being passed directly (hopefully) from Transmitter to Receiver. This chapter offers a different model, one with Speakers and Listeners. For us, human communication has everything to do with *interpretation*, with developing shared *understanding* and shared *meaning*. Transmitters and receivers don't care about meaning. People do.

- *We are each unique listeners, unique Observers.* Our unique way of observing, of interpreting has to do with at least three inter-connected, primary elements:

  ➤ Our life experiences (and more precisely, the *beliefs* we develop out of these experiences). We have beliefs about everything, and these beliefs live in language.

  ➤ Our moodspace or emotional space, emotional range.

  ➤ Our physical body, biology, posture and movement.

- *We are all necessarily "blind" in some areas.* This isn't good or bad—it just is. Because our listening has everything to do with our distinctions, our personal and social history, our moods and beliefs... we necessarily see some things quite well and completely miss others. Nobody has access to the way things are—we are interpreting and only have access to the way things are "for us."

- Our listening has a *big impact on the types of personal and workplace relationships we're available for.* And for non-hermits like us, our relationships have a great deal to do with our peacefulness, our productivity, our happiness.

## HOW-TO: TAKING NEW ACTION

1. Big Eye: *What are you telling yourself* about the notion that nobody gets things "like they are," that listening is interpretation, and that everybody is interpreting?

2. Big Eye: *What are you telling yourself* about the suggestion that we move away from having a "right/wrong" focus in many areas, and instead adopt something more akin to "works/doesn't work" or "powerful/un-powerful?" *Are you familiar with the "I'm Right" conversation*—does it show up a lot for you? If so, in what areas? What do you think some of the *costs of being in this conversation* might be?

3. Refer back to your SAMPLE SITUATION. Given this way of understanding listening and hearing, *what new possibilities or choices do you see* for improving the situation? *What new "moves" might you be able to make?* (Notice how some of these moves may be immediately visible to others, while others may not). Write these down.

4. Refer back to the BARRIERS TO LEARNING that, for you, may get in the way of making these changes and moving forward here. How can you overcome these barriers? What new stories, new actions, new interactions could serve you best here? *Enroll somebody else* in what you're up to.

5. *Share* what you've learned or noticed with someone close to you.

# Chapter 5

## MY FAVORITE MODEL:
## Observer–Action–Results

---

*"We see the world not as it is, but as we are."* [1]

Albert Einstein

*"Everything that is said, is said by someone."* [2]

Humberto Maturana
*The Tree of Knowledge*

---

Let's start with two basic questions:

1. How do we actually achieve the results (ANY results) we achieve? and
2. What actions are available to us, given that sometimes we—as individuals and as organizations—produce results that we'd rather not produce?

How each of us frames and understands this very basic process greatly influences even what we see as *possibilities* for improving whatever we say we want to improve. This section introduces my favorite model for showing how we achieve what we achieve, how we produce the results we produce, as individuals and as organizations. This is the simplest and also the most powerful way I know of understanding ourselves, our actions, and our results. If happiness (or more peace of mind, or better relationships, or improved productivity, or clearer communication) are the results we say we're looking for, this model can be used to help us see more possibilities for taking effective action.

This model, called the Observer-Action-Results model, was initially developed by Chris Argyris and Robert Putnam. It has appeared in articles and books by both and is a very influential model. It was introduced to me by Rafael Echeverria during a workshop, and I believe others have used it as well.

Once again, this model is all about how we do what we do, and get what we get. It's a wonderfully simple—yet incredibly powerful—way of understanding how we actually produce the results we produce in our lives.

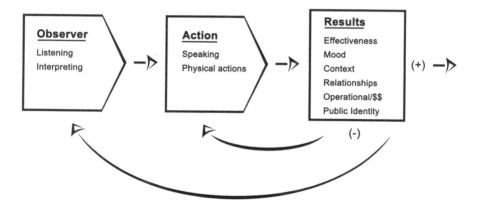

To start with, let's ignore the Observer part of the model and concentrate on only the Actions and Results. First, can we agree that the *results* we produce have a great deal to do with the *actions* we do or do not take? Most of us would say, yes, our results are strongly connected with our actions or lack thereof. Our results may include our happiness, our relationships, our financial results, our productivity, any outcome we're trying to achieve. We take actions and produce results as *individuals*, and we take actions and produce results as *organizations*.

Secondly, we see that our actions absolutely include our *speaking*—to ourselves and others. Much of our last section dealt with this, and this entire book is framed within the context of an active, generative nature of language and conversations. Of course, our actions also include purely physical actions.

Now, once we produce some results, we may assess these results as either positive (+) or negative (-). That is, sometimes out of our actions we produce results we want, and sometimes we produce results that we don't want. Again, this is true for individuals as well as organizations.

If we produce positive (+) results, then we feel confirmed in the action we took, and we'll probably take it again. And if we don't produce the results we want, we can take another action, and try again. If this doesn't work, we take another action, try again. And so on, until we (hopefully!) do produce the result we say we want. Chris Argyris has called this First Order Learning, and it's represented by the arrow suggesting more or new or different Actions, as shown below:

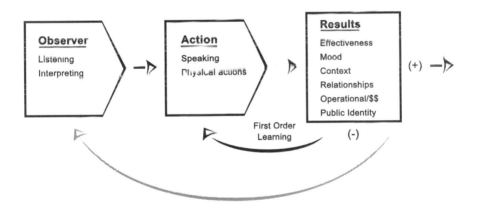

First Order Learning has to do with changing our actions (which of course include changing our speaking) for the purpose of producing new results. In some ways, First Order Learning represents our traditional approach to problem-solving. It implies that there is an objective problem "out there," and in order to solve it we must take actions which are effective in producing some desired result. It has everything to do with cause and effect.

Let's explore the *Observer* portion of the model now. Many of us have been in situations similar to this: You find yourself struggling with a problem, trying to figure out what to do, and it appears you've run out of options. You've tried several alternatives, none of which seemed to work, and you just don't see any more good possibilities left. At some point another person comes into the room, and in 5 minutes of conversation with you he or she offers a fresh new alternative, and you say "Oh, I didn't see it that way!"

Many of us have had this experience. We say that this occurs precisely because a new observer has appeared—someone with a different view, a different perspective, a different way of looking at something. Notice how all the metaphors here are *visual* metaphors—they have a great deal to do with the observer. They all point to a central claim of this model: ***Our results have a great deal to do with our actions or lack of actions. This is well-known. What's less clear is that our actions themselves have a great deal to do with the observer that we are, with how we "see things".***

What we don't often notice is that the way we observe, interpret, listen—the way we "see things"—comes *before* we take any action. That is, the way we frame a given situation tends to create a particular set of possibilities. Now, I may not know exactly which action I will ultimately take, but I *do* know that it will come from this set of initial possibilities! Others, who frame the situation differently, see other sets of possibilities, which lead to other actions.

Just because I may have exhausted all the possibilities I see doesn't mean there are no possibilities or options left. It just means that from the way I see things, the way I've constructed the situation, the story that I've built, from *my* perspective, through *my* beliefs, there are no possibilities.

*We are each unique observers*, unique listeners, unique interpreters of situations. We bring unique sets of concerns and stories to the table... and so what we see, what we observe, reveals more about us than about what's out there. What's important to notice is that many of us do not notice this! Back to the big eye. That is, many of us do not notice that we're observing in a particular way in the first place. We think we're seeing things "as they are." And we claim that this is not so, on two levels.

On the *biological level*, we claim that we *do not* and *cannot* see things as they truly are. We can only see and observe things as *we* perceive them. As we have learned from Dr. Humberto Maturana and others, there is nothing in the biology of the human being that can allow us to claim that we know how things truly are. All we know is how things are for us. We're all interpreting from the get-go. And on the level of our *language*, we can see how our distinctions, our traditions, our judgments and beliefs have everything to do with:

- what we *see*, and what we *can see*, when we look around; and

- what it *means* to us, individually and as part of the groups we're part of.

In this way of thinking, it's clear that the "reality" each of us sees has more to do with *us*—with *the observer we are*—than with what's objectively "out there."

The Grand Canyon looks different from the river than it does from the rim. *Where you stand matters*. The Observer portion of this model makes this explicit. We can now take a look at how we look at things. We can become an observer of the Observer that we are, and do so on purpose. Explicitly. If we don't like the results we're producing, we can bring our way of observing into the equation. We can flex the big eye muscle, and become conscious observers of our particular way of observing. Chris Argyris has called this Second Order Learning, and it's represented by the arrow pointing back to the Observer, as shown below:

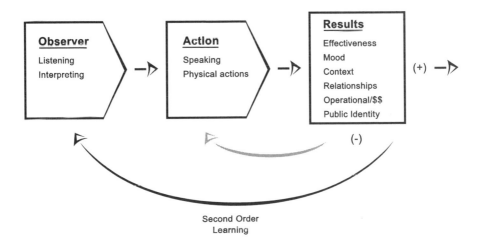

We agree with Chris Argyris that Second Order Learning holds the possibility for truly transformational learning, for making profound shifts in the results we produce. It is here that we become conscious of the impact that our particular way of observing has on our actions. From here, we are able to be much more conscious in designing new actions that have historically been unavailable (unseen or viewed as impossible) to us. By bringing our own perspective, our own way of seeing things, into the mix, we open possibilities that simply would not have existed under "the old way of seeing things." It is this *fundamental position of openness* that serves as the foundation for new possibilities.

*Of course, the whole notion of Second Order Learning makes no sense at all if we think the way we see things = the way things truly are! The whole idea of taking a look at how we look at things is of very little value if we're convinced that we see things "objectively" and "realistically" already.*

**It takes more courage to take a look at how we look at things than it does to simply try new Actions.** We claim that in a fundamental way, all my Actions are more or less the same. They're all coming from the same place, the same point of view, the same observer, the same perspective. But if/when we finally look at how we look at things, we then see that we have, indeed, had a particular "point of view" all along. Not *the* way to see things, but simply *a* way of seeing things. Moving forward here requires *courage* for most of us, I believe, because it involves *fear* for most of us. Not fear of being eaten by a tiger, but real fear nonetheless. I believe that this is because when we choose to look this way, at some level we know that we've expanded the playing field a bit, and that we're getting closer to the real stuff—the actual stories and interpretations—that are underneath a lot of our actions. We know we're getting closer to an area that has more to do with *who we say we are and how we say we "be"*—and far less to do with any of the particular things we may be doing.

※ ※ ※

Summarizing, we can say that if we *do* produce the results we want in our lives (+), we usually continue taking those actions that produced the effectiveness or the desired result. However, if we *don't* produce the results we want in our lives (-), we have three primary options:

1. Assume the negative results were caused by factors outside our control. *Do nothing*. Obviously, this is not a very powerful orientation.

2. *Change our actions*, including our speaking (called First Order Learning). This is usually included in our traditional problem-solving models and approaches.

3. *Change the way we look at things*. Call into question the observer that we are (called Second Order Learning). For us, this is the place of truly transformational learning and of greatly expanding our possibilities for action in the world.

This basic Observer-Action-Results model represents a profound shift in how we understand the role that each of us plays in producing what we produce for ourselves. Let's continue with some additional points about the observer.

We claim that we are each unique observers, but we are not detached, indifferent, or "objective" observers (as in the scientific paradigm). On the contrary, we are *concerned* observers. We are extremely invested in the way we observe (although it may be transparent to us). As unique observers, we each bring unique sets of concerns and beliefs to the table.

Are you the *same* observer that you were when you were 18 years old? That is, how many of us would say that we "see things" pretty much the same today as we did when we were 18? Most people we've met say that No, they are not the same observer as when they were 18, that they most assuredly do not see things now the same way they did back then.

I certainly see things differently. I used to think that people who hit mailboxes with baseball bats were pranksters. Now, I think they should be punished by death. (Just kidding!) But you lose a few mailboxes and it changes your *perspective*. It changes your *point of view*. The same event may occur now, and I absolutely don't *"see it"* the same way I did back then. I *observe* differently now. I am a *different observer* now.

Key question: *When did the change occur?* When did we go from seeing the world like we did when we were 18 to seeing it the way we do now? Was it one morning, we each woke up and *voila*, the world was all different? No—for most of us it was very gradual, every moment, every moment, every moment. The observer-that-we-are is constantly changing, gradually and sometimes not-so-gradually shifting and evolving and growing.

**Perhaps the term "human being" is not as appropriate as "human becoming."** We are each becoming a new observer, every moment of every day. This is not a strange or far-out statement, I believe—

merely an observation reflecting our own experience. I am still Chalmers, but I am not the same observer I was 5 years ago, and I'm not the observer I will be 5 years from now. Same goes for you. In this interpretation, we are each in a permanent state of becoming. And given a world in which constant change is occurring, I like this interpretation better than Popeye's.

This Observer-Action-Results model also denies Popeye. Do you remember Popeye's slogan? As I recall, the Popeye slogan is: *"I yam what I yam and that's all that I yam!"* Well, I am not who I used to be. I am not who I will be tomorrow. And neither are you. Human beings have a fantastic capacity for self-transformation, for learning, for growth. Through learning, we have the ability to develop competencies that we did not have in the past, then take actions we could not take in the past, to produce results we did not produce in the past. We can think about our thinking, and *choose* to think differently. We can talk about our talking, and *choose* to invent new conversations. While other creatures certainly communicate in some ways, as far as we can tell the communication occurs within the framework of that creature as a given. I've heard it put this way: Dogs and cats communicate, but for dogs and cats, their "dog-hood" and "cat-hood" appear to be firmly established! But humans, with our language, have the capacity to redesign our person-hood. In a very real way, we create out of what we speak.

Rafael Echeverria shared this perspective with us, and I will share it with you. To me, it's very powerful and captures in a succinct way what we're speaking about here: *We act according to how we are (and we do). But we also are, according to how we act.* There is a circular influence at work here. We act from our history, no doubt. But we can also act from out of our history. We can observe in a different way, we can learn some new distinctions and we can begin to see some different possibilities for new action. By taking *new actions* in the world, we generate a *new identity* for ourselves. By taking new actions which are inconsistent with our history, we can produce unprecedented, brand new (for us) results. We can become different than we were before. We can design anew.

In addition, as the startling conclusions drawn by the neurobiologist Humberto Maturana have shown, the taking of new action in the world *literally* creates a new structure within us, which then allows us to take

action and respond in new ways to future events. We are literally–not fig-
uratively–a different person after we take a new action. We are literally
becoming a new observer (a "human becoming") through the taking of
new actions. We are definitely *not* Popeye, and it can be proven biologically. Given that as living creatures we are structurally determined
(everything we do and can do in the world is based on what our structure
allows), this has fantastic implications on how we move and create results
in our lives.

❋ ❋ ❋

I have learned that *problems, possibilities,* and *solutions* are all a
function of the observer that we are. Think about it. The world doesn't
have any problems, in and of itself. People–observers–have problems.
What's a problem to one observer passes totally unnoticed to another. It
has to do with the different concerns of the different observers, the different distinctions and beliefs of the different observers. Different observers
produce or invent radically different possibilities, and from these possibilities produce or invent radically different solutions (actions). This is different than the common view that X or Y exists objectively or independently,
pre-given as a problem, and that what's needed is to first see it objectively
or rationally, "as it really is," then to solve it. This is different than the
notion that possibilities and solutions are "out there" waiting to be *discovered*. We say instead they are waiting to be *invented*–invented by
observers in conversation.

One of the points I remember Rafael Echeverria making is this: Many
of us *assume that people with whom we have difficulties are very similar observers as we are, except that they have bad intentions!* (Sound
familiar?) It's much more likely that they are very *different* observers,
that they have very *different* sets of concerns, very *different* distinctions,
and that they do *not* see things the way we see things. Don Miguel Ruiz, in
his book *The Four Agreements*, says it this way:

> *"We make the assumption that everyone sees life the way that we
> do. We assume that others think the way we think, feel the way we
> feel, judge the way we judge. This is the biggest assumption that
> humans make."* [3]

Our view emphasizes the degree to which what we "see" is connected to who's doing the looking, to the particular observer involved. In this way of thinking, it's natural and normal that you and I would not see many things in exactly the same way. To me, this has the effect of lessening the extent to which we quickly blame others and ascribe ill intentions to them. Because of this, I see it as a more powerful and effective context, a stronger and more adequate starting point for resolving differences and moving forward with others. I believe this is true for individuals, families, organizations, and even countries.

This way of understanding the observer also allows us to reinforce the distinction of *blindness* we introduced earlier. Being a different listener = being a different observer, seeing things differently and seeing different things. This refers to each of us being *necessarily blind* to certain possibilities because of our differences in background, experience, distinctions, traditions, learning. In very real ways, we *don't know that we don't know* these things.

This type of blindness is very widespread and considered quite normal. It's not bad that we have this type of blindness; it's only bad that we don't notice it. We will take different actions with people–we will form different types of relationships with people–if we notice this, than if we don't. We will interact differently, and we will solve problems differently. Can you see how being aware of this type of blindness sets a *different context* for relating and being together? It's a truly different starting point.

The world of accounting is not the same as the world of science. Accountants have a very different set of distinctions from which to view the world than do scientists. Accountants are very different observers than are scientists. Accountants have different histories and beliefs. Possibilities which are obvious to an accountant would not be available, not be seen, by the scientists. Or the farmer. Or the neurosurgeon. Or the person from a different region or country. And vice versa, all around. This is not "bad." It just is. What we see when we look out at the world has everything to do with our distinctions and our social histories. We are necessarily blind in areas in which we have limited or no distinctions. We are necessarily blind to the possibilities seen by others who come from different life experiences, traditions, beliefs, and practices. Will Rogers has a great expression that seems to fit here. He says: ***Everybody is ignorant, only on different subjects.***

124

Different observers are able to see some things clearly, while remaining blind to others. And so we can stop making others wrong simply because they have blindnesses we don't have. We can stop making ourselves wrong because we have our own areas of blindness. We can determine whether or not we're committed to get "un-blind" in an area or domain, and what that learning may involve. We can approach learning more effectively in organizations and schools. We can approach creativity and innovation differently in organizations, communities, and families.

In Peter Senge's *The Fifth Discipline*, the concept of mental models is very similar to what we're describing here. The sets of distinctions and beliefs that an accountant sees the world through may be radically different than those of an elderly African American grandmother from south Louisiana. And hers may be very different from those of a Moroccan rug merchant. These all may be seen as *mental models* or *mental maps* carried by these people and by all of us. In the book it is summarized this way:

> *"Mental models are the images, assumptions and stories which we carry in our minds of ourselves, other people, institutions and every aspect of the world. Like a pane of glass framing and subtly distorting our vision, mental models determine what we see. Human beings cannot navigate through the complex environments of our world without these 'mental maps'; and all of these mental maps, by definition, are flawed in some way."* [4]

Of course, we would further add that the term "map" or "model" may sometimes take us away from the root of the matter–that being the extent to which these maps and models are really stories, narratives and explanations–*all living in language.*

❋ ❋ ❋

*We keep searching out there for answers and pointing out there for blame... all the while looking through the very lens that is itself the source of our greatest potential for designing something new.*

**Footnotes:**

1. *The Expanded Quotable Einstein*; by Alice Capaprice; Princeton University Press; 2000.

2. *The Tree of Knowledge*, by Humberto Maturana, Francisco J. Varela and Robert Paolucci; Shambhala Publications; 1987.

3. *The Four Agreements: A Practical Guide to Personal Freedom*; by Don Miguel Ruiz; Amber-Allen Publishing; 1997.

4. *The Fifth Discipline Fieldbook: Strategies and Tools for Building a Learning Organization*; by Peter Senge, et al.; Doubleday/Bantam Doubleday Dell; 1994.

## SUMMARY—MAIN POINTS AND NEW INTERPRETATIONS

- Our *results*—personally and professionally—have a great deal to do with our *actions* or lack thereof. This is well-known. And when we say *actions*, we are talking about both our *physical actions* as well as our *language actions*, our conversations. What's less widely understood is that *how each of us "sees things"* has a huge impact on the actions we even see as possible in the first place. It also has a major impact on *how we actually do* whatever it is that we do. This is shown in what is called the *Observer > Action > Results* model.

- *Each of us is a unique Observer.* We can also say that each of us is a unique listener, a unique interpreter. And the observer that we are is *not fixed and permanent*; rather, each of us is in a constant process of shifting, of learning, of becoming a new observer. If we don't like the *results* we're producing at home or at work, we have 3 major choices:

  1. Do nothing (which is not a very powerful option).

  2. Take new actions (including physical and language actions).

  3. Take a look at how we look at things. Bring the Observer that we are into the equation.

- There is great power in becoming a better observer of ourselves; specifically, in *becoming a better observer of the way that we observe.* We each are already observing in our own particular way. The key question then becomes: Is the way that you're currently looking at things *working for you? Is it allowing you to produce the results you say you want?* (vs. being *right* or *wrong*). Because if not, you have the option of modifying, adapting, changing how you see things. You have the option of *choosing to become a different observer.*

- You are already the author of your own explanations, interpretations, and stories. You have the authority to invent new explanations, new interpretations, and new stories... ones that are more powerful, more helpful, and more consistent with the results you say you want. You have the authority, and you have the ability to learn how to do this. Once you notice, what's left is to make a new choice and enter into new learning.

## HOW-TO: POSSIBILITIES FOR
## TAKING NEW ACTION

1. Big Eye: *What kind of observer do you say you are?* That is, how have you historically tended to see things? Have you changed in this regard due to some life event? Or have you "always" been this type of observer?

2. Refer back to your SAMPLE SITUATION. Using the Observer > Action > Results model, we can say that this is a case in which you have *not* been producing the results you say you want. *Have a conversation* with someone close to you about this, paying particular attention to share "how you see it," as well as to your *underlying assumptions, conclusions and deductions that you made, that others may not have made.* This is *not* a conversation about right vs. wrong. Listen to feedback about other possible ways of seeing this situation.

3. Identify *one possible new action that becomes possible out of seeing the situation in a different way (out of shifting the Observer.) Enroll someone* to support you in being a beginner, being a learner, in taking this new action in the future.

4. *Share* what you've learned or noticed with someone close to you. Listen to their observations and perspectives.

# *Chapter 6*

## An Artificial Separation:
## Language/Emotions/Body

---

*"Sit up straight!"*

Grandma

---

What follows, I believe, is somewhat intuitive and self-evident for most of us. We know, have felt, and have experienced the connections which will be outlined here. Hopefully the value here will be to share these connections with you in such a way that you'll be more able to *use* your knowledge in *taking new action*. What I hope my contribution can be in this chapter is to present these in such a way—upon the foundation of language viewed as generative and creative—that you'll see more possibilities, more choices for producing what you want to produce in your life.

In the last chapter we introduced the notion that we are each unique observers; from how we "see things" we take action, and from our actions we produce results:

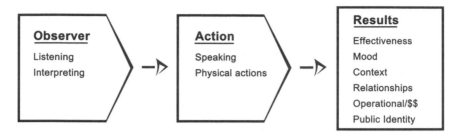

Let's start here: When we say we are each unique *observers*, we are not implying that each of us is a walking, talking eyeball. To us, the observer that each of us is can be viewed as a *bundle of congruency* among three separate but strongly inter-twined aspects:

- Our physical body (includes our biology as well as how we move)
- Our language
- Our mood/emotional states

That is, through the course of living as we've each been living, we've developed a coherency, a "way of being" composed of these three aspects, these three domains. Each observer—each of us, each human being, you and I and everyone else—may be viewed in this way:

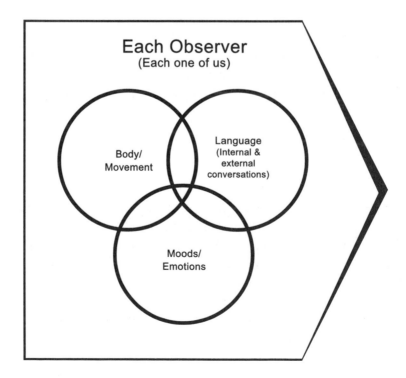

We can say that this combination, for each of us, is our own particular "way of being." Now this is in particular contrast to the widely-held notion that we are primarily *rational animals*. By the time I was an adult, I somehow had that in the back of my head—that we human beings are first and foremost rational animals and that the main thing that makes us human is our rationality. I don't remember anyone specifically teaching me that in any particular class. It just seemed to have been in the background of a lot of things I learned, heard, or picked up along the way. It's at this level that I'm sharing this new way of understanding with you—to offer it as a substitute for the *rational animal* way of understanding human beings.

Yes, I certainly can be rational, and I use rationality a lot. But when I look at it, there's a lot more going on with me, and with lots of other people, than rational reactions to situations and rational planning and rational decision-making and rational relationships and rational this or that. I can be rational, for sure, but to say that this feature is somehow the *most* primary, defining feature of human beings is, to me, contrary to my own experience. And once we look a bit more closely, it becomes clear that our ability to be rational is already resting on top of... you guessed it, language.

The *rational animal* interpretation, with its emphasis on our logic, also fails to fully take into account our emotional and physical sides. If we take a moment to reflect, we can all point to experiences in our own lives in which our emotions and our physical body have directly impacted—and continue to impact today—what we do, how we do it, what we say, and how we say it.

❋ ❋ ❋

*The claim here is that the separation many of us have been taught is an artificial one.* Language is *not* separate from our emotional life and our physical body and physical movements. Our "way of being" is one in which language, moods and emotions, and body are all linked and are all playing a part. We speak and we listen, but the speaking and listening are always supported or not supported by the emotions that we have available. Our speaking and listening are always supported or not supported by our range of physical motions, our capacity to move in one way or another, our physiology.

131

To me, the following is an excellent example of these connections. It clearly shows the ways in which our stories, our moods and emotions and our bodies are consistent with one another and linked together. And in particular, it highlights the importance of including all 3 domains as George—and the rest of us—look for possible actions to take in moving our lives in different directions. From Alan Seiler's book *Coaching To The Human Soul: Ontological Coaching and Deep Change—Vol. 1*, we read:

*"George was "shooting himself in the foot" when it came to promotion opportunities, as his performance reviews consistently highlighted the need for improvement in his communication with others. Early in the coaching conversation it was clear George was experiencing a major difficulty with delegation. More specifically, he was experiencing a communication breakdown in making clear and effective requests to others.*

*George reported that he often found himself angry with the people in his unit, and that he was often short and withdrawn in his expression of this anger. When asked what the anger was about he replied that he became angry when he felt that he had to ask people to do things, because they should know what to do and that it was an insult to him to have to ask. Further exploration revealed that this was a pattern of behavior he had learned in his childhood. George grew up in a household where a very strong and clear message is that you offend people if you do not know what to do for them, and that you should not have to be asked. In short, if you cared you would be alert, anticipate what they want and do it for them. Furthermore, a very strong and unstated message he also learned was that if you did not do this, your fundamental worthiness (as a human being) was questionable.*

*Thus, we could say that George had a very powerful story and associated beliefs in one area of relating to people. His story carried an expectation that not only should he be alert to what others want done without them having to ask, it also carried the unquestioned assumption that others should be as sensitive to him, especially as he was now in a senior position. We might be tempted to say that all he had to do was change the story and he could change his behavior. However, this story (occurring in language) is only*

132

*one aspect of his Way of Being. His story also had a strong emotional grip on him.*

*Needless to say, there was a fair bit of tension associated with his story. A lot of emotional energy was required to maintain alertness to the needs of others, and not have to deal with the question of self-worth, as well as deal with the insensitivity of others when they did not spontaneously notice what needed doing. The emotional consequence was that most of the time George lived in a mood of resentment. In other words, anger was almost permanently in the background, easily triggered when he felt he had to ask others.*

*However, this is still not the complete picture of how George had taken on a Way of Being with respect to delegation in the workplace. His story and his mood were also embodied; that is, he had configured his posture so that (i) he found it hard to ask people and (ii) when he did ask, his requests were very ineffectual."* [2]

And so everything we cover connected to language, internal and external conversations, stories, interpretations, narratives and beliefs is always within this context. It is always recognizing the *built-in connections* and *inherent relationships* among our language, our emotional capacity and range, and our physical body and movement. To me, this 3-circle model is more consistent with our own personal experience. Compared to the rational animal way of thinking, I see this as a far stronger model for those of us committed to taking new action and making lasting changes in our lives. I don't know whether it's Right or Wrong, but I do know that for me, it simply works better.

❋ ❋ ❋

As we've said, most of us already have an intuitive understanding of the connections which exist among our language, our moods/emotions, and our physical bodies. We have felt these firsthand, in a variety of situations. What may be unique about this particular way of looking is the claim that *each of these 3 aspects* may be used as the starting point, the "lever" for change and for designing something different. Each may be used to purposefully impact and influence—my favorite word here is *design*—the other two.

## Body and Movement

Let's start with Body—our physiology, our biology, our physical side—at a variety of levels. We begin with statements which are somewhat self-evident, but lay the groundwork for what's to come:

- We can only observe what our biology allows us to observe.
- We can only do what our biology allows us to do.

That is, the starting point for any observation I can make or action I can take is the biological structure from which I'm operating. This is so for each of us.

For example, my eyes only see certain wavelengths of light. My ears only hear certain wavelengths of sound. Any light waves or sound waves outside of those ranges go totally un-observed, unnoticed by me. We know, of course, that dogs can hear high frequency waves that humans cannot; same with elephants and low frequency sounds. We also know that the light we see is referred to as the "visible" portion of the spectrum. You and I are simply incapable—biologically—of hearing these sounds and seeing the other portion of what we call the electromagnetic spectrum. This doesn't mean that these phenomena don't exist. It simply means they are not available to us. We are interpreting no matter what, and we are interpreting from a particular human being biology.

People with different biological structures observe differently from each other. There are many examples we could point to, from degrees of color sensitivity and hearing acuity, to chemical or hormonal differences to other differences in how our physical bodies are. We claim that in all cases, *the observer is observing from a given biology* and that this biology *necessarily* defines the range of what's possible to observe.

As an aside, we may consider other creatures such as dogs, cats, snakes, bats, and insects. If we really think about this, we can see that what a "tree" is to a bat (in its world of echo-location) is different than what a "tree" is to a dragonfly (with its multi-eyes), which is different than what a dog experiences (with its dog eyes and dog nose) and what a snake experiences (with its heat-sensing capabilities) and so on. We can say, very clearly, that what each creature sees as it looks out on the world has a great deal to do with the biology from which that creature is operating. Said another way, what's "reality" appears to be species-dependent!

❋ ❋ ❋

Within this domain we include our cells and molecules, immune system and other bodily processes. We include our physiology and biology, and all of the interior interactions that occur and must occur in order for us to stay alive. A great deal is constantly going on related to how our bodies grow and react to the foods we eat (or don't eat), medicines and drugs we ingest (including caffeine, sugar, alcohol) as well as other parts of our everyday environment. Even at this level, we can clearly see the connections to our emotions, moods, and conversations. Anyone who's ever been afraid or nervous, for example, knows that heart rate, blood pressure and a whole host of other bodily functions are directly connected to our moodspace.

Also within what we're calling *body* are our *movement and posture*. That is, in addition to focusing on the "micro" (our biology, our cells, molecules, genetics, systems), we can also focus on the "macro" (how we physically hold and move our bodies through time and space). Here, we pay attention to and notice *how we carry ourselves* and *how we physically move* in the world. This includes:

- How we walk
- How we stand
- How we sit
- How we hold our head, chest and shoulders
- How we dance
- If we dance
- How we move, how close we get, our relative body positions—physically—to other people in personal, social, and work situations
- Our exercise habits and standards
- The range of physical movements that we're used to, that come easily and are readily available to us.
- The range of physical movements that we're *not* used to and are *not* available to us; that we have virtually no practice in, and have therefore not yet experienced.

Some of us exercise in some way, and some don't. Some of us do yoga, and some don't. Same with meditation, walking, and dancing. And there are infinite ways, of course, to meditate, to walk, and to dance. Some of us walk and sit upright, while others are much more slouched over. Some of us talk with others and square up, face-to-face, to have the conversation. Others tend to always be at an angle when interacting with others, assuming a much more sideways position. Some of us stand up in a crowded room to ask a question, and some of us stay glued to the chair. Some of us have a "personal space" that's measured in feet, while others measure theirs in inches. Some of us always look others in the eye, while others avoid eye contact at all costs. Some of us hug others, while others shake hands only. We could go on and on.

We're talking about our bodies and about physical movement, obviously. But by looking just a bit deeper we can see that we're talking also about much more. And this "much more" shows up precisely in our internal and external conversations, as well as in the range of emotions which are even available to us.

Any conversation about the body domain would not be complete without sharing with you the incredible contribution made by Humberto Maturana[1], the Chilean neurobiologist whom I've mentioned before. He provides solidly grounded, scientifically rooted evidence that says our commonsense understanding of perception and human capabilities need to be seriously reexamined. Dr. Maturana is truly a pioneer, on the cutting edge of new understandings of living systems—of which we human beings are certainly a part. Two of his key findings (referred to earlier) that have direct relevance for us are:

1. *Human beings are "closed systems" and are "structurally determined."* That is, what we are able to do has everything to do with our physical structure and systems, at a multitude of levels. What we perceive, the actions we take, and the reactions we have do *not* have very much to do with what's "out there." On the contrary, they have everything to do with what's "in here"—with our own individual structure, *our own mood/body/language combination.* In fact, we cannot and do not have direct access to what's out there. It's biologically, physiologically not available to us. All we have, all we know, is what we know and perceive as we react through our particular structure. What's out there serves more as a *trigger*, not as a *provider* or *determiner* of our experience. What we experience, how we react, and what we do is *not* primarily a function of the trigger. It's a function of *us*, of *our own structure.* (In this sense, a T-shirt I saw the other day makes perfect sense. It said "It's all about me!").

2. *Our structure is not fixed and permanent; instead, it's highly plastic and continuously changing.* Our new actions produce new neural pathways and new physical structures. By learning and taking new actions—*new physical actions and new conversational actions*—we produce a new structure. This new structure then enables us to take new physical and conversational action when the next trigger occurs, action we could not and did not take before. In this sense, our learning is truly embodied.

So the domain of Body, for us, includes our micro-level systems and molecules and processes, as well as our macro-level posture and physical movements. When we say Body, we're seeing each human being as Maturana does—each as a living being and so therefore each of us a closed system, each reacting to external events according to our own unique structure, our own unique combination or language/moods/body. What we "do" in any given situation has everything to do with how _we_ are, not on the external event or trigger itself. And when we say Body, we're understanding that we're each physically and physiologically always changing and growing—through each and every thing that we learn, say, feel and do.

Whatever each of us does during our time here, our bodies seem to always be present. So learning something about our bodies, and understanding some of the connections which exist between our physical-hood and our emotional life can greatly serve us. And learning something about our bodies and the connections to our internal and external conversations can greatly serve us—especially if we're interested in bringing about _new_ results in our lives, moving away from the status quo. This type of learning can greatly serve us if we're interested in designing a tomorrow that is different from yesterday.

## Language

This circle, the language circle, is the focal point of this book. However, our way of understanding human language is always within this context. Human language comes from human beings, and emerges as part of a "coherence" or congruent and inter-connected mix that includes our emotional lives and emotional patterns, as well as our physical body, biology and movement.

Our language includes our internal and external conversations, our listening and our speaking. It includes our every thought and our every story, complaint, opinion and conversation. As we said earlier, we are language beings. We are immersed in language as fish are immersed in water, and we each "live in language." Over the course of our lives, we begin to live in language and "dance" in language ways that are totally unique to our own way of being, totally consistent with and supported by our emotional energy and our physical bodies.

With language, we can now begin to see big differences in observation among individuals that share a very similar biology. In other words, there are much bigger differences in how people "see things" than can be explained solely on the basis of biological differences! Human beings may have very similar biological structures and at the same time produce wildly different interpretations or explanations of things. In our workshops, people with teenagers often report wonderful examples of this. This has to do with language, with different ways of interpreting, judging, declaring, and internal story-building.

This entire book rests upon a new interpretation of language—an interpretation in which language is *action*, is *generative*, is *creative*. It is in language that our distinctions, our assessments (judgments) and our stories live. We can frame language here by looking at 3 levels, each building on the prior:

- First, we can say that each of us—each observer—observes the world through a set of *distinctions* (remember our earlier discussion). Our distinctions live in language, such that an auto mechanic with distinctions in the domain of automobile engines observes something different than the rest of us when we're all looking at a car motor. Same with the forester looking at trees and the chemist looking through a microscope. Distinctions provide the starting point for observing. They provide the "things" we notice in the first place, when we look around. Give me new distinctions, and I'll see something different when I look out at the world.

- Second, we take a stand on what we see via our *assessments—our opinions* and *judgments*. (More to come on these in the next section). We are not purely neutral as to what we see and what we are likely to do. It is here that we orient ourselves one way or another in given situations, positioning ourselves in such a way that certain possibilities are opened and others are closed.

- And third, we tie it all together, we make sense of situations and events, we connect our assessments and opinions together with our *narratives* or *stories*. (And we are each the central character of our own story!) Each of us weaves stories around the events and observations of our lives, connecting elements and making sense of what's before us. And this we do in language. We generate these with our language. And it is through the "filters" or "lenses" of these distinctions, assessments and stories that we "see" the world.

To continue our theme, a key benefit of this way of understanding is that we can now separate our *explanations and stories* from the *events* of our lives. This is a huge benefit, opening the doorway to an entirely new set of options. Now we can see that the event belongs to itself, while my explanations and stories belong to me. My explanations and stories have to do with *my* way of listening and assessing and story-building. The event just *is*, while the explanations and stories can be examined in terms of the *possibilities for action* that each opens or closes. Our explanations (not the events) have everything to do with what we see as possible, what we actually do, and how we actually do it. And out of our actions, of course, we produce whatever results we create in our lives.

### Emotional State/Moods

The third primary aspect of our own particular way of being—of the particular observer that we each are—is our emotional state. Here, we find our moods and emotions. We find our own particular emotional patterns, emotional habits, and emotional range. Clearly, moods and emotions are tremendously important to us. They have an obvious and dramatic impact on how we live our lives, how we relate to ourselves and others, how we move through the world, and the results we produce for ourselves at home, at work and everywhere else. They have a great deal to do with our experience of living, with the "quality of our journey," regardless of where the journey may take us. They have everything to do with our happiness, our peacefulness, and our productivity.

We all have some commonsense understanding of moods and emotions, what they are and how they impact us. However, I'd like to share with you some alternative interpretations that I've learned. I'd like to offer some distinctions and a slightly different way of understanding moods and emotions, and point to ways in which this new understanding can serve us as we seek to design our lives. First and foremost, human beings are emotional beings. No matter what, you and I and everyone else is always in one mood or another. Apathy is a mood. Whatever mood or emotional state you find yourself in, rest assured—it's not *nothing*. It's *something*. And it's *already* impacting your thoughts, your internal conversations, your way of listening and your capacity to have certain types of conversations.

At a most basic level, *moods and emotions are pre-dispositions for action*. When I'm in a mood of resentment, for example, I'm simply very pre-disposed to get even, undermine, withdraw, or put a negative spin on things... no matter what the event or trigger. And when I'm in a mood of peace or ambition, for example, I'm much more likely to embrace or support... again, no matter what the external event or trigger.

Moods and emotions, tacos and burritos—the exact words we choose to use aren't so important. But in making this distinction with moods and emotions, we say that one of these is short-term and triggered by external events, and one of these is not. *Moods* are viewed as *long-term*, lasting weeks, months or years and are very much in the background. They are *not triggered* by some external event; they come "before" any events. They're *already there* when we interact in the world. They can be viewed as the predominant *predispositions to act* that we tend to find ourselves in *before* we actually take one action or the other. *Emotions*, on the other hand, are viewed as *shorter-term*, lasting moments to hours or days and are *definitely triggered by external events*. They are viewed as *temporary shifts* in our predisposition to act, and they are usually much more visible to ourselves and to others. And after the emotional shift which was triggered fades, we settle back down into whatever our longer-term moods are, our predominant way of being... until another trigger has us go to another emotion, and so on.

With these distinctions, then, we can say that being triggered into the emotion (short-term) of anger, for example, is quite different than living my life in a mood (long-term) of anger. Same with resentment, fear, anxiety, ambition, peace, all of them.

Our emotions and moods are *not separate* from the way we tend to "see things;" rather, they are strongly connected and utterly inter-dependent. We tend to interpret, to judge, to assess, to make up stories, that justify our moods and *make them right*.

Moods have a great deal to do with language, with our thinking, speaking, and listening. And as we know, moods and emotions also have a great deal to do with our physical bodies. In a number of ways, our moods influence our lives and our results. This is not "right" or "wrong." It just is.

And many of us are not very powerful observers of our own moods and the emotional spaces that we tend to live our lives in. Even if we do notice and want to make a change, we often are operating out of stories that are disempowering, grant the mood or emotion a great deal of weight and authority, endow the mood or emotion with qualities that make it appear to be impossible to manage, and ultimately do not take us in the direction of new action.

Are there any new moods that we need to learn, in order to go toward the result we say we want? And how do language and our physical bodies come into play, should we choose to move in this direction?

### Inter-Connection and Congruency of All Three

Let's look at each of us this way: Over the course of living our lives up to this point, we've developed a certain "coherent" combination of these three aspects. Over time, our stories *produce* a certain emotional space, and seem to be much more likely and available *to be produced out* of a certain emotional space. This emotional energy shows up in our bodies, as it impacts (at the outer level) our physical posture and physical conversations and (at the inner level) our immune system, cells, molecules, and other bodily processes. As we know, over time our emotional energy *will* show up physically. It's simply a matter of the type of impact which will occur. All three aspects are connected to each other, reinforcing each other, striving toward consistency with each other. When any one changes or shifts, the others begin the process of either "re-accommodating" to the new story or the new emotional state or the new physical movement or posture (in which case a new way of being emerges, a new observer comes forth)... or the process of "rejecting" the initial change efforts until whatever new story or new emotion or new physical movement is abandoned. In these cases, the "old way" is allowed to continue (in which case nothing has really changed, the same observer is present).

Let's look at some examples, as this congruency or connectedness is important to understand. It is the basis for a new understanding, a new interpretation of who we are. It's also the basis for a new capacity, the capacity to purposefully design how we "be" and who we "are" in the world. As always, try to keep coming back to yourself and how these connections show up for you. Remember, many of us are not very good observers of our own moods and emotions, and we may be even poorer observers of our bodies and how we carry and move them.

If you looked outside and on the sidewalk saw someone walking very slowly, shuffling along with a slumped over body, looking at the ground... what could you say about that person's mood and probably be correct? Most of us would say that such a person is sad, or depressed, certainly not joyful or playful. If you looked outside and saw a person skipping and leaping, what could you say about this person's mood or emotional state and probably be correct? We'd say this person is happy, playful, certainly not despondent or angry, for example. At a commonsense level, we all understand that these connections exist.

You can probably reflect on several instances in which you observed how colleagues or friends walked or sat down, and from that you were able to infer correctly about their mood or emotional state. Salespeople do this; parents do this; kids do this; we all do this. *We know this already*. Have you ever waited for the "right time" to ask a boss or colleague for something? Did you ever wait for the "right time" to ask your parents for something when you were younger? What do we observe to tell us when it may be the "right time?" And why do we do this in the first place?

We observe the conversations, bodies, and physical movements of others to make a connection to their mood. And we do this because we have a sense that as human beings, we're *not permanently open or closed* to ideas. Some days we're more open to certain suggestions, ideas, and possibilities than others. We're all constantly opening and closing possibilities, and this opening and closing is connected to—congruent with—our physical body/movements and to our mood/emotional state.

Even the term "attitude" was derived from physical observations, having to do with the physical angle, pitch, or position of an object in relation to the ground (an aircraft, for example). We've all had the experience, with ourselves and with others, that *attitude shows up in how we carry our physical bodies as well*. It's not just in airplanes. We have an intuitive sense of these connections, even though we may not have used the same words or models to describe them.

Have you ever felt better (mood) after exercise (body)? Most of us report that, yes, we have. But what if you waited until you felt better before going to exercise? Many of us would never get off the couch. When's the last time you danced (body) when you were angry (mood)? Usually those two do not go together. But if you're angry and start dancing and keep it up long enough, one of two interesting things will happen. Either 1) you'll stop dancing or 2) you'll stop being angry! (But the reason, of course, that we don't dance when we're angry is that we're *Right* about being angry!) Similarly, it's very hard to duck-walk, quack loudly, and stay resentful. Resentfulness does not stay in the duck-walking body very well.

*Please note—this is not to say that there's never a time to be angry, or that it's somehow "wrong" to ever be resentful or sad. We are not suggesting that all of us should only walk around in a mood of playfulness and lightness all the time, no matter what is occurring in our lives. That is absolutely not what this is about. What is important here is being better able to observe ourselves and our moods and emotions, and then make assessments about whether or not these moods (long-term) and emotions (short-term) we live in serve us or not. The purpose of this is to show the connections, the congruency, the linkages that exist among the three primary domains of body, mood/emotions and language. It is my purpose to introduce the possibility of more consciously designing one's moods, one's conversations, one's physical body, and one's results by taking advantage of the power inherent in these connections.*

If people in an organization have lots of conversations (language) that can be described as *bitching and back-biting* conversations... does this have anything to do with the mood of that organization? As we've discussed earlier, we say yes, these conversations have everything to do with that mood. Change those conversations, change the mood. Or change the mood some other way, and the conversations change. They're connected, they're congruent with each other.

You can change your mood by walking a different way (such as walking in a faster, more erect way, looking forward and outward... or walking in a slower, shuffling, looking down way). When's the last time you skipped? What mood would a short skip start to move you toward? You can shift your mood by shifting how you sit, how you hold your chest and shoulders, how you breathe. You can be an active designer of your own moodspace by purposefully *moving* your body in different ways, putting your body in different positions, such as in prayer, yoga, meditation and other practices. You can influence your emotions by changing your diet and exercise habits. And out of these shifts, you begin having different conversations with yourself and with others. Our bodies, our emotions, and our language are truly braided together. And so our ability to observe ourselves in *each* of these areas is key.

*From this point moving forward, we have three broad avenues— separate yet woven together—that we can explore, acquire new distinctions within, and use as a new foundation for our own peacefulness and productivity.*

❋ ❋ ❋

Have you ever had the experience of wanting to say No, understanding cognitively and logically that saying No was the best choice in the situation, yet somehow finding yourself unable to say it? How about wanting to stand up to make a certain request or say something, but instead, just sitting in your seat? We can come up with many examples of situations like these. This points again to this linkage, this deep and utterly inseparable connection. To focus solely and only on the language element is truly insufficient for us in real life. In fact, in real life the language element is never "alone." Our speaking and our listening are *always* supported by whatever emotional range is available to us at that time, as well as by our bodies and the particular range of physical movements that we have available to ourselves.

❋ ❋ ❋

One exercise we've done in our workshops is used to give participants a feel for what we've been talking about here. You can do this now, if you'd like, to give yourself the experience of congruency that we've discussed. First, sit in a chair with both feet on the ground, about shoulder width apart. Roll your shoulders forward and slump them over, as you look at the ground between your feet. Your posture should be one of slumped over, head down, looking down. Once you've achieved this position, say the following out loud, with enthusiasm:

- *I am so enthusiastic about tomorrow!*
- *My possibilities in life are fantastic, and I look forward to designing and creating great things!*

Most people in our workshops giggle and laugh immediately upon doing this exercise. We ask them why, and they say it didn't "feel right," that the slumped body didn't "go with" the words we asked them to say. In other words, the language and body were not congruent with each other. What would have been much easier to say, with that slumped over body? Most people say that things like "this stinks" or "when is this going to be over" or "nothing will work." These would have been much easier to say. These would have somehow rolled off our tongues with ease, given that body position.

Next, let's do the opposite. Stand up in a very straight body position, chest out, shoulders back, head up, facing the world this way. Imagine there's a string attached to the top of your head, pulling you straight up. Now smile broadly and say the following, in a loud and confident voice:

- *Nothing I do makes a difference.*
- *I have no options or possibilities. Things are hopeless, no matter what anybody does.*

In our workshops, most people report the same "disconnect" that they reported earlier. The standing-up-straight body simply does not "go with" this language. They are incongruent with each other.

We know this, but we somehow forget. We claim that *each of these three*—our body, our mood/emotional state, and our language—can be a domain of design. That is, we can purposefully invent new *conversations*, knowing that over time they will have the effect of influencing or designing a new mood. We can purposefully do something different with our *body* (walk differently, sit differently, stand differently, dance, meditate, exercise) knowing that, over time, this will produce different interpretations, different conversations, different available moodspaces. We can listen to music or do something else to purposefully change our *moods*, knowing that this will impact our listening, our interpretations, our language, our posture. This model has the advantage of explicitly providing three different domains of design, three different causal elements for use in creating new results in our lives.

Because moods (the way we're defining them) are longer-lasting than emotions, they have a more dramatic and lasting impact on our bodies. Are our bodies impacted by a *lifetime* of living in one mood or another? Does resentment live in our bodies and impact our bodies differently, over time, than does a predominant mood of peace or ambition? We say yes, and we have all seen evidence of this in ourselves and others. Consider the shoulder muscles, neck and facial muscles, back and spine, hips... consider how we walk, how we carry ourselves, how we sit, how we move, how we don't move... consider how *over long periods of time, we physically embody the mood.* We end up carrying it "in our bones."

This is why we say that any attempt to deal with or intervene on our prevailing mood or attitude simply *must include attention to our bodies and our movements* in order to be successful. In fact, we can even start here. But we also cannot forget *the language side*, because it's often the case that our internal narratives and stories—held as the truth—are precisely what we're using to justify our *not* doing any new things with our bodies!

Our experience in workshops is that the great majority of us already know this, we already know about these connections and congruency. For example, consider your relationships with people you say you care about. These can be professional or personal relationships, adults or children. How many of you would say that *if you saw one of these people walking or sitting slumped over, that you'd wish for them that they not do that?* Virtually all of us would. We have a sense that walking or sitting that way is connected to their internal conversations of who and what they are, and who and what they can become. It's connected to a moodspace of sadness or depression or resignation, and we know that this moodspace, over time, tends to close off possibilities and diminish relationships.

Maybe when grandma said "Sit up straight" she was really on to something important. This brings to mind two other claims shared with me by my friends and teachers at Newfield and Education for Living: ***Our bodies are not innocent. The way you stand is the way you stand in the world.***

❋ ❋ ❋

While many of us already know this, and already know at an intuitive level about these connections, most of us haven't taken full advantage of them in designing new *results* into our lives. To do this, we need new distinctions, a new framework based on this new understanding of language, coupled with *practice over time*. Here are a few examples and questions to consider:

- Have you ever noticed how your particular way of walking, standing, and carrying yourself is different from that of others? What differences do you notice? How do you describe your own way? Has it changed over time?

- Can you see how your predominant ways of walking, standing and carrying yourself are connected to your most-prevalent moodspace? To certain recurring internal conversations?

- Consider one important conversation that you say you'd like to have, but for whatever reason have been avoiding. What body would best support that conversation? That is, would you be standing tall, looking the person in the eye... or would you be slumped over, looking downward... or would you be sitting down, or what? Where would you be looking? How would your shoulders and chest be?

- Consider the same conversation as above. What emotion seems to be best for this conversation and most consistent with the body position and body movement you'll need?

- Are there any physical movements or motions that you avoid (dance, yoga, exercises, massage, sitting meditation, walking, riding a bike)? What stories have you created about that? Are these stories still true for you? Do they work for you?

- Are there any physical activities that you really love and participate in frequently? What is the impact of these on your mood? On your conversations?

- Are there any special places where you can take your body (beach, mountains, forest, lake) and produce an emotional shift, and a shift in conversations which are available?

❋ ❋ ❋

Many of us begin new actions, new undertakings with the best intentions. We think about whatever it is—whether it's a new conversation with a difficult employee, or with our spouse, or a presentation in front of a new group, or a big meeting in which we have a new key role—and plan for it and rehearse it over and over in our heads. Two observations:

First, rehearsing something over and over in our heads is NOT the same as actually practicing it! What's missing? Right—the body, the movement, the physical piece. We simply *must* put our bodies into it. (Learning = Time & Practice). This is why actually having the conversation with someone ahead of time or going over the presentation out loud, with a listener present, can make a difference. As can going to the new meeting room and familiarizing yourself with the layout, and so forth.

And secondly, how many of us *don't* practice ahead of time, and then find that our bodies freak out during the moment that we're doing the new thing? This shows up as knees knocking, heart pounding, higher pulse rate, sweaty palms, lump in the throat, tightness in the chest, dry mouth... all sorts of physical changes. Given our 3-circle model, and knowing that all 3 are inter-related, these body reactions really should come as no surprise. While our focus may be on having the conversation (language), we cannot avoid the fact that in order to have the conversation, our bodies—the physical side—will have a central role.

It's not a problem, in and of itself, that our bodies do what they do. This is simply the *event* that occurs. As we've talked about before, it's our *explanations* that really matter. Here's the key: *How do we interpret all these physical actions?* As I see it, there are at least *two primary ways of interpreting* our bodily reactions. Notice how different these interpretations are, as well as the *different future actions* (and therefore different future results) that are likely to arise from them:

- Interpretation 1: My body is doing this because I'm trying to do something I really shouldn't do. This is my body's way of saying run away, this is not for me, it's a bad situation and I made a big mistake by ever wanting to do this... and

- Interpretation 2: My body is doing this because it has little or no practice in this conversation or in this situation. This is my body's way of telling me that I'm a beginner here, and that more practice is needed for me to gain competence and confidence here.

We keep coming back to language, to conversations, and to interpretations—no matter what. And the invitation here is to always see our ability to invent and have new, more powerful conversations as *fully entwined* with our physical and emotional sides, at a number of levels. We can separate these 3 for convenience, to allow us to speak about one and not the other and to create some distinctions that can help us design new results for ourselves. But in the end, it is an artificial separation. In the end, we are always dealing with the unique blend, the ever-changing combination, that makes each of us the unique person—the unique observer—that we are.

**Footnotes:**

1. *The Tree of Knowledge*, by Humberto Maturana, Francisco J. Varela and Robert Paolucci; Shambhala Publications;1987.

2. *Coaching to the Human Soul: Ontological Coaching and Deep Change*, by Alan Seiler; Newfield Australia; 2003.

## SUMMARY—MAIN POINTS AND
## NEW INTERPRETATIONS

---

- *Language does not occur in a vacuum.* We cannot even talk about language without bringing 2 additional domains into the equation.

- We are each unique observers. We each interpret and "see things" in our own unique way. However, *the observer that we each are is composed of three separate yet tightly inter-woven elements:*
  - ➢ Our language (internal and external conversations)
  - ➢ Our moods and emotions
  - ➢ Our bodies, biology and physical movements.

- These 3 aspects are *dynamic and ever-changing.* They are *not* fixed and permanent. Each of these 3 impacts the other 2. Changes in our mood impact our language and our bodies. Changes in our conversations produce changes in our moods/emotions, as well as changes to our bodies and how we move. Doing different things physically has an impact on our language as well as our emotional state.

- *Each of these 3 can be our starting point* for bringing changes to our lives. We can take advantage of the power inherent in these connections. *We can purposefully make changes* in 1 area, knowing that the other 2 will be influenced as well. In this way, we can actively design ourselves.

## HOW-TO: POSSIBILITIES FOR
## TAKING NEW ACTION

- Big Eye: *What would you say is your predominant (long-term) mood?* That is, generally speaking, what type of moodspace do *you* say you're usually in? What type of moodspace do *others* say you're usually in?

- Big Eye: *How is the way that you carry yourself physically*–how you walk, sit, stand, interact physically, move yourself–consistent with your predominant moods?

- Big Eye*: Identify experiences you've had* in which shifts in your <u>mood</u> or <u>body</u> or <u>language</u> had an impact and influence on the other two.

- *Stand with your "normal" posture in front of a mirror. What do you notice* about how you stand and how you carry yourself? Look at your shoulders, your neck, and your back. Notice your chest and your head and your arms, how they are normally held. *Can you think of specific ways in which your normal posture reflects your "normal" mood and your "normal" conversations?* Write these down.

- *Assume a body position of standing slightly more erect than whatever is normal for you,* one in which your shoulders are slightly further back and your chest slightly further out than normal. Make sure your neck and head are a bit more erect than usual, eyes facing forward and outward. What do you notice? Try practicing this posture for a week, noticing yourself as you walk and sit and interact.

- *If you practice this* for a week, what do you notice? *If you do not do this practice*, notice what stopped you. Refer to BARRIERS TO LEARNING.

- *What do you say about your historical nutrition and exercise practices?* Do they support you or not? What would be required in order for you to move into learning in this area?

- Find music that you love, music that moves and inspires you. *Play it more often than normal.*

# *Chapter 7*

## WE SPEAK OURSELVES INTO THE WORLD

---

*"He who loves wisdom must investigate many things."* [1]

Heraclitus (540BC–480BC)

---

In the previous chapter we shared a model in which language (speaking and listening, internal and external conversations) is seen as being not in a vacuum, but instead is seen as being fully inter-related and connected to our emotional space and physical body/biology. And at the beginning of the book we made a big claim—that our language has to do with *Action*, with *coordination of action,* with *creating* and *generating* (vs. merely communicating with others about how things are). This is the broad new interpretation upon which everything else I'm sharing with you rests.

In this chapter, we go from this broad interpretation of language toward the *specific actions* that we say we're involved in with our language. That is, if language is action (as we say it is), then *what exactly are the actions we take?*

Remember our conversation about the power of distinctions? *These are distinctions in language,* which represent new possibilities for taking

153

action and producing results in the world. Building directly on the work done by John Searle [2] and J. L. Austin [3], and especially Fernando Flores, we offer that no matter what, when human beings are speaking, this is the "universe set" of possibilities for speech acts:

1. Assertions
2. Assessments (a special type of declaration)
3. Declarations
4. Requests
5. Offers
6. Promises

Every conversation among human beings involves one or more of these. Said another way, in this interpretation, all human speech is either a declaration, an assessment, an assertion, a request, an offer, or a promise. Everything that we do with our language falls within one of these categories.

In this way of thinking, every conversation—private and public—you have ever had was full of these and only these. And every conversation you ever *will* have will be full of these and only these. We claim that what's needed for those of us looking to produce new results in our lives is to gain competence in these speech acts. These are what we call *distinctions in the domain of language* that—like the forester in forestry, the auto mechanic with car motors, and the wine connoisseur with wine— allow us to see possibilities, take purposeful action, and produce desired results in a given domain. However, in this case, the domain is huge. The domain is far bigger than forestry, auto mechanics, or wine. *The domain is language*, and we claim that it encompasses virtually every aspect of our lives. New distinctions in this domain bring the possibility of seeing ourselves and others anew, and literally redesigning who we are in the world. Conversely, having no distinctions here often leads to actions which many of us would say are not desirable and do not bring happiness or desired results.

These 6 distinctions are the actual vehicles, the actual mechanisms that we use as we do *whatever* it is that we do. What's needed are awareness, understanding, time, and practice. So let's take a look.

**Footnotes:**

---

1. *Diogenes Laertius: Lives of Eminent Philosophers*, by Diogenes et. al.;Harvard University Press; 1938.

2. *Expression and Meaning, by John Searle;* Cambridge University Press; 1985.

3. *Linking Language to Action*, by J.L. Austin; Cambridge University Press; 1962.

# Chapter 7

## SECTION 1.

## ASSERTIONS AND ASSESSMENTS

---

*"Assertions have to do with what is so. Assessments have to do with what is possible."*

Julio Olalla

---

Let's begin this way, with two statements:

### *I am a man.    I am stupid.*

Our key question is: *What's the difference between these 2 statements?*
(Women usually come up with different responses than men here!) Let's
add a few more examples. Please examine all the statements in the **left**
column below. What do we traditionally call these sorts of statements? In
our everyday speech, what do we call these?

| | |
|---|---|
| *I am a man.* | I am stupid. |
| *Bubba is the CEO of AA Corp.* | Bubba is a strong CEO and good leader. |
| *The book weighs 8 pounds.* | The book is heavy. |
| *Ann is 5'11".* | Ann is tall. |
| *It's 68 degrees outside, with no clouds.* | The weather today is great. |

Most of us would say that we usually call the statements in the left column "facts" or something to this effect. I agree, and would like to introduce a new distinction which can be understood as being very close to our traditional understanding of facts. We say that every statement in the left column is an *assertion*. This is one of the new distinctions to be brought forth in this section.

With assertions, the speaker is committed to establishing what is "true" and what is "false"—for him/herself as well as for the community of listeners. Assertions can also be seen as the so-called facts of life. They are where language is *most descriptive and least generative.* Let's look now at the **right** column below. What do we usually call these types of statements?

| | |
|---|---|
| I am a man. | *I am stupid.* |
| Bubba is the CEO of AA Corp. | *Bubba is a strong CEO and good leader.* |
| The book weighs 8 pounds. | *The book is heavy.* |
| Ann is 5'11". | *Ann is tall.* |
| It's 68 degrees outside, with no clouds. | *The weather today is great.* |

Most of us call the right column statements "opinions" or "judgments" or "subjective" statements. I agree, and offer the distinction of *assessment*. This is the other new distinction which will be brought forth in this section.

We say an assessment is a speech act in which the speaker defines how he or she relates to the world or to a specific event. With assessments, it's "good" or "bad" or "right" or "wrong" or "tall" or "short," etc. Here, the speaker is committed to *taking a stand* on what he/she observes, coming to some opinion or choice or *judgment* about what is being observed.

**As non-hermits, our ability to keep <u>assertions</u> and <u>assessments</u> separate, distinct from each other is critical.** Absolutely critical. In many ways our language traps us here, because it appears that the statement "Bubba is six feet five inches" is the same sort of statement as "Bubba is tall." In our traditional understanding, it appears that 'six feet five inches' and 'tall' are both properties of Bubba. We say no! But our collapsing together of these very different types of statements has consequences on the actions we take, the types of relationships we form, and on the results we produce. Let's explore a bit here. While assertions are close to what we traditionally call "facts," and while assessments are close to what we traditionally call "opinions," there are key differences worth exploring.

Some examples of assertions and assessments: *The room is 65' by 98.'* Assertion or assessment? It's an assertion. It's either true or false that the room is 65 x 98. Any objective third party with a tape measure could prove the true-ness or false-ness of this statement. Let's say in this case that it's a true assertion, that the room indeed is 65 x 98.

How about this statement. *The room is 1,000,000' by 2,000,000.'* Assertion or assessment? In this case, it's still an assertion, but it's false. The objective third party with the tape measure does his thing, and guess what—the room is NOT 1 million feet by 2 million feet.

Assertions can be true or false and can be verified by an objective third party who has the distinctions involved. We already have the distinctions "feet" and "inches," so it's possible for us to prove whether or not the room is indeed 65 by 98.

For example, in order to say whether or not it's true that the computer's combobulator has been degaussed and requires an upgraded fuse pack, the third party would have to already possess the distinctions combobulator, degauss, and fuse pack. Armed with the appropriate distinctions, one could then say whether or not the assertion is true. Without the distinctions, one could not verify the true-ness or false-ness of the statement. As Jeff Spring has said, without the distinctions, all I may be able to do in these sorts of situations is ask, "How does that translate into dollars?"

How about these statements: *The room is spacious.* Or *The room is cramped.* Assertions or assessments? These are assessments. Opinions.

Judgments. And what if I also said, "All right, let's get to the truth here. I want the bottom line. Is the room really spacious or is it really cramped? What's the final truth about this?" Some people may respond immediately with, "The room is cramped" while others may just as quickly say, "Well, anybody can see that this room is spacious." And others may say "It depends." *This is a key point—we say that the **room doesn't have a property, in and of itself, of spaciousness or crampedness.*** The room just is. All it has are its assertions. Spacious and cramped are not properties of the room. Whether or not the room is spacious or the room is cramped has everything to do with *who's doing the looking.*

So while assertions belong to the thing being observed (in this case, the room), we say that assessments *belong to the observer.* And this is a fundamental, crucial difference. It makes a huge difference in how we build relationships, work and be together, solve problems, gauge progress and interact, at a multitude of levels.

We could go on and on with examples. "The car is sporty." "The car is boxy." Well, which is it? Is the car really sporty or is it really boxy? We say the car doesn't have a property, in and of itself, of sportiness or boxiness. The car just is. I say it's sporty, while Mr. Ferrari may say it's boxy. Again, these are assessments. They belong to the observer, not to the thing being observed.

How many of us know people who act as if their assessments (personal opinions, judgments) are assertions (facts)? Many of us do—this is a common phenomenon. No surprise here, given our traditional understanding and education in this area. Our observation is that many people who live as if their assessments are assertions have difficulty in forming healthy, mutually respectful relationships with the other non-hermits in their lives. They come across as self-righteous, opinionated, stubborn, arrogant. Said another way, their actions in language *generate this public identity* for themselves, and usually this public identity is not what they're trying to create. **Our first key point involving these distinctions is this:**

- *Assertions belong to the thing being observed and can be true or false.* An objective third party can always verify the true-ness or false-ness of the assertion.

- *Assessments belong to the observer, and in many ways reveal more about the observer than they do about the thing being observed.* There is always room for another assessment. No third party may ever "prove" an assessment true or false. They are simply personal judgments made by different observers out of different standards, beliefs, moods, and experiences.

❋ ❋ ❋

Let's also notice this—we assess everything! We assess people, plants, buildings, shoes, jobs, weather, movies, traffic, everything. We seem to be assessment machines, producing assessments at every turn. This *isn't good or bad,* it's simply part of living in language. But since we produce such volumes of assessments, our claim is that we can develop some *competency* here, we can become more capable of making solid assessments and therefore move *into the future in a more grounded way,* providing us our best chance for producing the future results we say we want. **This brings us to a second major point about assertions and assessments:**

- *Assertions are descriptive and "factual" and have to do with the past and the present.*
- *Assessments have everything to do with the future,* and can be viewed as "stepping stones" toward the future.

Let's explore more here, because it's this *future* impact of assessments that is often unseen and is at the heart of many of our issues. Example: *Bubba missed three meetings in a row in October.* This is an *assertion,* and it can be proven true or false. Let's say in this case it's true. If a camera was in the meeting room, it would not have seen Bubba at those three meetings. Can you get a sense that this statement just sits there; it's a statement of something that already happened and it's describing that situation. It has no particular emotional flavor.

How about this: *Bubba is unreliable.* This is an *assessment,* and can you now feel it swing toward a prediction of Bubba's future behavior? I am now "orienting" myself toward Bubba in a certain way. For example, if I have the assessment in the present that Bubba is unreliable, and in the future he becomes available for selection to my team, guess who I don't select... Bubba. Why? Because of my assessment that he's unreliable. My assessment of him in the *present* served to influence my *behavior* towards him (in this case, that of not choosing him) in the *future.*

Is it possible that Bubba could have missed the same three meetings (same assertions) but I could have instead assessed him as reliable? Yes, of course this is possible. In this case, my assessment of *reliable* would orient me in such a way that in the future, I may choose Bubba for my team. Our key point here is that regardless of whether the assessments may be "positive" or "negative," they all serve to *influence our interpretations and actions* in the future. Sometimes the influence is minor and insignificant, and sometimes the influence is huge and is at the heart of everything.

Back to the first assessment of *unreliable*. Key question—when did Bubba go from being "reliable" to "unreliable?" Was it when he missed the first meeting, or was it the 3 in a row that did it? Or was it 2 in a row in a one-month period? *What are my standards for reliability?* If you miss 1 meeting do I assess you as unreliable? Or is it 3 in a month? Or 6 in a year? What is it? This has to do with what we call *standards*. The reason different people have different assessments about the same event or situation is that different people have different standards. The real problem is not that we have different standards, of course. The problem is that they are often hidden and unspoken. Conversations for the purpose of sharing standards are extremely important and powerful conversations to have, for personal as well as professional relationships. And these are precisely the conversations which are often missing.

What is my standard for "effective?" For "appropriate?" For "efficient?" For being a "good" husband? For "laziness?" And have I shared my standards with my wife? With my colleagues? With my boss? With my subordinates? Can you begin to see that we often make many assessments about many things, influencing our future interpretations all the while, while not having any declared standards and not being aware that this is happening. (Standards live as declarations, a very powerful and generative speech act. We'll cover declarations in our next section.)

To continue, if I assess Bubba as unreliable, what actions from him will I readily see in the future? What will I absolutely notice about him? *I'll notice every single time he's late, no matter what the reason.* Make sense? And guess which actions of his I'll miss or write off as an exception or aberration... you got it—Bubba being on time.

One reason for this may go back to the background conversation of "I'm Right." I want to be right about my beliefs (in this case, that Bubba is unreliable) and so this influences how I interpret things that haven't yet

162

happened. We tend to interpret so as to make ourselves and our beliefs right.

❈ ❈ ❈

Consider this scenario. Two 3$^{rd}$ grade teachers, Ms. Smith and Ms. Jones, are pulled aside by the principal before the beginning of the school year. The principal says "Ms. Smith, you've got the most seniority here and have been named Teacher of the Year. Congratulations—you're getting a special Honors class this semester. We've taken the top 5% of students from the other classes and combined them into our first ever Honors class. Have a great year. I know it'll be exciting, challenging, and fun for you and for these excellent students."

The principal then turns to Ms. Jones and says "Ms. Jones, on the other hand, you have the least seniority at our school and we've decided to do another pilot. In this case, we've decided to pull out some of the lower-performing and behavior-problem students from the regular student body and combine them in a remedial class. We're tired of this small minority of students disrupting and slowing down the general population, so we've decided to create classes just for them, kind of "out of the way," and see what happens to the other classes without their influence. Now I know you didn't sign up for this, but this is all we've got for you this semester. Do the best you can, and we'll try to get you a regular class next semester."

Get the picture? Now, in reality, *both teachers get regular classes.* Both are assigned *normal, randomly selected* groups of 3$^{rd}$ graders, just like always. Make a prediction—what do you think happens, in Ms. Smith's class and Ms. Jones' class, over the course of the semester? You guessed it—Ms. Smith's class *are* the honors kids. Ms. Jones' kids *are* the poor students and behavior problems. And they have evidence to prove it:

In the "honors" class, little Susie's standing on her desk, flapping her arms is viewed as a glorious display of spontaneous creativity... while little Ann's doing the same thing in the "remedial" class is seen as disruptive behavior. In the "honors" class, if a student fails a test, it's "oh, little Johnny failed a test... wait, 3 more kids failed... to have 4 honors students fail may mean that I need to do something different with the pre-requisites or with how this topic is structured in the material...". On the other hand, if little Johnny and 3 other kids fail a test in the "remedial" class it's

163

"Look, I knew you weren't gonna pass it anyway, we've gotta move on, open your books to the next topic."

We claim that it's not the kids' behavior alone that influences the teachers' experience. Rather, it's that behavior occurring against the already-held assessments that produces the particular interpretations. For us, this is the mechanism underneath what we commonly call the "self-fulfilling prophecy."

Maybe it's not so much *"I'll believe it when I see it."* Maybe, in real life, in a wide variety of situations, what is actually more prevalent is *"I'll see it when I believe it."* And this takes us back to the whole topic of beliefs. The great majority of all our beliefs are assessments, not assertions. They belong to us, as observers, and do not have so much to do with how things really are.

We say that our assessments say more about *the observer* than they do about *what's being observed.* Consider these examples: One teacher says little Johnny is stupid. The other says little Johnny is rambunctious. I listen, and still don't know very much about little Johnny. However, two teachers have just now revealed themselves, shown themselves, to me. One teacher may teach my child, the other I will not let near my child. My partner and I are driving along and I look out the window and say "Look at that huge mountain." He looks out and says "Where?" "Right over there" I reply. "I still can't see it... oh, you mean that little hill!" Obviously, what's a huge mountain to me is a hill to Mark. I grew up in south Louisiana, and so to me, anything over the height of an overpass is a mountain. We aren't describing the landscape as much as we are revealing ourselves and our standards (which are often hidden and unspoken).

A woman in a workshop relayed a story to us about her return from a visit to Hong Kong. This woman was about 5'4" tall, and she returned and announced jubilantly to her friends "I'm not short—I'm medium!" What had happened? Had she actually grown during the trip? Of course not. She was with a group of people, over a period of time, who simply had different standards for tallness and shortness. Again, with assessments, we reveal ourselves more than we describe.

This points to the *social nature* or *social influence* of assessments. When I make an assessment, it's true that I'm making it as an individual human being. What's not so obvious is the impact of where, when, and how I was born and raised and live have on the standards and assessments I make. Many of "my" standards are actually the standards of my community. I simply picked them up as I went, never consciously or actively declaring them myself. We personally didn't get to choose these standards. They were part of the history of our community when we arrived, and we simply adopted them as our own. And they continue to influence us today.

Let's also notice that assessments are *historical*. That is, the standards with which we make assessments change over time. This becomes very apparent in the world of sports, where a 4-minute mile used to be "world-class" or "excellent," and now runners routinely post times in that range. Or the records in many sprints, pole vaulting, throwing and jumping events. Or what's now considered "very big" or "really strong" for NFL linemen or NBA centers. Consider also fashion, where what's "in" or "pretty" or "trendy" obviously has a great deal to do with when the assessment is made. We could go on and on. The underlying standards change over time, so therefore the *assessments* that are produced *change over time*.

❋ ❋ ❋

The story about the 2 teachers shows how our assessments of *others* impact our interpretations and interactions, which strongly influence our relationships and results. And back to the big eye, this often occurs without our noticing that this is happening. We also say that our assessments about *ourselves* have the same power. Consider the following story.

Little Johnny's in the 2nd grade and is restless at school, doodling during math and generally being distracted and not involved in the lesson. His teacher comes up and sees the doodles he's drawn and says "Little Johnny, how could you do something so stupid? You know we're supposed to be doing our lesson. Go the principal's office." Little Johnny goes home that day and wants to play with his big sister. He goes into her room and accidentally knocks off the CD player, which falls to the floor and breaks. She says, "Johnny, look what you did, you can be so stupid. Play somewhere else." He goes downstairs and wants to help his mom so he goes into the kitchen and starts helping her dry the dishes. He drops one on the floor and it breaks. Mom's had a long day and is tired, and she says "Johnny, that is so stupid. Just go in the other room, I'll finish by myself."

This goes on for a few years, and now Little Johnny's in the 10th grade. The teacher puts a problem on the board and says, "Class, this problem is in a new area and is a tough one. Who can try to answer it?" Key question:

Does Little Johnny raise his hand? No. Why not? Most people answer with "because he's stupid." More correctly, he sees himself as stupid. He assesses himself as stupid, but doesn't see it as an assessment. He sees it as the Truth, as a fact, as the way things are. Flash forward to when Johnny's 25 years old and working, and a promotion to supervisor position becomes available. The manager says they're going to promote from within, and anyone wishing to apply should have their application on his desk by Tuesday. Does Johnny apply? No. Why? Because (he tells himself) he's stupid. Again, more accurately, he's holding the assessment—the belief—about himself that he's stupid, and he doesn't see it as an assessment. He sees it as a fact.

This is a clear case of someone living as if an assessment (stupid) is an assertion. We say that there's no such "thing" as stupid. Stupid isn't a thing, it's an assessment. Show me stupid. Where is it? It's not as if right behind my spleen is my stupid. You got 1 pound of it, Bob got 4 pounds, and I'm out of luck because I happened to get 10 pounds of stupid. But Johnny lived as if the assessments others made about him were actually the Truth about him. He lived as if his own assessments about himself were actually the Truth about him. In both cases we claim nothing is further from the truth. Stupid is not a permanent, fixed feature or objective characteristic of Johnny's personhood. Stupid is an assessment, made first by others and then by himself, about his actions or lack of actions in a given domain. Change the actions, change the standards, and the assessments will change. They're not permanent, fixed, facts or features of his personhood. They're assessments, always open to revision and updating.

Of course, Little Johnny didn't interpret this way when his teacher, sister, and mom said those things to him. His interpretation was "I'm stupid." And this is consistent with how a great many children and adults interpret. When I was first introduced to this, I remember thinking about how important the words we say to our kids are. I still think about this as I'm parenting my own children now.

❊ ❊ ❊

**Let's move now into our next key point about assertions and assessments:**

- *Assertions* are not influenced by moods and emotions.
- *Assessments* are greatly influenced by moods and emotions.

I may report that it's 68 degrees, no clouds, and 20 percent humidity no matter what mood I'm in. But you'll never hear me say "it's a great day" unless *I'm* in a good mood!

Recalling our three circles drawing, we see the connection between mood/emotion, body, and language. Here we can clearly see the *connection between moods and language*. This connection shows up strongly, precisely in the *assessments* we produce. Reflect a moment. It's easy to recall situations when the assessments we came up with about a given event or situation were connected to the mood we happened to be in at that time. We already know this, though sometimes we don't see it so clearly. If I happen to be in a moodspace of happiness (let's say my daughter just found out she got a perfect score on a difficult test), I will absolutely react to an event—let's say a flat tire—differently than if I was already in a mood of resentment or "overwhelm" when the flat occurred. I will also react to—interpret—conversations differently. We can all point to numerous situations in which this has occurred.

We can also see the connection, starting with observing a person's assessments and working the other way. For example, imagine you're with a person over a long period of time, and this person consistently produces assessments of "that won't work" or "no, I'm sure that's not going to work out well" or "nothing will make a difference in that." What mood would you say this person lives in and probably be correct? Most of us would call it pessimism or resignation, certainly not joy or elation. The connection between moods and language shows up very strongly, very clearly, in our assessments.

You want to know something about your mood? Take a look at your assessments. You want to consciously design a different mood? Take a look at your assessments—particularly your competency to ground your assessments (which we'll cover shortly) with true assertions, as well as the way you declare standards for observing that are shared with others. For example, if I'm in a mood of resignation I may have lots of assessments that "this won't work." What's possible is to have a conversation with someone in which I share my assessments, as well as the grounds for making the assessment and the standards from which I'm observing.

✳ ✳ ✳

We often *"borrow" others' assessments* about people that we've never even met. For example, let's say that at work I know Bob but don't know the newest employee named Bubba. One day, Bob may say to me "You know, Bubba is a good employee and all that, but he's kinda lazy and seems to be pretty arrogant about how he does his reporting." A few days go by and in the hall I see Bob and another man walking toward me. As we approach, Bob says "Chalmers, I'd like to introduce you to our newest employee, Bubba." What's the first thing that goes through my mind? "Oh, here's lazy and arrogant Bubba." And often, once I get to know Bubba, I have very different assessments of him. He's not lazy or arrogant to me—I may have very different standards than Bob does. Or Bob may not be a competent observer of Bubba. But it doesn't matter—we do it anyway.

We've worked with school systems quite a bit over the last few years, and we see this phenomenon also with kids. Third grade teacher Ms. Smith may say to fourth grade teacher Ms. Jones, "Oh, I see you're gonna get Little Johnny next year. You better buckle up—he's a real troublemaker." Now, to a certain degree we can all understand the reasonableness of sharing information. But the key point to observe here is that it's very possible to do this without being conscious of the influence it has on how we interpret, form beliefs, and take action.

One gentleman at a workshop shared this story with us. He was the incoming manager to an office of about 40 people or so. The outgoing manager offered to take him to lunch to "let him know exactly what he was inheriting." The incoming manager politely declined, saying he'd like to get to know the employees in his own way. In this way everyone would have a "clean slate" to start with.

❊ ❊ ❊

Let's say I'm walking down the street in a new city, and someone passes me and says "ugly tie!" and I hurl myself into the gutter, devastated. This is an example of my granting to the universe the *authority to assess me* in the domain of my clothes. On the other extreme is giving *nobody* the authority to assess me, in any domain. This shows up as a profound predisposition to not let anyone else give me their authentic experience of me, to share their assessments about me with me. This, in turn, robs me of information that could be very valuable for me to have, for with it, I could then choose to take different actions and design a different result or public identity. Or not. But either way, I'd get to choose. I'd not be blind anymore.

My wife could say "I think you were rude to Ms. Jones at the party" and I may say "I wasn't rude–she bumped right into me." Or a colleague may say "You know, I think how you steered that meeting wasn't exactly what we were looking for" and I may respond with "Well it certainly wasn't my fault. I stuck to the agenda and everybody else just got distracted." We could go on and on. Here are 2 important questions for all of us:

- Who do you give the authority (permission) to assess you?
- And in what domains?

These are powerful questions to reflect upon, because the answers don't have to have an "all or nothing" flavor. I heard somewhere that one component of wisdom had to do with who you choose to listen to about specific aspects of your life. I agree with that. And let's be clear–in some organizational settings, others *do* have the authority to assess you whether or not you like it or think it's fair or right or whatever. Consider the army. The drill sergeant absolutely has the authority to assess the private in the domain of his/her clothing, manner of walking, talking, in a great many areas. But passers-by on the street do not. In many organizations, bosses do have the authority to assess subordinates' performance, and a variety of approaches are in use today (some absolutely more effective than others). But that same boss may not have the authority to assess the subordinate in the domain of his/her hobby, woodworking.

Another example–I give you full permission to assess me in the domain of this book. I'm a first-time author, and I have a great deal yet to learn about writing. So your feedback about the content, context, flow, value, connections from topic to topic, and so on are very valuable to me. I request your assessments here, and I value them. And with all respect, I do not give you the authority to assess me in the domain of my yard. You may drive by my house, have lots and lots of assessments about my landscaping and lawn, and it's incredible how much I just don't care what those are! And let's be clear–I'm not saying that you won't have assessments in this area. You may have them, I just won't care what they are.

**Do you want to know something about yourself? Ask someone else.** Do you have anybody in your life who will give you the "straight poop" about your actions? That is, someone who–with your permission– gives you the benefit of their best thinking–they give you their actual assessments. This means they won't withhold the assessments, even if they predict that you won't like what you hear. I say it's a great thing to have a relationship that includes those sorts of conversations. I believe it's a real blessing to have a relationship in which others are *truth-ful* with you, though this doesn't mean that they have the *Truth* about you. In this way you get to design your own public identity.

For example, I may have requested that 3 people give me feedback about my performance in a meeting, or during a family/group situation. They may each be totally honest with me, and yet at the same time, each provide me with a different assessment, a different perspective, about my behavior. One may have seen me as very assertive, another may have seen me as arrogant, and the third may have seen me as confident and knowledgeable. Each is being truthful, fully honest with him/herself. The key, of course, is that each is coming from his or her own set of standards, beliefs, experiences, moods, and so on.

If *1* person I trust reports that I appear rude, that's one thing. However, if *7 out of 10* report this, that's quite another. As related to feedback about how we're showing up, we say that:

### Assessments are never the truth, but they may be useful.

Does this make sense? In this setting, these assessments are extremely valuable in allowing each of us to create a more powerful public identity, and out of that, healthier and more mutually beneficial relationships. They're valuable because they represent valid information about how I'm being perceived, about how I'm showing up. They're valuable because they give me information I can then use in making a choice—with both eyes open—about the actions I will take in the future. They aren't the Truth about my personhood, they aren't permanent and built-in features of my being, but they nevertheless may be very valuable to me, as a non-hermit.

The example above pointed to the *usefulness* of others' assessments. Without awareness, however, of the notion of *permission to assess* and *assessments in certain domains,* we can also see how assessments made by others can trap us and limit our possibilities. For example, in personal situations we often give those closest to us great permission and latitude in assessing us, *even in domains in which they may not be competent to do so.* Think about it. Many of us can point to cases in which adults are still driven to the point of unhappiness by the assessments of their parents. Or when parents are extremely triggered and driven by the assessments of their children. Or spouses with each other. I've heard it put this way, describing this tendency to grant those close to us tremendous permission to assess us: *"I love you and I give you permission to define who I am."*

Our claim is that we can all be more conscious here, more deliberate in who we give permission to assess us and in which domains. The reward for doing so, I believe, is more peace and less resentment in our lives.

※ ※ ※

Have you noticed that we tend to assess others based on their *behavior*, but tend to assess ourselves based on our *intentions?* I don't have access to your intentions or concerns, all I see are your actions in the world. And these are what I use as the basis for my assessments. On the other hand, I know my own intentions and concerns I'm trying to address. Even in cases in which my actions produce upset or negative consequences, I may continue to use these intentions as the basis for assessing myself. Others around me, of course, don't have access to these and so they simply assess me based on my actions. It's possible that we can generate very different assessments out of the same situation. And without sharing our standards and having a conversation, it's also possible that this phenomenon can repeat itself and serve to damage our relationships and our results.

※ ※ ※

Socially (for us non-hermits), certain expectations also arise when we make assertions and assessments. When we make *assertions*, it is expected that

1.  The assertion is *true*, and

2.  We can and will provide *evidence* to support what we say, if asked.

Language generates and creates, not just describes. Make a bunch of false assertions and over time, you will absolutely generate a public identity for yourself of "liar." Consistently fail to provide evidence to back up the assertions you make, same thing.

While assertions can be *true or false*, assessments can be *grounded or ungrounded.* That is, assessments can be consciously connected to facts, behaviors, and standards or not. When we make *assessments* (and we make lots of them), it is socially expected that we have some grounds for making the assessment; that it's not just coming out of thin air. Consider: how do you assess people who seem to always come up with opinions or judgments that appear to have no basis in fact? (What we'll call ungrounded assessments). Most of us assess these people as "flaky" or "out of it" or "odd," not very powerful public identities to have. And if we find that someone is making lots of public assessments and doesn't have any grounding for them, we begin to think differently and relate differently to that person.

So let's talk about *grounding our assessments.* Whether or not we're able to ground our assessments has an impact on our public identity, as we discussed above, and also on how well we're able to move into the future and produce what we want to produce. Grounding assessments is a very valuable practice to develop, as assessments show up in virtually every area of our lives. And let's repeat—we make tons of assessments and assessments are not bad. We assess and we must assess, in order to navigate and move through the world. Who to marry, who to avoid... when to make the business deal, when to postpone... what to eat and what to purchase... when to cross the street, when to stay put... we are assessment machines.

So given this, and the influence our assessments have on our future, we say that *developing some competency in making grounded assessments* is very helpful and valuable. Since we're making assessments *anyway*, and since they're carrying us into the future *anyway*, let's at least do the best we can to connect our assessments to facts. To make an assessment grounded, follow the following steps:

1. **Clarify for yourself "why" you're making the assessment in the first place.** *For the sake of what* **am I making this assessment?** Usually it's for the sake of some possible future or interaction. If you can't come up with a "why," then the assessment you're making is probably purely "recreational" and can't be grounded. This is not to say that we won't or don't or shouldn't have recreational assessments; only that they're inherently ungroundable.

2. **Clarify for yourself the standards that you're using to assess.** If you say someone is "reliable," then what are your standards of "reliability" against which you're judging this person? What are your standards for "good" or "excellent" or "rightness" or "laziness" or

172

"timeliness" or "high quality" or "supportive" or "risky" or whatever? This step requires that we at least notice whether or not we have consciously set standards in these areas.

3.  **Purposefully come up with actions or events (assertions) that you can point to that support your assessment.** In other words, what are the actual behaviors, actions, or facts that you've observed and compared against your standards in order to come up with the assessment you've got? Do you have any firsthand information, or are you trusting other observers' reporting of observable facts? Note—be careful of the tendency to try to use other assessments to ground the first assessment. (For example, you can't ground your assessment that I'm unreliable by then assessing me as sloppy—those are both assessments, not an assertion in sight).

4.  **Purposefully try to come up with actions or events (assertions) that point to the *opposite* assessment.** Even though you may assess a person as "unreliable," are there any situations or behaviors or actions or events in which he or she has been "reliable?" Is it possible to find observable facts that seem to point in the *opposite* direction of the assessment you've got? If so, what does this mean?

5.  **Ground the assessment with other people—share your assessment with others,** especially the way in which you've gone from observation to assessment. Note—this is not about trying to get others to agree with you. Maintain a mode of openness and inquiry in this conversation, as this can be one way to build trust and lay a foundation for solid relationships. It can also be an excellent source of feedback about the effectiveness and consequences of using our current standards.

❉ ❉ ❉

Remember what happens when we practice—well, we claim that we *develop habitual ways of making assessments,* and over time we get very competent in assessing in that manner. We settle into moods, and these moods influence and shape the types of assessments we make. There's nothing wrong with this, of course. But back to the big eye, let's just be aware that this is happening so we can be at choice about the assessments we produce, and the results that are being influenced out of that.

But just because you and I come up with the same assessment, and can ground it, that doesn't make it "right" or the "Truth". And even if you and I and 1000 others come up with the same grounded assessment, that wouldn't make it "right" or the "Truth," either. All we could say in that case is that you and I and the 1000 others are observing from a very similar set of standards. We simply "see things" in the same way. We can simply say that in this case, all the *observers are similar* to each other. We can't and don't say that our similar or identical assessments mean we have access to the "Truth" or "the way things really are."

❊ ❊ ❊

Most of us very quickly assess people when we see them and meet them. We are judging people very quickly, in many situations, personal and business-related. And to navigate successfully in the world, we must assess, to be sure. *But if I'm busy judging you all the time, I miss you.* I truly miss what you have to offer if I'm always busy producing assessment after assessment about you. I truly miss what others have to offer if I'm constantly and quickly making assessments about them and about everything else. Maybe one benefit of noticing this tendency is to allow us to simply begin to *reduce the number of "recreational assessments"* that we make. Or, at minimum, to slow down our assessment-producing mechanisms, to not be so quick in creating judgments (especially recreational ones). It's been my experience, and the experience of many others, that some measure of peace can be achieved in this way.

Should you choose to move in this direction, basic action steps will be:

1. Notice when you "automatically" generate a recreational assessment about someone or something (big eye). The recreational assessment will usually be in the form of a spontaneous internal conversation, one that seems to just happen on its own. Many of these also seem to have a "negative" flavor about them.

2. Don't beat yourself up; just notice what's going on.

3. Breathe deeply and slowly, down low in the tummy, through your nose.

4. Let the assessment go. Turn your attention elsewhere. Know that in this moment, you are making a conscious choice to design your own mood.

5. Practice (repeat steps 1, 2, 3 and 4) as necessary.

❀ ❀ ❀

Distinguishing assessments from assertions in the way that we're doing here also makes it easier for us to take a key step—that of maintaining the *difference between "true" and "Truth."* When I say something is *true*, I am making an assertion. As such, I am willing to provide *evidence* to back up my assertion if you ask for it. But when I say something is *Truth*, something entirely different is occurring. In this latter case, I make no such offer to provide evidence. In this case, I am claiming to have somehow privileged access to How Things Really Are and am claiming to serve as the conduit through which this Truth flows. I make no offer to provide evidence—instead, in many cases, I make a *demand for obedience.* Think about it, through history and across time zones, in personal relationships and in relationships among different nations and different cultures.

Consider your own experience and your own relationships, at home and at work and everywhere. Whenever people claim to have the *Truth*, a demand for obedience seems to follow closely behind. This happens in relationships of all sizes and types. And in every case, the impact on relationships and results, at a variety of levels, is enormous.

- We observe, we take action, and we produce results in language. *Assertions* and *assessments* are two of the six "language acts" which we use to do what we do, get what we get (and ultimately, it seems, *be* what we *be*).

- Keeping assertions *distinct and separate* from assessments is critical. They produce very different things and lead to *very different results.* This is especially tricky because in our traditional ways of thinking and speaking, we've used them in similar ways. Most of us have grown up *without* having such a clear distinction drawn between the two.

- *Assertions* are the "facts of life" and are where language is least generative and most descriptive. They can be true or false, and are verifiable by a 3rd party. They belong to the "thing" being observed, and they tend to have a *past* or *present—a very descriptive—* orientation. Make a bunch of *false assertions* and over time, create the public identity of "liar." The *assertions* we make are not impacted by our mood or emotional space.

- *Assessments*, on the other hand, are extremely generative and creative. These are our highly personal judgments and opinions, serving to orient us toward or away from future actions and results. We make a lot of assessments about virtually everything. *Assessments* are not good or bad, they just are. *Assessments* have a very strong future orientation, influencing future actions and ways of seeing. The *assessments* we produce are very strongly connected to—and consistent with—our mood or emotional space.

- *Assessments* are never "true" or "false." As personal judgments, they can never be "verified" like assertions can. They can be *grounded* or *ungrounded.* Grounded assessments are made *with conscious awareness of standards and of assertions*—that is, specific criteria coupled with observable behavior. Grounded assessments are powerful because they're connected to facts in a stronger way and therefore allow us to more successfully move into the future. We can all learn to make grounded assessments. Make a bunch of *ungrounded assessments* and over time you will create for yourself a public identity of "flaky" or "out of it."

- *Assessments belong to the observer,* not to the thing being observed. They reveal more about the observer and the observer's standards, than they *describe* about anything. Our *assessments* about ourselves, about others and about everything have a direct impact on how we feel, how we interpret, how we act, and how we interact with others.

## HOW-TO: POSSIBILITIES FOR
## TAKING NEW ACTION

1. *Can you recall situations in which people you were with* clearly did NOT have the distinctions *assessment* and *assertion*? What was it like, being with these people, over extended periods of time?

2. Big Eye: *Can you recall times in which <u>you</u> operated without these distinctions,* in situations involving other people?

3. Refer back to your SAMPLE SITUATION. List some *assessments* you have about yourself, the other person or people, and any other key entities involved. For each one (+ or -), *identify how that assessment influences* future interpretations, actions, and interactions. For example, out of this assessment what are you *more likely* to do or think or say? What are you *less likely* to do or think or say?

4. *How did you come up with these current assessments? Are they grounded or not?* That is, what are the *standards* you used and what are the *assertions* you used in order to come up with the *assessments?*

5. *Identify—being specific—what "improved" or "better" results would look like* in your SAMPLE SITUATION. Use assertions or new behaviors which can be verified (vs. more assessments) when describing. In other words, what are the *assertions* you'd have to see before you made the assessment that X is "better" or Y has "improved"?

6. Refer back to any NEGATIVE INTERNAL CONVERSATIONS you identified earlier. These are full of negative self-assessments, of course, which may or may not be grounded with standards and assertions. *Have a conversation with someone close to you* about these. *What standards*, if any, are you using when assessing yourself? How come you're using the standards you're using? Do others share this standard? *What observable data*—what assertions—are you using to ground the assessments? Is more information available? If so, what does it mean?

7. Big Eye: What are the *moods* that for you seem to be the *launch pad for making* the negative assessments, or seem to be produced after making the negative assessments? How do these moods impact your other relationships and interactions?

8.  Can you see the impact of *learning* on your ability to shift, to create better results and more positive self-assessments? What are the new actions you say *you'd like to be able to take, but are currently not taking?* Here is where learning comes to the rescue. *Declare yourself to be a learner,* to be a beginner, in that particular area. If possible, enroll someone more competent than yourself to be your teacher.

*Chapter 7*

## SECTION 2.

## DECLARATIONS

*"We, therefore, the Representatives of the united States of America...
solemnly publish and declare, That these United Colonies are, and of
Right ought to be Free and Independent States;"* [1]

Declaration of Independence
United States of America

*"Whether you say you can, or say you can't... either way, you're right!"*

Anonymous

---

If assertions are the speech acts with the least generative or creative capacity, then *declarations* can be viewed as the *most generative, most creative.* We can contrast them this way: With *assertions, first comes the world and then comes the word.* We use assertions to describe what is already so. They are dependent upon the existing world. But with *declarations, the word comes first. Then the "world" follows.* We use declarations to generate new possibilities, new action, new results in the world.

181

These are _not_ dependent on the existing world—they bring a new world into existence. In our view, assessments (see previous chapter) are a special type of declaration. As such, as we have seen, they have the creative power of all declarations—very different from the descriptive characteristic of assertions.

**Declarations are speech acts in which the speaker—out of nothingness—brings forth a new world of possibilities, a new way of seeing things, a new playing field on which to play.**

Declarations produce a new context and are closely connected to leadership (organizations) and our ability to guide and design our own lives (personal). With our declarations, we bring forth new worlds and invent new possibilities. More than any other linguistic act, we claim that declarations are what generate our reality. Matthew Budd, author of _You Are What You Say_, says it this way: *"A declaration is an utterance in which someone with the authority to do so brings something into being that wasn't there before."* [2]

Let's start with a brief look at our most famous declaration—the Declaration of Independence. We say that the primary purpose of the Declaration of Independence wasn't to describe anything. What the Declaration of Independence did was create possibilities and shift context. Notice these specific parts of the declaration:

It was declared that *"..these United Colonies **are**, and of Right ought to be Free and Independent States;"* and that *"all political connection between them and the State of Great Britain, **is** and ought to be totally dissolved;"* (my emphasis). This is not describing—this is declaring into being a new situation, a new relationship, a new context. After this declaration, something (a new country) became possible and very likely, and something else (continued colonialization) became very unlikely. Now, after this declaration much work remained in order to fully realize the declaration, but notice how the declaration opened the space of possibility, created the new context in the first place.

Again, this new context that was declared into being had the impact of changing how future events were interpreted! Without the declaration, certain colonial and British movements and actions would have been interpreted one way. With the declaration, these same future actions are interpreted very differently.

In a very real sense, our country was *declared into being*. For that matter, all countries and organizations that I'm aware of are declared into being. Somewhere in the archives is a charter or original document upon which those authorized "hereby declared..." and in so doing, brought forth the new country or organization.

President Kennedy declared that "America will put a man on the moon within this decade," and indeed it happened. Kennedy had the power (authority) to make such a big declaration and have it not be dismissed as wishful thinking or a pipe dream. He declared new possibilities, created a new context for action, one in which new actions and new results occurred. As this declaration shows, to declare has *more to do with starting a process and creating something than it does with merely naming a goal or objective.*

The parent who says "No more TV after 9:00" is creating a new context with her declaration. Before this declaration, little Johnny could watch TV at 10:00 and nobody raised an eyebrow. But after the declaration, his same actions show up as "wrong." The reason? The context is different. Context isn't physical, but it's real. And it's generated, in language, by our declarations.

❋ ❋ ❋

So we've said here, and earlier in the book, that declarations create or shift context. Before we go further, let's further define and clarify what we mean by "context" and "content." We say that context is very, very important for relationships of all types—personal and professional. Context can be critical for individual success, marriage/family relationships, as well as for success in organizations. Webster's defines *context* in the following way:

- *the parts of a discourse that surround a word or passage and can throw light on its meaning*
- *the interrelated conditions in which something exists or occurs*
- *the environment or setting.* [3]

Another way of looking at the first part of this definition is to view *context* as *with-text*, or as "that which goes with the text." The context "surrounds" the text (goes with the content) and provides the background against which a particular meaning is generated. Change the context, change the meaning of the content. In our example, little Johnny watching TV at 10:00 can be viewed as the content—the event, the fact, the action. When the context was changed by the parent's declaration, it had the effect of shifting how that same event gets interpreted. And we claim it is very powerful to notice this and do this consciously.

We can also view context as the background environment or setting, although in this case we aren't referring to the physical environment or physical setting. While the physical environment can certainly be part of the overall context, we're focusing here on how our declarations create a non-physical environment or background. And we call this the mood or "atmosphere" or "culture" that lives within relationships, families, organizations, communities, even nations.

Think about these situations and of the real impact of context on the given person, relationship, family or organization:

- Over a period of time, a person regularly declares "I'll never get ahead, things never go my way." This is the context that is set for him or her, practically on a daily basis. Does this have any impact on his results? On how she interprets events that happen? On how he moves through his activities, relationships and interactions? We say yes, it does. Any of the many different, ordinary events which happen in a normal day will likely be interpreted in a negative way, and be seen as "proof" or "evidence" that things never go her way and that she'll never get ahead. And even seemingly positive events will be interpreted simply as exceptions, aberrations, or the calm before the storm.

- A newly-married couple declare to one another that they want their new relationship to be characterized by the following: mutual respect; true partnership; openness in communicating; and love. Does their having this conversation and sharing their commitment and understanding of what actions constitute mutual respect, true partnership, openness in communicating and love *have anything to do with their ability to actually create it?* We say yes, it does, in a big way. By setting such a context, they create from this day forward a background against which their future actions will be interpreted. They create from this day forward a setting that serves to actively *support* them in actually bringing about what they have declared for themselves.

- An organization's leaders publicly declare a new mission statement and new set of goals and priorities. In addition, over time they continue to participate in and have others initiate *conversations* at all levels in the organization about the new mission and priorities. In these conversations, people ask questions, engage in dialogue, possibly make changes to the goals and develop a strong, *shared understanding* of where we are and where we're going. Here, we can say that the leaders have generated a *new context*, one in which X is now important (where Y used to be) and Z is understood as the most overarching mission. Does this context have anything to do with the *results* produced by the organization? We say yes, it does. In fact, we say that the degree to which the context is indeed shared throughout the organization has everything to do with coherency and consistency in decision-making, with trust and empowerment, and with aligning all the organization's resources so that everyone is "on the same page" moving forward.

So effective *leadership*—at the organizational as well as the personal level—has a great deal to do with creating and maintaining a certain context (and not another). Successful *relationships* are often built out of conversations in which we share our views and ultimately come to some mutual understanding, make some mutual declarations, about what we're committed to bringing forth—and how we're committed to *be*—with each other.

The longer I live, the more I become convinced of the power of context. It's not physical, but it's real. In virtually every setting, every situation, every relationship, context is important for results. And have you noticed that *conversations for the sake of setting and sharing context* are sometimes conspicuously missing in personal and professional situations? Maybe what we need to do is invent some new conversations.

❋ ❋ ❋

We can also see how declarations are *closely connected with moods*. For example, in a mood of ambition I am likely to make very different declarations and set very different standards than I will in a mood of resentment or resignation. This combination has a great deal to do with what we call our *horizon of possibilities*. I like this term because it presents a wonderful visual metaphor, of a sweeping landscape before us. A big, broad horizon, way out there and beckoning us, full of possibilities and choices... as opposed to a narrow, shrunken down view, seemingly closing in from both sides, limiting possibilities and choices. This horizon, used this way, represents the future and the universe set of possible actions, leading of course to possible results.

What's important to notice is this: our moods certainly influence the types of declarations we're likely to make. And at the same time, the making of new declarations has the impact of shifting our moods.

❊ ❊ ❊

We claim that with our declarations, we do four primary things, take *four primary actions* in the world:

- We open or initiate
- We close or conclude
- We resolve
- We evaluate (with our assessments)

Let's introduce each of these, along with a few examples. As we're going through these, notice the ways in which new or different declarations can be the tools—and are often the starting point—for designing changes into your life.

**Declarations that open or initiate:**
- "We, the people of the United States of America..." brings into being a new context, and a new possibility for a creating a country.
- "We, the board of directors (or owners), declare..." creates a new organization.
- "Hello, my name is..." opens or initiates a relationship.
- "From this day forward, we're going to..." opens or initiates a new way of doing things together
- "Starting tomorrow, I will..." sets a new direction, creates a new context
- "I love you" sets a context of partnership, mutual legitimacy, care.
- "Our mission has shifted to include..." sets a new context, a new direction for an organization.

- "No more TV after 9:00..." sets a new context at home.
- "I don't know" opens a space for learning to occur.
- "You're hired" initiates employment.
- "I'm grateful for..." opens possibility for joy, contentment.
- "This (X) isn't working..." declares a "breakdown" into being, causing a break in the "status quo" or "auto pilot" of doing what we were doing. Generates the possibility for purposefully inventing new actions to produce new results; generates the possibility for new learning to improve actions and results.

**Declarations that close or conclude:**
- "I'm sorry" closes a chapter with someone (and also opens a new one).
- "I forgive you" concludes an event and closes the resentment that has accompanied it (also opens a new context for the relationship).
- "Thank you" declares that I'm satisfied with your fulfillment of some promise to me; closes a commitment cycle.
- "You're fired" closes employment.
- "The meeting is adjourned" finishes the meeting.
- "Our relationship is over" ends a relationship.

**Declarations that resolve:**
- "We the jury, find the defendant..." resolve questions about guilt or innocence (regardless of what *actually* happened).
- Yes (every decision is a declaration.)
- No
- In
- Out
- Ball
- Strike

**Declarations that evaluate (assess):**
- Right
- Wrong

- Good
- Bad
- Lazy
- Thrifty
- Helpful
- Arrogant
- Fat
- Skinny
- Tall
- Short
- Shy
- Outgoing
- Timely
- Late
- Pretty
- Ugly
- Effective
- Ineffective
- Efficient
- Inefficient
- Acceptable
- Unacceptable
- (We could go on and on... remember our chapter on assessments).

In the above sets of examples, declarations are creating *openings* or *closings*, they are *resolving* and *evaluating*. Our declarations serve to open possibilities or avenues. They allow something to begin to happen, as well as to close, or reach completion with something that happened in the past. Our declarations serve to resolve issues and enable us to move forward, and they greatly influence the quality of our journey along the way. This *opening* or *closing* or *resolving* or *moving* is not physical, of course, but it's very real. It has everything to do with our experience and with the actions we take in the world.

Declarations that resolve or evaluate have the impact of orienting us *toward* certain possibilities and interpretations, and *away* from others. Once we decide something, we move in one direction and not another, embracing one set of possibilities, and not another. And declarations that evaluate we call assessments, as we discussed earlier. These are like "stepping stones" to the future. They orient us one way or another in our action, and therefore greatly influence our results.

For organizations and for individuals, declarations can operate like the *rudder* of a boat. The boat (organization or person) changes directions as a result of those with authority declaring one thing or another. Declarations are how we identify our priorities and commitments to the future and how we bring certain ways of being into existence (self-worth, well-being, dignity, among others).

Let's take a look. We say that the following are *key declarations*, having significant impact on our lives, our results, and our happiness. We'll explore each one in turn:

1. Yes
2. No
3. I don't know
4. I apologize
6. I forgive you
7. Thank you
8. I love you
9. I am...
10. This is not working

## Yes and No

We mentioned earlier that the simple act of saying Yes or saying No has a great impact on our lives. I say Yes, and I commit myself to some action, I move this way, with these possibilities now open and these others now closed. I say No and I commit myself to different action, I move the other way, with a different set of possibilities opened and another set closed. Truly a generative act, saying Yes or No. We say that every decision is a declaration. Every decision, every choice moves us and orients us one way or another. Many of us have heard this line before: To not choose is a choice. To not decide is a decision. We agree.

Do you know anyone—maybe yourself—who has difficulty occasionally saying No? Many of us have experienced this, and for some it's not occasionally. Not being able to say No translates into more than simply not being able to utter a word or two. We say that this is connected to power, and ultimately to our dignity. *Here, we claim that not being able to say a certain thing (in this case, "No") = not being able to be a certain way (in this case, assertive, designing my life, with dignity).*

Try to imagine a person of dignity who also happens to be unable to say No to any request made of him or her. It's difficult, isn't it? (*In the practice of ontological coaching, the underlying conversations and interpretations which are behind the action of not saying No are explored and shown to the coachee, who then may begin inventing and practicing new, more powerful interpretations*).

Not being able to say No also translates into a way of living that is extremely widespread and pervasive in our world. Have you ever found yourself "stressed out?" (In workshops, the vast majority of hands immediately go up). Well, it may be connected to this. We call it being "overcommitted" or "living in overwhelm," and it seems to be everywhere. I make 27 promises (by saying Yes to others' requests), and I forget that I'm already sitting on 43 commitments I haven't yet fulfilled. And now I get to be stressed out and resentful. I get to be unhappy. This is real. I know about this firsthand—how about you? I've recently begun to practice declining, and I'm slowly getting better. It's all time and practice, coupled with perhaps a new interpretation of what No means.

What does No mean to you? Many of us tend to equate No to "rejection." In other words, we think that by saying No to someone, we're rejecting them. Or better yet, we think that when others say No to us, they are rejecting us. We say something different. We say that *No isn't rejection of a person. It is simply a decline of a request.* The person and the request are separate. When I say No, I'm simply declining your request, I'm not rejecting you. Have you noticed that the traditional understanding of "No = rejection" is very widespread and pervasive, even though no one actually sat us down and taught us that on purpose? What's available is to adopt a different interpretation of No, one that can serve us and support us in designing the results we say we want. We'll also talk a little more about No later on, as we cover promises and agreements.

## I Don't Know

Perhaps no declaration is as important for learning as this one. As we discussed earlier, we say that *I Don't Know* is a required first step for learning to occur. It generates a space for learning, opens a context for learning, where one was not present before. Remember any experiences when you may have been trying to teach someone, and the learner thought they already knew it? How much learning takes place? Not much. The context is all wrong. No matter what you, the teacher, try to do, it's unlikely that learning will occur. Not in that context.

And how important is learning, given that we live in a world characterized by relentless, ongoing change? We say it's tremendously important. For individuals and for groups of all types. Learning is absolutely connected to results, to happiness. Anything that has a lot to do with learning has a lot to do with results. For us, ignorance (I Don't Know) is not the opposite of learning—it's the threshold of learning.

Many of us do not have much practice in saying I Don't Know, so we haven't developed a lot of competence here. Also we can observe that in many organizational, family, or relationship situations it may not be okay to say I Don't Know. In these cases, it's likely that I Don't Know is interpreted to mean (by either the one saying it or those listening) "I'm stupid" or "I don't care" or "I don't want to know" or something else, but it is apparently not interpreted to mean "I'm available for learning". What may be missing are conversations about learning, how to bring it about, as well as granting ourselves and others permission to be a beginner at something. We have the authority to do so.


## I Apologize

This powerful declaration serves to "clean up" broken commitments and acknowledge mistakes. (Again, not to physically clean up anything but to linguistically take care of a relationship). In our work with organizations and individuals, we have repeatedly encountered situations in which promises have been made and not kept, and no apologies have occurred. And in other situations, there has been great misunderstanding and uncertainty as to whether or not promises were actually made, as well as to whether or not they were fulfilled to everyone's satisfaction.

Imagine a situation in which someone breaks a promise to you, but does not acknowledge it and does not apologize. Does that action have an impact on your relationship with him or her? For most of us, the answer is yes, it definitely does. Why is this? Well, the answer may vary depending upon the type of promise broken and the context in which this occurs. We say it's because language conveys commitment, and puts in motion events that would not have been put in motion otherwise. Can you see how when I make a promise to you, that changes things? You then begin to do something else, confident that I will uphold my end of the bargain and do what I said I would do. And if I don't, it's likely that your public identity, your financial results, your other relationships (among other things) may be damaged.

In organizational settings, leaders sometimes make promises and, from the perspective of employees, do not follow through and do not apologize. In our view, this has a big impact on the "mood" or "culture" of the organization. It also greatly influences how employees listen to (interpret) anything that is spoken by the leaders from that point forward. Usually it produces resentment and cynicism, two moodspaces not very conducive to the learning, innovation, and creativity that's needed for success today. But if leaders are made aware of the broken promises, and if they make sincere apologies (and sometimes public apologies), the listening of the employees is quite different. And it's the listening—the interpretation—that matters moving forward.

In personal settings, the power of *I Apologize* is quite evident. Simply reflect on your own experience—on the times in which you have sincerely apologized to someone, and they have accepted your apology, or vice versa. This language act is an act of relationship building, of relationship healing, of closing and opening. It acknowledges and allows a chapter to "close," while creating space for a new playing field to open up in front. Conversely, consider the relationships open to someone who never says "I'm sorry" or "I apologize." Consider the way such a person may "dance" in that relationship and of how his or her partner may respond over time. Consider the public identity likely to be generated by such a person. This all has to do with the creative, generative power of a sincere apology.

Who has never made a mistake? The answer is Nobody—we all have. Well then, unless we all are planning to live our lives all by ourselves, this declaration can surely serve us.

## I Forgive You

Continuing on our previous point, we all make mistakes. Is it possible that you'll go through your whole life and in doing so, never encounter someone who makes a mistake that involves or impacts you? Probably not. *But of all the declarations we'll discuss, perhaps this one has the most direct impact on our mood and on our ability to find some peace in our lives.*

People mess up. It appears to be a very widespread phenomenon. Sometimes they don't even know they messed up. Bubba may be perfectly happy and content, sleeping gloriously well at night, and I'm over here deep in resentment because he did something to me that I'm convinced he shouldn't have done. And to boot, my resentment doesn't stop at my relationship with Bubba. No, it seems to also bleed out and touch lots of my other relationships, even those that don't have anything to do with this guy. Sound familiar?

Forgiveness is a powerful declaration, one that allows a chapter to close and another one to open. The other person may not even know, or need to know, about the action of forgiveness. In this context, *forgiveness is not for the other person*. It's for the person doing the forgiving. For this is the person who is suffering.

Like all declarations, *I Forgive You* is highly generative and creative. And whether or not we forgive has a great deal to do with how we interpret forgiveness. Let's explore. Forgiveness may be defined as a declaration in which we say: *What you have done to me caused me harm and damaged my possibilities. I do not condone this, and I do not give you permission to do this again. I choose to forgive you, to let go of these conversations. I now will focus my attention and my awareness in other areas, rather than continuing to live in these conversations about you and about what you did. I choose to move forward with my life. I revoke my promise to somehow, some way, get you back. I choose to move into some peace and out of this resentment.*

By forgiving, we bring one chapter to a close and open a new one. We are "moving forward" in a real (but non-physical) way. We are "shifting" out of something and toward something else. Has this been true for you? In cases in which you have forgiven someone, have you felt this? Many of us have. It's not physical, but it's real.

Now, what common interpretations or beliefs do we have about forgiveness that make it *unlikely* that we'll forgive someone? Said another way, what do we tell ourselves about the other person or about forgiveness that make it *difficult or unlikely* that we'll actually forgive? Here are some interpretations we've shared and learned in our work:

- "But I'm right"
- "They don't deserve to be forgiven"
- "If I forgive, that means I condone what he did"
- "To forgive is a sign of weakness"
- "To forgive means I'll forget, and I'll never forget..."
- "I won't forgive him because I want him to still suffer"
- "Forgiving her lets her off the hook"

Sound familiar? You can probably come up with others, too. We say that these interpretations are not very powerful. (This is key - notice how we're *not* talking about whether or not the above interpretations are "right" or "wrong." The focus here is on the *actions, interactions,* and *results* these beliefs lead to). These beliefs need to be updated in order to serve as the starting point for different actions. What's important to notice is that from the above interpretations (or beliefs, or stories), the action of forgiveness is *not* likely to occur. And because the action of forgiveness doesn't occur, the results (benefits) of forgiveness are not available, either.

One root word underneath forgiveness means "to refuse to hold." Beautiful—*to forgive is to refuse to hold,* to let go, and what we refuse to hold is our *resentment* toward someone, our promise to "somehow, someday get even." What we let go of are recurring negative assessments ascribing intentions and blame to others, and at the same time casting ourselves in the role of the victim. What we let go of is an orientation in which we're predisposed to withdraw, distrust, find fault, and avoid intimacy. Resentment is an incredibly powerful and negative moodspace, one that we have all visited a time or two (or more). I believe that if more of us shifted our understanding of forgiveness, we'd be able to move through setbacks, suffering and difficulties in a healthier, more productive way.

I have heard it put this way: *pain is biological, but suffering is linguistic.* I don't need to have pain in order to suffer, and I can have pain without the suffering. Forgiveness deals directly with the suffering. The *single most powerful tool* that I have discovered for designing well-being in my life is the declaration of forgiveness. It applies to my work and social life as well as my home life. A great many people in our workshops report the exact same thing, and for all of us it seems not to be a one-time thing. It's a process. It requires ongoing awareness, commitment, and practice.

*I can declare forgiveness, but I cannot declare forget-ness.* That is, forgiveness is a conscious process involving new declarations on my part. Forgiveness is a choice. On the other hand, I cannot choose to "never remember" something. I cannot declare that a particular memory will not be "served up" to me from time to time, or that I'll be reminded of an event or situation occasionally, even when I'm not consciously trying to do so. What I *can* do, however, is choose how I respond, how I react, how I move. This is the key, and it all happens in language.

Forgiveness brings peace. It's just that simple. Show me a person in your life that you say is peaceful, and I'll show you someone who doesn't have a list of 10 people they haven't forgiven. Maybe, for non-hermits, there is no peace without forgiveness. And maybe our ability to forgive *ourselves* is at least as important as our ability to forgive others. In addition to bringing closure and a new context to our relationships with others, we say that forgiveness can also bring dignity, self-worth and self-acceptance into being. This is another key situation in which not being able to <u>say</u> a certain thing = not being able to <u>be</u> a certain way

Don Miguel Ruiz, author of <u>*The Four Agreements*</u>, offers his perspective on the power of declaring forgiveness. He says:

*Forgiveness is the only way to heal. We can choose to forgive because we feel compassion for ourselves. We can let go of the resentment and declare "that's enough!".. I will no longer be the Victim."... That's the beginning of the free human. Forgiveness is the key."* [4]

One of my all-time favorites songs is by Don Henley, and is entitled <u>*The Heart of the Matter*</u>. I agree—I think it really is the heart of the matter. He says it so well, with these lines:

*There are people in your life, who've come and gone*
*They let you down, they hurt your pride*
*You better put it all behind you, 'cause life goes on*
*You keep carrying that anger, it'll eat you up inside*
*I been trying to get down to the heart of the matter*
*But my will gets weak, and my thoughts seem to scatter*
*But I think it's about forgiveness, forgiveness*
*Even if you don't love me anymore* [5]

Caroline Myss, author of <u>*Anatomy of the Spirit*</u>, has a great deal to say about the power of forgiveness, including this passage:

*Forgiveness is not the same as telling the person who harmed you "it's ok," which is more or less the way most people view it. Rather, forgiveness is a complex act of consciousness, one that liberates the psyche and soul from the need for personal vengeance and the perception of oneself as a victim. ... the consequence of a genuine act of forgiveness borders on the miraculous. It may, in my view, contain the energy that generates miracles themselves.* [6]

Forgiveness—of ourselves and of others—is directly connected to moving out of resentment and designing some peace within our lives. This powerful *language act*, the declaring of forgiveness, is central to our ability to close previous chapters and begin new ones. It may be the most powerful language act available to those of us seeking the experience of happiness, the experience of peacefulness in our lives.

## Thank You

Thank you is an acknowledgement of the contribution or kindness of another. Difficulty in declaring Thank You when someone gives us a gift or goes out of his or her way to do something for us will obviously have a negative effect on those relationships. We will begin to show up as ungrateful and find that many people aren't so interested in being with us. This, of course, isn't an issue for people who never interact with anybody, but it becomes important for the rest of us.

Thank You can also be seen as a declaration of acceptance that brings closure to a transaction, usually a promise or agreement of some sort. For example, when someone brings us the lunch we ordered at a restaurant, we usually respond with Thank You. This brings closure to their part of the promise (to bring you what you ordered), leaving your part of the promise to come (paying for your meal). By responding with Thank You, it's often interpreted by the other person to mean "everything is ok, they've accepted what I delivered."

Thank You is also connected to moods, in a powerful way. **We claim that the moodspace of joy is connected to gratitude.** Think about it. It's hard to imagine someone in a joyful mood who isn't grateful for something. It was taught to me this way: *If you're looking for more joy in your life, begin by declaring gratitude.* We can declare gratitude to the universe, at any time, for any reason, or for no reason. We can declare gratitude for being alive, for being able to walk or talk or think or hear or see or climb or hug or whatever. At any point in our day, we can simply stop and declare our gratitude to God or to the universe for the many good things in our lives. And in so doing, we can consciously move toward more joy in our lives.

I've also heard statements of gratitude put this way: *Any day vertical (or above ground) is a good day!* I believe virtually all of us have some things to be grateful for. The only question is whether or not we notice them and acknowledge them.

### I Love You

If we are talking about happiness for non-hermits, then *love* is certainly a topic that needs to be somewhere in the mix. There are obviously many ways to look at love and many different ways in which the same word is used. We can love our spouse, our children, our job. We say we love a certain sports team, and we say we love pastrami sandwiches. We have romantic love and we have platonic love, love of music and love of God.

Here, our focus is on people and relationships and results. Let's start by considering a relationship between two people in which *I Love You* is never actually spoken out loud. We claim that *saying* it is very different from *thinking* it. Saying it is very different from knowing it. To say I Love You is an act of relationship building and shaping. It is an act of context creation, as it creates a space that was not there before. And it definitely includes our body and emotional domains.

Let's go back to the big eye. Notice if there are loved ones in your life that you haven't actually said *I Love You* to in awhile. Why not? What is the story you have, out of which you don't say I Love You? Can you feel little body reactions in yourself simply as you think about the prospect of speaking those words to that person? We may be out of practice in this regard, and we may not have known this step is available as a direct relationship-builder. We may also know at some level that by saying I Love You we'll shift the relationship, change the context. And we may or may not want to do that.

One of the most interesting ways of looking at love that I've ever heard is from Humberto Maturana, the pioneering Chilean neurobiologist. His definition of love is: *The radical acceptance of the other as a legitimate other in co-existence with me.* [7] At first I found this way of looking at love extremely odd, but over time it's grown on me. Clearly, this is different from the popular view of romantic love. Here, the focus is on our declaration of acceptance and of legitimacy. We declare our acceptance of another human being as being "legitimate" in his or her co-existence with us. To me, the words "true and equal partner" come to mind. Think about the implications of such a declaration. Declaring such a context, to me, immediately brings about a space of mutual respect and acceptance. It also allows space for us to make requests of each other, and maintain flexibility and openness in designing how we do what we do together.

This way of looking at love seems to also speak about *ethics*, how we choose to be and live with each other on both the individual and collective levels. This definition of love—focusing on *acceptance* and *legitimacy*—makes it possible to greatly expand the circle of people that we "love," doesn't it? It seems to me that somewhere along the line we've gotten a Hollywood version of romantic love in our heads, and that anything that doesn't look like that is seen as evidence that we're not doing something right.

Eckhart Tolle, in <u>The Power of Now</u>, says much the same thing (though in a different way) as he's discussing moving from unhealthy relationships to something better. He says *"The greatest catalyst for change in a relationship is complete acceptance of your partner as he or she is, without needing to judge or change them in any way."* [8] Of course, we're now dealing with our incredible propensity for making assessments, many of them made very automatically, out of habit, as if they just form by themselves. And as we discussed, a great many of our assessments are purely recreational, not able to be grounded, but they influence the future, they influence how we interpret, they influence how we interact, nevertheless. The first step is to notice that this is happening. Then and only then can we begin to choose, and to practice, something different.

I haven't seen this play, but I love the title. It captures in a very concise way a fairly common dance that we do. The play is called: ***I Love You, You're Perfect, Now Change!*** [9] A friend shared this next analogy with me, in a humorous way—it has to do with men and women, love and marriage. It was told as somewhat of a joke; however, it does seem to hold up in a fairly sizable number of cases: *Many men enter marriage with a secret, private conversation that the woman will <u>not</u> change. And many* *women enter marriage with a secret, private conversation that the man will!*

Have you noticed that men and women also tend to say I Love You in different ways? For example, many men say I Love You by bringing home the paycheck. Or by taking out the trash. Or by keeping the yard and exterior of the home kept up. One of my teachers noted that if we want men to begin being more "open" in expressing themselves vocally, we could start by remembering that many men have not had much practice in this area at all. Many men have lived virtually their whole lives without actually saying I Love You. This request may be one of asking men to do something that they have never done. This doesn't mean we shouldn't move in this direction—only that many men will absolutely be beginners at the outset.

I certainly had not had much practice fourteen years ago, when I told my parents I loved them. I always had loved them, and they knew that, and I knew that they knew that, but I just hadn't said it to them since I was an adult. I knew I wanted to tell them, and my body immediately began to freak out. My heart was pounding, my hands were sweating, I had the nervous shakes, all from simply thinking about what I was going to say. Clearly, my body had not had any practice doing this. I struggled through and told them, face to face, that I loved them. My heart pounded and my knees knocked and I just did it. And I say that this has been part of our redesigning a relationship that, as adults, is deeper and more fulfilling than what we had before. We're now more comfortable (practiced) saying it to each other, and our relationship is different and to me, far better because of it.

## I Am..

This is the beginning of the declaration of who we say we are in the world—what we can call our identity or "self". We can call this a *primary declaration*, and it is at the heart of the practice called ontological coaching. In this sense, ontological coaching is defined as coaching people in their "way of being," with particular attention to the observer, language, moods/emotions, and body distinctions. It's the type of coaching done by those who have pioneered this work, as well as by me and others who have followed in their footsteps.

A great deal of suffering, we claim, comes from human beings operating out of certain primary declarations that do not serve us very well and are not conducive to the actions and moods that would move us in the directions we say we want in our lives. And often, the "root" declaration is not visible to us at all. We don't see it. All we see is that we seem to keep making the same mistakes over and over again and attracting the same type of people and situations to ourselves time and time again. This is where coaching comes in and where the coach creates a space (in conversation) for the coachee to begin to see these underlying declarations and interpretations for what they are—declarations and interpretations, not as the truth. From here the coachee can see the impact these have on his or her actions, and can begin to invent (declare) and practice new ones. For if all this time I've been operating with one interpretation or primary declaration that I made up about myself long ago (which now, I'm beginning to see, doesn't serve me very well), *why can't I invent a new one now that serves me better in going where I say I want to go?*

People who make significant changes in their lives usually start with a language step. This step often takes the form of a personal declaration, a new I Am statement about who we say we are. For example, consider the shifts made possible when we declare for ourselves the following:

- "I am an honest, loving, and contributing man."
- "I am a strong and ethical leader."
- "I am a human being, and I matter."
- "I am a powerful teacher.""
- "I am a good friend."
- "I am a worthy and loved woman."
- "I am a forgiven and accepted man."
- "I am an ambitious, passionate woman."
- "I am a courageous, forgiving and authentic man."

Think about what these mean, what these feel like saying out loud, what these feel like saying to yourself, what sort of new context would be in place. These and many others are truly the key initial acts of creating a new way of being. I like the expression in Neale Donald Walsch's <u>Conversations With God</u> books that points to our ability to choose, to declare, and create who we are in the world: *we all have the power to declare and bring about "the grandest version of the greatest vision we ever had about ourselves."* [10]

With new personal declarations, I'm still Chalmers... but the Chalmers that I am is different. You're still you, but the you that you are is different. And *we speak it into being*. We declare a new context for ourselves and our lives. We're not human *beings*, we're human *becomings. This is what this book is all about*. What do we choose for ourselves? What do we declare? What will we bring forth? **Because if we're going to do it at all, we're going to do it in language.**

Consider the declaration "I'm shy". We all know people who, at one point or another in their lives, have characterized themselves in this way. But let's look a bit closer. Where is shy? What is shy? The traditional view says that it's part of our "personality" and that some of us are naturally outgoing and some of us are naturally much more reserved. I certainly do not doubt the influence of our biology and genetic makeup. My 3 kids are truly different from each other, and they've been different since they arrived. And at the same time, we all know people who make truly significant changes in their lives, well after their childhood is over. Maybe this has been the case for you. Maybe this is the old nature–nurture debate, in different clothing... I don't know. But my understanding is that in real ways, the jury is truly still out. There appear to be biological influences as well as interpretation-related influences in many, many areas. Given this, we say it's prudent to at least examine different interpretations and their consequences—especially if we want to produce *different* results than those we're producing now.

First, we can see that when I say "I'm shy" in the present, that this influences my future. It is a declaration, so it's like a stepping stone, carrying me into the future as it influences *what I'm likely to do* and *how I'm likely to do it*. Example—I'm at a dance, I'm shy, and I want to ask a young lady to dance. Will I do it? Probably not. Why not? Because I'm shy and shy people don't ask young ladies to dance. Shy people hang out at the edge of the gym, so I guess that's what I'll do. After all, I'm shy. Here we can see a case where my declarations and assessments about myself limit my possibilities.

As an exercise, it may be valuable to reflect a moment to see where you may be doing the same thing. Virtually all of us do this to ourselves, to one degree or another. To me, the key in this type of reflection is to have my main focus be on *just noticing*, and not being so quick to judge and beat myself up about what I see.

Let's say that I decided that I was really committed to dancing with young ladies, and I declared myself a beginner at dancing. I got some lessons, and I practiced. I watched a lot of music videos and danced by myself in my room. Then at the next dance, even though my body was freaking out, sweating, knees knocking, and feeling terribly uncomfortable... I took the action of asking someone to dance, she says yes and we dance. Or she says no, I ask someone else, and this time she says yes. Then maybe I ask her to dance again, or ask someone else to dance, and we dance again. Over some time, learning takes place, and I'm much more practiced and competent at dancing. Let's say at some later date you come into the gym and see me dancing. *Am I still shy?* No—now I'm confident, or outgoing, or whatever. All *assessments*. All about my *actions* or lack of actions, not about *me*. None of them are permanent descriptions of my personhood. They are all assessments, judgments, made by different observers out of different standards, moods, and beliefs.

If I choose, I can take some action with this new understanding of shy. I can declare myself a beginner at dancing, get a teacher, enter into learning, practice, and develop some competence. Does this mean that all people are equally comfortable and equally competent at dancing? Of course not. What it does mean is that *by holding the assessment 'shy' as only an assessment, I open possibilities for action that are not available with traditional interpretations.*

With the traditional understanding of shy as some permanent feature of who I am, what am I to do if I want to produce different results? I can't go to the local supermarket and purchase 50 pounds of un-shy. I do not know the Truth about this matter. But I do know that if I have the *interpretation* that I'm shy (or stupid or whatever) and if I hold that it's some *permanent feature* or *biological characteristic* of who I am, this interpretation limits my possibilities for designing something different. This interpretation—this *declaration held as the Truth—can* paralyze me. This interpretation usually does not lead to happiness, especially if I want to produce some *change*, some *new result* in my life.

It also seems to me there's a tendency for many of us, given the infinite number of stories that we could invent, to make up stories that disempower us. Or limit our possibilities. Or even paralyze us into non-action. Do you see this also, sometimes in yourself and sometimes in others? We develop habits of interpreting, we settle into moods, and we may not even notice that this is occurring. We may even get self-righteous about our stories, to the point that we don't even see them as *our* stories anymore. And finally, we may not have conversations with others in which this is talked about and shared. All of this is very much connected to our well-being, our happiness.

### This Is Not Working...

This type of declaration points to what we call "breakdowns" and dealing with the breakdowns in our lives. This distinction, originally developed by Fernando Flores, is very powerful and is truly central to our ability to design our own lives. Simply put, a *breakdown* is an unexpected "break" in the normal flow of what I was doing, in the normal routine of my day. Breakdowns may initially seem to be all "negative," but they are *not positive or negative* in and of themselves. Here's a great way to understand whether or not a breakdown has occurred: *If you hear yourself suddenly say "oh shit," rest assured that in almost every case, a breakdown is present!* Not all breakdowns begin with such a salute, but many do.

More specifically, breakdowns are *unexpected interruptions in the fulfilling of a commitment*, whether that commitment is:

- Going to pick up a gallon of milk that I said I'd get
- Getting to the meeting by starting time
- Meeting this quarter's earnings projections
- Resolving the issue by Tuesday at noon
- Managing the project team
- Processing the system test results
- Serving as a volunteer on the PTA committee
- Doing a great many other activities that, in some way, shape or form, involve others.

Also, notice the extent to which virtually everything we do, on a daily basis at home or at work, can be seen as *actions we take in order to fulfill some prior commitments we have made*. Now these prior commitments may be explicit or implicit, short-term or long-term, personal or business-related, but they are there. For most of us, we can say that we live in a "web" of commitments.

When a breakdown occurs, we are no longer functioning on "autopilot" in taking care of one commitment or another. That is, we are no longer operating in *transparency*. For example, have you ever driven all the way home, and when you arrive home have no memory whatsoever of the particulars of the drive home? You don't remember the intersection you turned at which you made the wide left turn, don't remember the stop sign at the corner or whether any other cars were even there... you simply find yourself at home. This is an excellent example of what we call *transparency*, and it seems to show up in our lives whenever we do anything that has even a little repetitiveness involved. Transparency is a fact of life for many of us; it's not bad, it just is.

In this way of thinking, transparency is actually connected to *competency*. For example, beginning drivers don't have much transparency—they remember everything, and everything they do must be done with full conscious awareness. The steering wheel and clutch pedal are very present for them, as are the accelerator and gauges, while for experienced, highly competent drivers, these seem to recede into the background.

Well, breakdowns are *breaks* in the transparency. We're now fully conscious, fully aware, fully choosing. And what we do in moments of breakdown is *absolutely critical* to the results we produce. It's in moments of breakdown that we're putting our "rudder" into the water on purpose and steering ourselves one way or the other on purpose.

Here are common examples of breakdowns being declared, at home or at work situations. You can probably think of many others:

- "Something about this is off track"
- "Something's wrong"
- "This is no longer satisfactory"
- "Stop—let's step back and look at what we're doing"
- "This is enough"
- "This is too much"
- "This is not acceptable"
- "This represents a major new opportunity"
- "This represents a major new threat"
- "That's a problem"
- "Things can't keep going like they're going in area X"
- "I need to learn about Y"
- "We need to do something about Z"

Let's explore a few additional points about this distinction that we're calling *breakdown,* because 1) we all have breakdowns; and 2) the way we manage and move through our breakdowns has a huge impact on our ability to create peacefulness and productivity for ourselves.

- The universe doesn't have breakdowns. People do. Different observers have different breakdowns. What's a huge breakdown for one observer (one person) passes totally unnoticed by another. Different observers come from different concerns, and they observe from different distinctions.

- Breakdowns are not good or bad. They just are.

- Breakdowns may "happen" to us—the external world serves them up for us—or we may proactively declare breakdowns into being.

- We can each declare the status quo to be a breakdown. In organizations, this depends on levels of authority and the type of breakdown being declared. In our personal lives, we have the authority to declare any aspect of it to be a breakdown. Often, this is the first step toward real change, learning or improvement.

- Declaring a breakdown sets a *new context for action*—for individuals and for organizations.

- Breakdowns are inevitable and are simply a fact of life. *The point is therefore not to attempt to avoid all breakdowns;* rather, it is to gain competency and ability to deal effectively with the breakdowns which occur, as well as to gain practice in declaring breakdowns proactively as a way of moving ourselves toward the results we say we want.

- We address our breakdowns through conversations, and *all conversations are not created equal.* Some conversations absolutely move us toward taking care of the breakdown, and some do not.

For example, in many cases right after "*oh (expletive...!)*" we are automatically "thrown" first into a conversation in which everyone shares their own stories, their own personal assessments, of why the thing happened and what it means. This isn't necessarily a bad thing at all; in fact, it can be very useful. But if we *stay* in this conversation forever we'll *never actually move* toward resolving the breakdown. At some point we have to take new action. This requires a promise, a commitment, an agreement... not a collection of assessments and judgments. These new conversations are precisely the *actions* which are needed to resolve breakdowns and "move" in the world.

How we handle breakdowns impacts us in many areas. A big part of my identity—how I identify who I am—has to do with my actions in handling the inevitable "breakdowns" or "problems" or "issues" in my life, and the story I've built around my way of doing this. For example, if I navigate and handle breakdowns successfully and consistently, I seem to make up one type of story about myself. And if I'm constantly running into trouble, having lots of activity but little new results, I make up another story about myself.

Notice again that how I identify myself is always *a story I have about myself.* This story is full of explanations and declarations ("I am...") and personal assessments. As we've seen, in our own lives and in the lives of others, this story can be very empowering and supportive of our ability to deal effectively in these situations, or it can be disempowering, even paralyzing. Sometimes our story—which we make up as a *result* of not being effective in handling a type of breakdown, for example—is then turned around and used by us as the *cause* of our not being able to handle the breakdown! Around breakdowns and everywhere else, our ability to observe *what we're up to in language* can be the difference between successfully producing the results we say we want—or not.

❄ ❄ ❄

Moving away now from breakdowns and our *9 key declarations*, let's make a few additional points about declarations in general:

- While assertions can be *true* or *false*, declarations can be valid or invalid.

- What makes a declaration valid or invalid has to do with the *authority* granted by the community to the one making the declaration.

- Difficulty in relationships—both professional and personal—may have to do with "fuzziness" or un-clarity about *who gets to declare what.*

Two people can say the same thing (same words), but the power of the declaration only comes into being if the person declaring has the authority to do so... or the strength (force) to back it up. I can stand on the street corner and declare that the new priority for ABC Department Stores in the new millennium will be tires and automotive services. I can declare this until I'm blue in the face, and guess what? The world is not different. But what if the CEO of ABC Department Stores, along with their Board chairman, came on TV and said the same thing? In this case, the world *would* be different.

I can pretend I'm a preacher, priest, rabbi or judge and say the same words a preacher, priest, rabbi or judge says, and even have two people go through the motions and say exactly what they're supposed to say at a marriage ceremony. And when I say "I now pronounce you husband and wife," they aren't really married. The world isn't really different. But if someone else "with the authority vested in them" says the same words, then the people *are* really married and the world *is* really different.

In many ways, authority is socially granted. The authority to marry people, judge people (juries), commit resources, go to war, create policies, set boundaries, shift directions and priorities within organizations or governments, set boundaries and standards within the family unit, all are socially granted, by our society, our institutions, and our organizations. Notice, however, that the early American colonists did not have the authority to declare independence. At that time, only the British Crown had that authority. In the end, the colonists had the force to make their declaration valid. There certainly was no guarantee that a new country would come to be. What is clear, though, is that *without the initial declaration it certainly would not have happened*.

Are we clear about *what we get to declare*, in situations involving others? Have we *agreed* with our partners and colleagues on where the boundaries are? In our work, we see a lot of these conversations missing. And in many of these cases, we see recurring breakdowns and problems connected with this unclarity.

And perhaps more central to the point about creating the experience of happiness—are we clear about *what we get to declare for ourselves* as individual human beings? Let's take it totally out of the realm of workplace dynamics and stay squarely with each of us, as creative, growing, and learning human beings. We say that each of us has the authority to declare:

- what public identity we will create for ourselves
- the kind of life we will lead
- who and what we are
- what's important to us

- our own personal standards
- what's acceptable to us and what's unacceptable to us
- how we will be treated in order to remain in personal or professional relationships.

And so on. Have you ever known someone who did not believe that they had the authority to declare these things about themselves, and therefore did not declare them? Has this ever been so for you? Does this have anything to do with the results we achieve? With our well-being, our peace, our effectiveness? We say yes, it does.

Perhaps nothing is more powerful than a person publicly making a *new primary declaration* about who he or she is, and who he or she is not. Of course, much of the power also comes from the letting go of the old (usually unspoken and unseen) stories and declarations of invalidation, un-acceptance and powerlessness. The new context has a powerful influence on our mood, our interpretations and our movement in the world. This is precisely what ontological coaching is all about, and is the basis for the tremendous, transforming power it represents.

We all have the authority to make declarations in the area of our *personal standards*. Our standards greatly influence how we assess situations, ourselves and others. This, in turn, plays a big role in how we then come to identify a great many things that we "need" to do in our lives. Consider these major "domains" of our lives:

- family/spouse
- work/career
- social/friends–relationships
- play
- body/health
- spiritual/religious
- mood/attitude
- money/finance
- learning/education
- dignity
- world/larger connection.

Our standards (or lack of standards) in each of these areas tend to reveal themselves in the types of assessments we make, and in the actions we take out of those assessments. Our standards come before the assessments, underneath them, in all the areas listed above. The previous section dealt with assertions and assessments, and we showed how it's very possible (even likely) that different people will produce different assessments about the same thing or event.

For example, I see horrible traffic, and Bubba thinks it's just fine, actually flowing pretty well. I say we need 3 months savings in the bank for emergencies; Jean says we need 1. Or I say the presentation was excellent while Pat says it wasn't so hot. I say this way of disciplining kids is best, and Terry says something else. I say the room is comfortable while Sarah says it's way too cramped. I say I'm fat while Bill sees me as average. I say attending certain conferences is valuable and worthwhile, and Ian says they're useless. We could go on and on. A key point is that *we are each making assessments out of some standard, and our standards are declarations*. We declare them into being for ourselves, whether we notice this or not.

We each operate out of our own standards of reliability, tallness, laziness, effectiveness, appropriateness, sportiness, you name it. And then the generative power of declarations kicks in, because from that point forward, the standards are used as the basis for interpreting. And out of those interpretations come the assessments of unreliable, short, not lazy, very appropriate, boxy, and so on.

One reason we focus so much on assessments is because they carry us into the *future*. Our assessments are how we "take a stand" on things, how we "orient" ourselves toward future interactions with people and events. And what are *often hidden*, *often unseen*, and *seldom spoken about* with the very people with whom it could make the most difference... are the *standards* out of which we generate our assessments. In fact, in many cases, our standards are hidden *even from our own view*. We don't see them clearly and may not remember ever declaring them consciously. *But based on the assessments we keep making, we know they must be there.* Can you see how this must be so? Here is where the power of coaching comes to the rescue, in the form of conversations that can allow us to 1) take a look at and 2) begin to declare new standards for ourselves. Here's the key: *As long as they remain hidden, they've got us; we don't have them.*

A key standard which we all have, though we may not see it so clearly at times, has to do with how we allow others to treat us. One expression I have heard that comes to mind here is:

### We teach people how to treat us.

In other words, our actions or inactions with people have the effect of "teaching" them what's okay and what's not okay in being and dealing with us. We allow people to treat us in certain ways, right up until they violate the standards we have set for ourselves related to how we will be treated. This shows up in how we hold people accountable for promises they make to us, as well as in the way we allow people to treat us verbally and physically.

Consider cases in which physical or emotional abuse occurs within a relationship. In this way of thinking, the person being abused may allow the abuse to continue, even over long periods of time, as long as it remains at or below a certain level. This certain level is the person being abused's *standard* for abuse. It can even be seen as a story in which a certain amount of abuse is considered to be "deserved." Up to and including that point, no action is taken. But once that point is passed—that standard is violated—new action is taken by the person being abused. And a new lesson is learned, in our dance together.

❈ ❈ ❈

Assertions, assessments, and declarations all carry a *social commitment* with them. You recall that when you or I make an *assertion* in the world, we are entering into a social commitment that:

1. the assertion we make is true, and
2. we'll provide evidence if requested.

If we continually make false assertions in the world, and if we continually are unable to provide evidence if requested, we generate a public identity for ourselves as "liar." And we do this whether we're aware of it or not.

Now, when we make *assessments*, the social commitment is:

1. that we have the authority to make the assessment, and
2. that we have some grounds (assertions; facts) to back up the assessment.

210

Should I continually make assessments about people or events without any firsthand information and without being able to connect my assessment to any assertions, I begin to generate a public identity for myself as "flaky" or "odd." People begin to think I'm off in la-la land, making assessments that seem to be quite different from those of others, and that don't seem to be tied to or connected to anything. And again, this occurs whether I notice it or not; it's social, it's part of what happens when we live life as non-hermits.

And so with *declarations*, the social commitment is:

1.  that the speaker does, indeed, have the *authority* to make the declaration; and

2.  that the speaker *will act consistently* with his/her declaration.

This authority is socially granted. If we continually make declarations in the world that we're *not authorized* to make, we generate a shift in our public identity. We soon begin showing up as "bozo" or "out of it" or "loony" or whatever.

And if we *act in ways that are inconsistent* with our declarations, we get to show up in the world as "hypocrites." Said another way, we generate the public identity of hypocrite. And usually, people who show up as hypocrites (especially leaders who show up as hypocrites) have a negative impact on those around them, as well as on the quality of their own personal relationships.

There are many instances in *relationships, families, organizations and communities* in which people make declarations, fail to act consistently with them, and then find that a mood of cynicism or resentment has been produced. (I believe the same thing happens with us, at the individual level. We produce resentment and cynicism for ourselves when we keep our declarations private and then don't act consistently with them). I believe there are missing conversations which, if they occurred, could help greatly.

For example, leaders could follow their declarations with requests to colleagues to call it to their attention if, in the coming days or months, it appears that the leader is acting inconsistently with his/her new declaration. Something like *"OK, guys, I've just made a public pledge that this product is our highest priority, and that our employees will be treated as full professionals. I know we've all done some things in the past that we're not looking to continue here. I also know that sometimes I'm not*

211

*a great observer of myself. Like many of you, I'm a beginner at some of this. What are some specific actions that we know, right now, we'll need to start doing (or stop doing)? (Discuss and identify). I also have a specific request for all of you. I request that should you see me saying something or doing something that seems out of line with this, that you bring it to my attention as quickly as possible. Do you agree? (Get agreement). Thanks. Here's how you can reach me...".* Doing this = being *very committed* to following through, to actually bring the new declaration into being, to actually make it so.

Sometimes the big eye doesn't work so well for us and we don't see ourselves the same way others do. Sometimes, having these other perspectives can be extremely valuable. Armed with this feedback, now I get to choose whether or not to continue acting as I have been. I get to choose which new actions I may take, knowing the impact on my public identity and the mood of the organization are at stake. The alternative (not having this information) is not a very powerful alternative. It limits what I see, which limits what I can do.

We can do the same thing in our personal lives. It is much more likely that I will follow through with a personal declaration if I have enrolled others around me to support me in acting in line with it. By keeping these declarations to myself and only thinking about them (but not speaking them out loud), I limit my effectiveness and my chances for success. What's possible is to *let other people know what you're up to.*

Invent conversations for the sake of sharing declarations and it seems to *up the ante.* Now, my partner knows what I'm up to and my identity is at stake. I can ask her for support and feedback along the way, and we can have a true team effort in getting there. The alternative (*not* having these conversations, not sharing what we're up to with those close to us) will absolutely not lead to the same results. It's not wrong—it's just not as powerful, especially if two of the results we want are a stronger relationship and more consistent achievement of our own goals.

**Footnotes:**

1. *The Declaration of Independence of the United States of America;* July 4, 1776.

2. *You Are What You Say: A Harvard Doctor's Six-Step Proven Program for Transforming Stress Through the Power of Language;* by Matthew Budd, MD and Larry Rothstein, Ed.D.; Crown Publishers; 2000.

3. *Merriam Webster's Collegiate Dictionary;* Merriam Webster Editorial Staff; 1994.

4. *The Four Agreements: A Practical Guide to Personal Freedom;* by Don Miguel Ruiz; Amber-Allen Publishing; 1997.

5. *The End of the Innocence*, by Don Henley; audio CD; 1989; Geffen Records.

6. *Anatomy of the Spirit: The Seven Stages of Power and Healing;* by Caroline Myss, Ph.D., Three Rivers Press, 1996.

7. *The Tree of Knowledge,* by Humberto Maturana, Francisco J. Varela and Robert Paolucci; Shambhala Publications; 1987.

8. *The Power of Now*, by Eckhart Tolle; New World Library, 1999.

9. *I Love You, You're Perfect, Now Change;* audio CD; Varese Records; 1996.

10. *Conversations with God: An Uncommon Dialogue;* Books 1, 2, and 3; by Neale Donald Walsch; G.P. Putnam's Sons Publishing; 1996.

## SUMMARY—MAIN POINTS AND
## NEW INTERPRETATIONS

- *Declarations* are very powerful, very creative language acts. With our declarations we open and close possibilities, resolve issues, shift the context, shift directions, and bring into being what was not there before.

- The power of a declaration to bring about something new is *connected to whether or not the speaker has the authority* to make that declaration. In organizations, authority is granted formally. Same with politics, our judicial systems, and in many other areas.

- For individuals, *we say we each have the authority to make certain declarations* for ourselves, no matter what: who we are and who we're not; what our standards are in a myriad of areas; where we choose to go with our lives; how we choose to live and be; and so on.

- *Assertions* can be true or false. *Assessments* can be grounded or ungrounded. *Declarations can be valid or invalid.* Whether or not a declaration is valid or invalid is based on whether or not the person has the socially-granted authority to make the declaration. Make a bunch of invalid declarations, and produce a public identity of "bozo" or "looney."

- *Whether we act consistently with our declarations or not* has the effect of producing a public identity for ourselves of "high integrity" or "hypocrite."

- *Declarations are very connected to moods and emotions.* Like moods, our declarations influence and color our "horizon of possibilities." Out of certain moods, some types of declarations become more likely. And when we make certain declarations, we seem to also influence and produce certain moods.

- *Every decision is a declaration.* Every Yes and every No. And with these declarations we are *not describing how things are;* instead, we are moving and taking action in the world.

- The declaration *"I don't know"* creates a new opening for learning. *"I forgive you"* dissolves resentment, brings closure, and makes peace possible. *"Thank you"* acknowledges generosity and makes joy possible. *"I'm sorry"* takes care of the past and sets a new background, a new context for the relationship. *"This (X) isn't working anymore"* declares a breakdown into being. When we *declare something to be a breakdown* for ourselves, we have declared acceptance and at the same time have created a new context. This new context serves as the necessary starting point, the key first step, toward taking new actions and producing new results.

## HOW-TO: POSSIBILITIES FOR
## TAKING NEW ACTION

1. Refer back to your SAMPLE SITUATION. Consider whether or not improvements may be made by *paying attention to declarations.* For example, is there misunderstanding or fuzziness about *who* gets to declare *what?* If so, a conversation to produce a new agreement here may be the next step. Are people *not acting consistently* with declarations previously made? Are they aware of this? Are people making declarations that they *don't have the authority to make?* Have *you* declared (publicly or privately) this SAMPLE SITUATION to be a breakdown? If you've declared it to be a breakdown in private, can you see any benefits which may come *as a result of also declaring it publicly?* Are you and others involved open to learning, or not? Is it okay for you and others involved to say *I don't know?* Is the present situation connected to "un-cleaned up" past events? Would sincere declarations of *apology* make a difference? Who should make them? Would sincere declarations of *gratitude* make a difference? Who should make them?

2. *Have a conversation* about this with someone close to you. Speculate and identify any possible new actions, new declarations, new conversations which may be helpful here.

3. Refer back to any NEGATIVE INTERNAL CONVERSATIONS you identified earlier. Can you spot any declarations that *you've historically made—often about yourself, your abilities, your prospects, your future—which are now starting to not serve you* anymore? Or can you see any declarations that historically you *have not made,* but that *if you did make them* some positive results might occur?

4. *Make at least one new declaration* that you say will support you in moving out of a NEGATIVE INTERNAL CONVERSATION. Identify specific actions on your part that you say would be consistent with the new declaration. *Share the declaration and new actions with someone close to you,* and enroll the person in supporting you in acting consistently with your new declaration.

5. On a regular basis, take the time to *identify things that you are grateful for. Declare your gratitude—say Thank You—to God or to*

the universe for these blessings in your life. *Declare your gratitude—say Thank You—*to people in your life for the positive contribution that they are.

6. Big Eye: Are there situations you can think of in which, for whatever reason, *you fell down on fulfilling a commitment* you made? If so, have you offered a sincere apology?

7. Big Eye: Identify for yourself any people who you believe have "wronged" you and *that you have not forgiven. Have a conversation with someone close to you* about this, and about the possibilities made available by the power of declaring forgiveness. *Speculate* about what may be holding you back, and about what might need to happen in order for you to move forward and to forgive.

*Chapter 7*

## SECTION 3.

## REQUESTS AND OFFERS

---

*"You miss 100% of the shots you don't take."*

Wayne Gretzky

---

We've covered assertions, assessments, and declarations. Let's now explore the language acts we call *requests and offers*. These will serve as a lead-in to *promises* and the remainder of the book.

Much of what's involved in this chapter involves both requests and offers, although to keep things simple we'll be speaking primarily about requests. But in virtually every situation, what we say about requests can be said about offers. The only difference, of course, has to do with who is committing him/herself to take some specified action and who is doing the accepting or declining. Let's explore.

We say that requests, offers and promises are the speech acts that *directly* involve other non-hermits and actually bring forth non-hermit-hood. I can be alone, making assertions and assessments and declarations. But with requests, offers, and promises I'm *by definition* having conversations with others, coordinating future action with others.

This point is critical to understand and may be so close we overlook it. *Human life, for the vast majority of us, is all about coordinating action with others, in an incredible variety of ways.* We do what we do with and through others. The results we get in all areas, including our well-being, have a great deal to do with the way in which we *coordinate action* (do things) with others. Requests, offers, and promises have everything to do with this basic and pervasive connection. So let's start with a question: *Do you make requests in your life?*

Many people respond with Yes, of course. Many people say they make many requests, every single day. Lots of people say they make frequent requests. The great majority of us make at least some requests. Think about this. Think about the requests you make at work or home, in business or personal situations, even though you may not formally call them requests. Human beings make requests all the time, in a huge variety of situations. So to set this up, we can say that requests are absolutely part of our lives.

Second question: *Why do you make requests?* Or *why does anyone ever make any request?* Clearly, people make specific requests for specific reasons. I'm looking for a broader answer here. I'm inviting you to look at the whole phenomenon of making requests in the first place—what is going on such that anyone would ever make any request? Is it possible to look at the whole category of requests this way?

We say this: *We make requests when we have an assessment that the future is going to unfold in a certain way, and we don't like that. We want the future to unfold in a different way than it seems to be heading by itself, and in order to put things in action to bring this about, we make a request. Requests are profoundly creative!* For example, let's say I'm a teacher, and I have the assessment that if nothing happens, the future is going to unfold in such a way that I'm going to end up grading 150 essays by myself. I don't like this, so I make a request of my colleague to assist me. She accepts my request, and now the future unfolds in a better way, from my perspective. A future that includes my grading 75 papers due tomorrow works better for me than a future that includes my grading 150 papers!

Or I may have the assessment that the future, if left to its own devices, will unfold in such a way that my grass will not be cut. It will just grow and grow. I don't like this, so I request that Bubba cut the grass. If he accepts, the future now is different, and I like it better the new way. Or I may believe that if nothing happens, my company will continue doing Process A or Procedure B the same way in the future. I don't like this, as I see opportunities to do things better. I request that the appropriate people get together to discuss possibilities. I may offer to lead or coordinate the conversation. A new possible future has just been initiated.

Make sense? This is not the only way to view requests, of course. But to me, seeing requests in this manner has a way of focusing on how we can exercise some power to influence the future. We can invent the future in this way. We can intervene on what we think the future will look like, and put in motion events which may lead to results we say we're looking for.

We also see another way in which language—in this case, requests—generate and create. This is related to *public identity*, with the collective assessments others have about us. Public identity has to do with who we "are" in the world, with how we show up for other people. This is important, because that's who the world interacts with. That's who the world talks to, hires, fires, deals with, and enters into relationships with

Consider this. Have you ever been in a situation in which you wanted to make a request, but didn't? Something stopped you, either fear or worry or whatever, but you didn't do it. Now bring to mind a similar situation in which you *did* make the request. It may have been hard, but you somehow did it. Notice how different those situations were, for you and for others. Our claim is that when you make a request, you're not just making a request. You are shifting who you "are" in the world. Whereas before you may have been a person who lets something like that pass without saying anything, now you're a person who stands up and makes a request. You are seen differently by others. You *are* different to them. You *are* different.

Consider the differences in these 2 relationships:

- In relationship A, one person does what he or she does, and this is not what the partner was looking for. It bothers the partner. But the partner *never makes a request* to discuss it in any way. The behavior simply goes on and on.

- In relationship B, one person does what he or she does, and again this is not what the partner was looking for. It bothers the partner. In this case, however, the partner *makes a request* to have a conversation to talk about it.

That conversation, in turn, may include a request that the person begin doing X or stop doing Y in a certain way. If the request is answered with a Yes, a commitment is made and the first step is taken toward inventing a new future.

We can talk about balance in the relationship, we can talk about the context of the relationship, we can talk about dignity in the relationship, we can talk about the results of the relationship. All of these come up as we reflect on these two relationships, one of which includes requests and one of which does not. What would you predict—physically and emotion-ally—for the partner who never makes the request? Many of us have enough experience here to say he/she would likely be resentful, perhaps frustrated and ongoingly out of sorts. And it's also likely that this is not what the partner was intentionally trying to create for him/herself!

What would it be like for any of us to make requests, and always be turned down? I'm talking 100%. How would you characterize a situation in which someone gets No for an answer in every single request that's made? Well, most of us would say it would be pretty lonely, not very good at all. In such a case, I would do everything by myself. I'd go to the store by myself, do my job by myself, go fishing by myself... do it all, by myself. Welcome to *involuntary hermithood*. For most of us, welcome to unhappiness.

We can say that when we make requests in the world, we do so because we want to invent a new future and to do that we've got to get a few Yes-es. It is important to us that we get positive responses to our requests. Without Yes, we don't have a promise or commitment to do any-thing different. Without Yes, we don't have anybody supporting or help-ing us. Without Yes, we are greatly limited in what we can do in the world. So a question becomes: *How can we make requests in such a way that people say Yes?*

This is *not* about manipulation, or in any way hiding or not sharing information so that the other person is damaged or misled. This *is* about distinctions that allow us to more clearly see some "underneath" aspects of this interaction. And once we see some new things, we can do some new things, take some different action.

Here's the claim: *Not all requests are created equal.* Some requests are more effective than others. Some requests, by virtue of how they're made and what they include, have the effect of producing the results we say we want. And what we all seem to be looking for is <u>shared understanding</u> that leads to <u>shared commitment</u>. With shared commitment, we're moving forward and designing our lives—at home and at work. So let's take a look—what do we mean when we say *effective request?*

To set this up, you may want to do this little exercise. Think about a request that you have been avoiding, that you say you'd like to make but for whatever reason haven't made. Or think about a request that you have made in the past, but for whatever reason you didn't get the result you wanted. If you'd like, write it down so you'll be able to take a look at it as we go along. Once you've done this, you can check your request to see which, if any, of the elements below may be worth investigating further. We say that these *six key elements* can help make our requests be most effective.

### Elements of Effective Requests (or Offers)

- Committed Speaker
- Committed Listener
- Future Action and Conditions of Satisfaction
- Timeframe
- Mood of the Request
- Context

Let's explore each one, and notice how different our conversations—as well as our results—could be.

### Element 1—Committed Speaker

First of all, someone needs to make the request. Most people don't respond very well to anonymous requests (words written on a wall, for example) that can't be attributed to anyone. So if I'm making a request of you, there are some actions I can take to make myself a committed speaker. For example, instead of throwing my request over my shoulder to you as we pass in the hall, I can stop and we can look directly at each other, face to face. I can say "Bob, whenever you've got a minute can we talk about the ABC? It won't take long, but we'll need to have a little time to

think through some things because there's a request I want to make..."
Then Bob and I can either move to the edge of the hallway right then, or
set up a time in which we can have the conversation.

We say a committed speaker does <u>*not*</u> do this: Make a request of you,
as I'm sticking my head around your office door, while you're jotting
down notes and eating pizza at the same time. I can instead say, "I've got a
request I'd like to discuss with you—is it possible for you to stop what
you're doing for a moment?" A committed speaker puts his or her body
into the request. A committed speaker takes the actions, whatever these
may be, needed to *generate a committed listener*.

Referring back to the exercise and your own request: In the request
situation you've identified, were you a committed speaker? If not, what
can you do differently in the future in order to become one?

### Element 2—Committed Listener

A committed listener is one who is <u>not</u> talking on the phone with
someone else, jotting down notes and eating pizza. Obviously, such a person is not able to give us his or her full attention. A committed listener is
one who demonstrates solid eye contact, who is present and aware, and is
not actively engaged in something else. As I'm striding down the hall,
focusing on something else I've got to do, I'm not going to be very committed as a listener as you sling your request over your shoulder toward
me. Can you think of times in which you've made requests to less-than-
committed listeners? What were the outcomes of these?

Referring back to your own request: Did you have a committed listener? How will you produce one next time?

### Element 3—Future Action and Conditions of Satisfaction

Here, we share what we want the listener to do (future action) and
something about the standards we want him or her to apply while doing
it (conditions of satisfaction). For example, I may say "Son, I want you to
cut the grass. I want you to cut <u>our</u> grass, and to cut <u>all</u> of our grass. I want
you to use our lawn mower to cut the grass, and our lawn mower needs to
be turned on the whole time. Also, I want you to edge our lawn using our
edger, and I want you to edge 100% of the perimeter of the yard. When
complete, please wash the mower and edger in our driveway using our
hose. Put the hose back on the rack on the wall, and after the sun dries
the mower and edger, put them back in their respective spots in the
garage. Then close the garage door."

Or I can say "Son, I want you to cut the grass." Here's the key—*if you're getting the results you want by making vague requests, by all means continue making vague requests!* Honestly. That's the bottom line, isn't it? Ultimately, it's all about getting the results you want or not. There's not a *right* way or a *wrong* way to make requests. But there are ways that are *more powerful* than other ways. It's all about results.

In many situations, why don't we provide the type of detail and conditions I provided in the above lawn mowing example? We ask this question in workshops, and people respond with:

- Not wanting to insult their intelligence

- Assuming they already know all those details

- Not having enough time to spell it out in such a way

And I don't disagree. These are all valid concerns, they could be very valid interpretations. And yet we still come back to the issue of results. Are you getting the results you say you want from your requests? If not, maybe a place to look is here. Are we asking for what we really want? *Are we generating shared understanding or not?* Anyone who's ever requested that a 10-year old boy "clean up your room" knows that it's very possible to have radically different standards and radically different understandings of what constitutes "clean!" Remember, there's no such thing as shared <u>commitment</u> without shared <u>understanding</u> coming first.

Let's briefly discuss the situation above, particularly a situation in which we *don't* ask for exactly what we want because we don't want to insult the other person's intelligence. This has come up a number of times in our workshops, in many situations. But if we're still committed to getting a good result out of our request, what "moves" are available to us? *Two powerful moves* which are available to all of us, in many situations (not just this one) are:

### *Speak into your concerns.*
### *Declare yourself a beginner.*

That is, speak directly into your concern about not wanting to insult the other person's intelligence. And declare yourself a beginner at having the conversation in this way. Both are utterly sincere and legitimate. It may sound something like *"Bob, I'm not entirely sure how to proceed here so let me just share with you what's going on with me. I want to be specific in requesting your involvement in X, but I have a concern that the way I'm going to ask it is going to insult your intelligence, and that's not at all what I want. This project is new for me, I haven't had too many conversations like this, and I really want us to be on the same page with it. Are you okay with me being specific here, even in areas where it may seem obvious, so that we can make doubly sure we're understanding this in the same way? As uncomfortable as it may be, I think it'll end up giving us a lot better starting point for moving forward and avoiding misunderstandings later on," and so on.*

What exactly changes when you speak into your concerns and declare yourself a beginner? *The context changes.* A new context is now present, one in which a new listening on the part of the other person is much more available. Think for a moment, and I'll bet you can come up with a variety of situations in which such a context can be helpful—at work or in personal situations.

Another reason that we sometimes don't ask for what we really want is that *we don't want to be declined.* We're fearful that if we ask for what we really want, the other person will say No. To avoid this (which we probably interpret as "rejecting me") we make really fuzzy and nebulous requests, allowing lots of room for mis-interpretation and mis-understanding, ultimately, not leading to the result I really want. Does this sound familiar?

It's also possible that we have an interpretation that we really *don't deserve to be requesting,* that we really don't have permission or authority to make such a request. Out of this interpretation, it's easy to see how we could tend to be vague in requesting, leading to all the things that happen when one person thinks we agreed on one thing, and the other thinks something entirely different.

In any event, we say that being specific and clear and precise in this area can serve us, *especially during the initial parts of a relationship.* Over time, as we get to know each other and develop a stronger *shared background of obviousness,* we can ask for things with less detail, and still expect the other person to fully understand.

For example, if I say "May I have a glass of water?" I don't need to also say "and I don't want water taken from the ditch outside." It's *obvious* I don't want ditch water! In our culture, it's obvious that someone requesting water in a glass is requesting it for the purpose of drinking it and that the water needs to come from the drinkable supply, not the ditch or sewer.

We have all had this experience, of being new to a job or situation and knowing that the way people make requests of us as "green beans" is different than how they'd make the same request of a 20-year veteran. Conversely, we may have been the veteran in the organization when a new person is hired. Same thing. We simply don't have a strong shared background of obviousness yet, so we need to provide more specifics in our requests if we expect to generate the same level of understanding— and the same ultimate outcome.

The problem often is that *what's obvious to me isn't obvious to you.* So we say it's prudent to assume, especially at the beginning of relationships, that very little shared background of obviousness exists. Then, over time as we get some history of successful requesting and following through under our belts, we can accurately assume that big chunks of meaning get transferred with very few words.

Have you ever requested that someone else "be more supportive?" Or has someone else ever requested that of you? What's really involved here? What would a camera see me doing as I'm *being more supportive*? Because it's possible that what support is to me, is micro-management or over-involvement to you. We can see many cases in which requests are made that people be more "supportive" or more "creative" or more "open." And while many of us have an intuitive understanding of what is meant, it's quite possible that the other person doesn't share this with us. And before we enter into a promise about something we aren't on the same page about, we say it's better to have the conversation up front. Then I know what I'm agreeing to do, and can do a better job of actually doing it.

It's wonderful to be able to say very little (or sometimes, nothing at all) and have the other person consistently understand a big amount of meaning in our requests. This is usually reserved for those in long-term relationships and is developed over time and with lots of practice. And even here, the invitation is to always be open to the possibility that you could inadvertently be interpreted in a way differently than that which you intended.

## Element 4—Timeframe

Let's say I get back from my trip and I look at the yard, which obviously hasn't been cut. I say to my son "What's going on with the grass? I thought we talked about this—you were going to cut it." And he responds with "I'm getting around to it." What was missing in my request? Right—the *time*. *When* do I want it done? *When* do we want others to do what we want them to do? Sometimes the background of obviousness may fill in the timeframe. And sometimes it doesn't. Again, back to results. If you're getting the results you want by not including an explicit timeframe, then certainly continue not including it in your requests.

Here are some interesting ways in which we bring timeframe to our requests in less-than-effective ways:

- "....and I'd like it *as soon as possible*."

- "... and that's needed *as soon as you get a chance*."

- "... make sure that's done *in a timely fashion*."

- "... to be done *promptly*."

Do these sound familiar? We say this: if you really don't care when someone fulfills your request, ask them to do it *as soon as possible*! At least this way, you won't have any expectations of it happening anytime soon.

Again, what's *as soon as possible* to me may be very different than what it is to you. By asking for something by 3:00 PM tomorrow afternoon, however, we now have a much clearer understanding of what is being requested. Now, the listener may accept or decline or make a counter-offer, or may commit to get back to me about it in 10 minutes, but in any event there is a much stronger level of shared understanding.

### Element 5—Mood of the Request

When we say "mood of the request" we refer to the emotional space or "moodspace" that the speaker happens to be in, as well as the emotional space that the listener happens to be in. Obviously, the way the listener interprets and responds is not separate from the mood he or she happens to be in at the time. And, as the speaker, it's easy to see how my mood will absolutely impact *how I get listened* in the request situation. Many of us know this already—*how* we say what we say is often more important than the *words* we choose. **The right conversation in the wrong mood is the wrong conversation.**

Being able to flex the big eye muscle and observe when we (ourselves) happen to be in one mood or another can definitely serve us. We can take steps to design a mood that's more conducive to what we want to accomplish, or we can simply take time out and wait till "the time is right" to make the request. But a word of caution here: Some of us live in moods for years and years, during which time we'll continuously find that the time is <u>never</u> right!

On the other hand, being a better observer of *others'* moods can also serve us. If we see that the other person is in a mood of anger or sadness, for example, we can speak into it. We can ask if something is wrong, and if later would be a better time to have this conversation. Again, many of us do this already and without consciously thinking about it. And some of us do not, bulling forward anyway, asking the request in the same way that we would've had the person been in a mood of joy. And in the latter case, probably not producing our desired results.

## Element 6—Context

Let's turn our attention now to the context of the request. Many of us do this already. We don't simply walk up to a colleague and say "Will you help me with the float?" without providing some background information, especially if it's likely that the other person isn't intimately familiar with the situation. Usually, we begin with something to set the stage, like "John, as you know we're both on the PTA float committee and we've got to get the preliminary design for the Christmas float done by next Monday. I'm really tied up today and tomorrow with this other project, and I see from the worksheet that you're involved here. Are you available Friday afternoon to get together and help with our design work?"

We set the context, we inform the listener of what else is going on in the background or what else has occurred in the past, in order to give the listener a more broad or more adequate perspective on what the request means and how it fits into the bigger picture. Again, many people do this without really thinking about it. Others consciously make it happen. We say that no matter how it happens, it can be helpful in preparing the other person to listen to what you have to say, in the way that you want them to listen (interpret) it.

These six elements can be helpful as you begin to be more purposeful about your own requests. And they may also be useful as you listen to the requests others make of you. In these cases, you can listen for specifics in the actions you'll be committing to take, as well as for a shared understanding of timeframe.

❊ ❊ ❊

Another observation about requests—specifically, about *requesting that others support us in keeping prior commitments or in acting consistently with prior declarations*. We claim there is great power here. In the last chapter, dealing with declarations, we had an example of this. After the declaration comes the request for support in acting consistently with it. Specifically, the request is for feedback if others observe some actions which seem to be inconsistent or out of line with the declaration.

Many good things result from this. We can now be much more aware and conscious about our public identity, about how we "show up." This allows us to be much more conscious about purposefully designing actions that lead to certain public identities, and not others. In turn, this leads to more fulfilling and healthy relationships and results. Practicing these types of conversations—requesting support and then listening to others give me their assessments and perspective of my actions—has the impact of making us more competent, over time, to have them. They become less and less scary, difficult and awkward. They become much more ingrained into "how we do things," into the context of an organization or a personal relationship. And context matters.

Requests also carry with them *social commitments*, just as declarations, assessments, and assertions do. For requests, two social expectations are created:

- That *we are sincere* in asking for what we're asking for; and

- That *we will declare satisfaction* if what we ask for, is delivered.

Our sincerity shows up in how we follow up (or don't follow up) with those making promises to us, and what we do with what we're given. And should we consistently *not* declare satisfaction—even when others *do* fulfill their promises to us—we can expect problems and relationship difficulties to quickly arise.

❊ ❊ ❊

As we leave requests, let's consider one final point—how many of us have resisted making a request, or not made a request, because we have this internal conversation: **"*I shouldn't have to ask you that!*"** This comes up in workplace and personal situations. We observe something we'd like to change, but we don't make the request because we think the other person should already know or the other person should just do the new behavior on their own, out of "common sense" or something like that. Does this sound familiar?

This is a wonderful example of a key choice that we all have: ***Do we want to be right or do we want to be happy?*** That is, we can be so right, so incredibly right, about how we *shouldn't have to ask* the other person to change his or her behavior, or clothes, or to stop doing this, or start doing that. And out of this position of "right-ness," we don't make the request and so don't bring about what we want to bring about. Usually we then simmer in silent resentment, continue to find evidence that supports how right we are and how wrong the other person is, and still nothing is in place to bring about a new result!

Or we can make an effective request, produce the result we want to produce, and achieve some degree of satisfaction. We can ask for what we want. We can take responsibility for what *we* can do, and operate more out of the *works/doesn't work* orientation and less out of the *right/ wrong* orientation. The choice is ours.

## Offers

Much of what we've discussed so far in this chapter applies equally to requests and offers. Certainly the 6 elements of effective requests can be seen as the 6 elements of effective offers. Just as we make requests in order to get a Yes, leading to a commitment (promise) which leads to our coordinating future action, we make offers for the same purpose.

However, there's another aspect of offers that's also important, and in some ways sets offers apart from requests. Offers are connected with *career* and with *business* in ways that requests are not. For example, one way to look at a career or a business is as a *set of coherent offerings*, made to the public ongoingly. Taxicab services offer to carry passengers from one location to another for set fares. Tax preparation services offer to provide assistance, for a fee, in the areas of personal and business finance. Oil companies offer petroleum products to the market for set prices. Car makers offer vehicles and service. We could go on and on.

When you become associated with a coherent, related set of offerings, we can say that you've built a career. Change the offers you make to the world, you change your career. For people looking for a job or a life change, perhaps this way of looking at offers can be helpful. Maybe one way to think about what I'd like to do, is to think about what I'd like to *offer*. And this way of thinking takes us to the notion of *concerns*. Offers are made to address concerns. Broadly speaking, this is the function of business—to offer goods and services that address the concerns of people. This is also the function of non-profit and other organizations. They make different offers, because they're committed to addressing different concerns.

So we may ask ourselves: What concerns that are "out there" in the world already would I like to address with my offers? Or what concerns are not out there yet, but I believe soon will be? And what specific offers would I like to make to address these new concerns? *Listening is obviously important here*. Also, where are the boundaries of my competence to be able to offer this or that? What new learning is needed in order to become competent enough to do this or that? And so on.

Making offers publicly—and keeping commitments consistently—have a very positive impact on our public identity, of course. We begin to build this identity and become associated with our ability to address these concerns. Individually, this identity may be connected with our careers or our personal relationships. Organizationally, this identity may be connected with our business success or failure. And in both cases, we're directly dealing with our productivity, our peacefulness, our happiness.

### SUMMARY—MAIN POINTS
### AND NEW INTERPRETATIONS

- *Requests and offers* are language actions, speech acts, in which *other people are necessarily involved in our bringing about some new action* and producing some new results. *Making requests (or offers) is seen as a very creative act,* in a number of ways. First, it puts in motion new actions and new commitments, which are the basis for doing things—*any* things—with other people. Second, a person who makes a request or offer that he or she historically has not made *is a different person.* In these cases, we show up differently to others around us, and we ourselves are different observers than we were before. Choosing to make different requests or offers than we used to make is choosing to *be* different than we were before. *To never make any requests or offers* is to not participate in actively guiding or designing our own lives.

- *As non-hermits,* we all make many requests at home and at work and everywhere. The only reason we make any requests at all is because we think the future—if left to its own devices—will unfold in a certain way, and we don't want it to! Requests and offers, if accepted, generate a new today and a new tomorrow. Requests are the front end of creating a commitment or promise *on the part of another;* offers are the front end of creating a commitment or promise *on our part.* And how we make and manage promises, commitments, agreements has a huge impact on our productivity, our peacefulness, and our results.

- *All requests are not created equal.* Some requests are more effective than others. That is, some requests are more likely to be accepted than others. Some requests lead to a clearer and more solid understanding than others. Some requests are the starting point for working and doing things well together, while others are the starting point for misunderstanding, resentment and poor results. Elements of what we call *Effective Requests* and *Offers* include:
  - ➢ Committed speaker
  - ➢ Committed listener
  - ➢ Future action and conditions of satisfaction

> Timeframe

> Mood of the request or offer

> Context

Paying attention to these 6 elements can greatly serve us in making effective requests and bringing about the results we want in our lives. Sloppiness here is often a big part of the problem in situations involving misunderstandings and claims such as "so-and-so didn't do what he or she promised" or "so-and-so never listens," among others.

• Some degree of a "background of obviousness" always exists between the speaker and the listener. That is, some things may be considered "obvious" by <u>both</u> the speaker and listener, in which case solid mutual understanding is reached *without* certain specifics, details, and descriptions. However, in many other cases *what's obvious to one person isn't obvious to the other.* In these cases, paying particular attention to the Future Action and Conditions of Satisfaction element, as well as to the Timeframe element, can be very beneficial.

• *Shared commitment only comes after shared understanding.* Shared understanding is produced in conversation, and is at the heart of why we pay so much attention to our requests and offers, and how they can be made to be more effective.

# HOW-TO: POSSIBILITIES FOR
# TAKING NEW ACTION

1. Refer back to your SAMPLE SITUATION. Notice the *assertions* which you say must be in place before you'll say the situation is "better" or "improved." Are there any *requests or offers* which are needed in order to *bring about new actions* that would lead to these new assertions? In other words, in order to "improve" or "make better" the SAMPLE SITUATION, what new actions need to take place? What new steps need to be taken? By whom? When?

2. Are requests needed for someone to *start* doing something? To *stop* doing something? To *continue or change* how he or she is doing something?

3. Are any *requests* needed in order for someone to make a new declaration? Or for two or more people to *have a conversation in order to reach agreement* about who gets to declare what?

4. As a guideline, remember to *consider each of the 6 Elements* of Effective Requests or Offers.

5. If possible, *practice making important requests* with someone else ahead of time.

6. Big Eye: *Notice your internal conversations* (as well as your body and emotions) as you consider making an important request you haven't historically made. Are these internal conversations serving you, leading you to results you say you want? Remember any BARRIERS TO LEARNING which may pop up for you, and determine how you will move through them. If possible, enroll someone close to you for support in your learning.

# Chapter 7

## SECTION 4.

## PROMISES, COMMITMENTS, AGREEMENTS

---

*The woods are lovely, dark and deep*
*But I have promises to keep*
*And miles to go before I sleep*
*And miles to go before I sleep* [1]

Robert Frost
*Stopping by Woods on a Snowy Evening*

---

Perhaps more than any other action we take or move we make, the way that we deal with *promises* (or *commitments* or *agreements*) has a profound impact on our relationships and our results, in our business and personal domains. For those of us who are not hermits, promises are pervasive and are found in virtually every aspect of our lives. Promises, commitments, agreements... whichever term we use, the claim is this: *They are directly connected to our relationships, our public identity, our*

237

*effectiveness, and our personal well-being.* They are directly connected to a great many of the results we produce for ourselves in the world.

Have you noticed that promises are pervasive? They're everywhere! Remember, human life for the vast majority of us is all about coordination of action with others. For those of us who have jobs, who go to school, raise kids and have friends and families, carpool and do volunteer work, travel and do things with others, promises are everywhere. Every time someone says Yes to any request, a promise is created. Our whole social fabric and structure, our whole economic network, are held together by promises—promises between businesses and organizations, as well as those between individuals. What does it say on the bottom of your credit card slip? For most, it's something to the order of "I agree to pay." Somebody promised to do X work for Y pay; somebody promised me a seat on the plane in return for certain dollars and under certain conditions; somebody promised to turn my cable on between 10 and 2; somebody promised to pick somebody else up at 7:00; or to have the Jones file completed by due date; or to take input A and perform action B on it before sending it as output C to the next department; or to serve as president of the club or coordinate the carpool schedule. Promises and agreements and commitments underlie *everything* that we do with others. They are the *most basic* level, the "actual action" that we use in very different ways, as we do what we do in the world.

And this is so close, we sometimes miss it. But once we begin to see it more clearly, a whole new world of possibilities opens up to us. Let's continue with a story.

In this story, I'm a single guy, living in Nashville a few years back, and I decide to attend a conference. This conference was about leadership and communication and was in Knoxville. At the conference I meet a young lady named Betsy, who is also single and a consultant and seminar leader. We talk for awhile about seminars and flipcharts and sessions we like or don't like at the conference, and eventually the conversation turns to more personal things. We talk about our families and schools, what we're into outside of work, hobbies and interests, and so on. After awhile I think to myself "Hey, we've been talking over an hour. I'm kinda liking this person!" I find out that she lives in Knoxville, and I get up the courage to ask her out. I say "I'm sometimes in Knoxville for business. Would it be okay if you and I had dinner together the next time I'm in town?" She says okay, and gives me her name and phone number.

This is on Sunday, as the conference is winding down. Back in my office the next Tuesday, I think "Hmmm... I think I may need to go to Knoxville this weekend" and give Betsy a call. We set a date for 7:00 pm Saturday night for me to pick her up for dinner, and she gives me directions. I say "hooray" (to myself), I write the directions down and continue on with my week.

Saturday arrives, and I'm pretty busy. I've got a bit of work to complete before leaving, and some unexpected emails arrived that required a response before Monday morning. I know that it takes about 3 hours to get to Knoxville, our date is for 7:00 pm, so that puts me at 4:00 for departure. But I'll need some extra time, so I should really leave around 3:30 or 3:45 or so, just to give myself a bit of a cushion. I'm busy right up until 3:30, finish up quickly, and get on the road a bit before 3:45.

I'm cruising on I-40 east toward Knoxville, when about halfway there I notice a little green sign on the edge of the highway. It reads "Welcome to Eastern Standard Time." Without any hesitation whatsoever the following conversation occurs in my head: "Oh shit!" (Notice—evidence of a breakdown.) Well, I just lost an hour. I speed up, thinking that maybe I can make up most, if not all, of the lost time. I get to the outskirts of Knoxville, reach into my pocket for the directions to her house, and they're not there. In my hurried departure, I left them at home on the counter. I also realize I've forgotten to recharge my cell phone battery, which is dead. I remember vaguely the directions and the address, something like 4545 Whispering Pines or Whispering Winds. And also hey, I'm a guy—I don't have to ask for directions! Like all men, I'm pretty sure I have a built-in internal navigation system that allows me to get to my destination without the unnecessary hassle of asking someone else for directions. Anyhow, after driving around and around for awhile, not finding her house, I look down at my watch and it reads 7:40. Our date, remember, was for 7:00.

Let's switch the scene to her, at her house. What's going on with her? What are some of the internal conversations going on for her? What is she telling herself at this moment? Some possibilities may be:

- "He's not coming—he stood me up."
- "What a loser he is."
- "What a loser I am."
- "He better have a good excuse."

- "Maybe I gave him directions that were confusing."
- "I hope his car didn't break down."
- "I wonder if he got into an accident."
- "Why hasn't he called?"
- "Why do I keep ending up with guys like this?"

You can probably think of more. Now let's switch back to me, driving around and not finding her house. What's going on for me? What are some of my internal stories? Some possibilities may be:

- "Where is it? How could I have been so stupid and leave those directions?"
- "I know it's close, maybe just around this corner, or just around the next corner."
- "What kind of story can I make up?"
- "I've blown it, and I really liked her."
- "What a bad way to start a relationship. I'll never get over this terrible first impression."
- "I'm gonna be late again. Why can't I ever be on time anywhere?"
- "What's wrong with me? I keep doing this kind of thing."
- "Maybe I should have asked for directions."

Look at all these stories, for her and for me. And *what is the one fact we can point to here*? The one fact—out of which all these stories got generated—is this: *I made a promise, and I broke it.*

We claim that how we manage our promises has a great impact on our public identity and on the type of relationships we form. In particular, we see the following four aspects as being specifically impacted by our making or breaking commitments:

- Trust
- Relationship
- Success
- Self-Esteem

Let's take our date example. Is her *trust* for me going up or going down? People in our workshops all report that her trust is on the downward march. This *relationship*, that was created a week ago in language, is also on the decline. How about the *success* of just this first date—looking up or down? It also is going downward. Finally, how about her *self-esteem*? Going up or down? And let's also say that unknown to me, the last 3 guys she had dates with stood her up. Is her self-esteem going up or down? It's going down.

How about me? Am I trusting myself as a guy others would want to date? No. From my perspective, which direction is this new relationship headed? Down. Am I feeling very successful at this moment? No. And how about my own self-esteem? Going in the down direction. All of these—trust, relationship, success, self-esteem—all are diminished. These are predictable results directly caused by the action of making and breaking a promise to another. This is a "no win" situation. Neither party has anything pointing in the upward direction.

We can also begin to go "unconscious" in this regard: if I've broken 457 promises in the past, what's one more? The more we break commitments, the easier it is to keep breaking them, until we reach the point of no longer being fully conscious when we make them. In these cases, we aren't even fully aware of all the outstanding promises we have, which obviously makes it far more likely that we'll not keep them.

We can summarize this, so far, with the chart below:

# Agreements

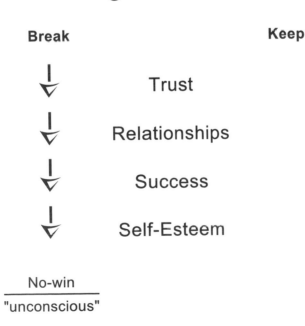

**Break**                    **Keep**

Trust

Relationships

Success

Self-Esteem

No-win

"unconscious"

241

Consider a situation in which someone breaks a promise to you, and then some time passes when you don't see the person. Then, after a year or two, you see this person again. What's one of the <u>first</u> things that goes through your head? For many of us, it's remembering that the person broke a promise to us. And it seems to happen even if the person is a friend.

What do many of us want to do if we have broken a promise to someone, and then soon afterward, we see that person walking right toward us in a hallway or on the street? Many of us want to duck into a room or closet; some of us even cross the street. All to avoid the person to whom we've broken a promise. Think of it this way—if you break enough promises to enough people, and then begin to avoid all these people, welcome to being by yourself quite a lot. Those people will also tend to avoid *you*, and will certainly avoid doing things—*coordinating action*—with you. Break enough promises, and we end up doing whatever we do, by ourselves. It's a fairly sure and well-proven path to involuntary hermithood.

If you have a choice, will you work with or be with or play with people who break promises to you? Probably not. Same goes for me. We know this very well—our making and keeping or making and breaking promises has a giant effect on who we "are" in the world. These actions have everything to do with how others see us, with our public identity. And it is our responsibility to take care of our public identity.

Many of us are not aware that this is happening, as many of us are sloppy in our making of promises. We say Yes casually to others' vague requests, or we make promises that we have a sense we aren't going to keep, but in that moment it seems like the most expedient thing to do. We say:

- "Yes, dear, I'll be home at 6:00" and then something comes up and we don't make it till 7:30.

- "I'll take you fishing this Saturday, Bobby" and then something else happens, likely connected to work, and we end up not going.

- "I'll take care of that, Joe" without fully understanding what we just agreed to. We're in a hurry and we don't clarify our understanding, and maybe we don't focus on it well enough to ever write it down. It never makes our to-do list and so it doesn't get done.

In each of these cases, we can point to how trust, relationship, success, and self-esteem are all diminished—for both the one making the promises, as well as for the person on the other end. And if we do this over time, we can predict the (usually unspoken) responses of people to whom we've broken promises. In these cases, our public identity is already such that other people listen (interpret) insincerity even as we're making the promise itself. Their internal responses to the three promises above include something akin to:

- *"That's BS. You won't be home then."*
- *"That's BS, Dad. Something always comes up. We won't be going."*
- *"That's BS. He's not gonna do it. I better make other plans to handle this."*

❉ ❉ ❉

Let's return to the story before making a few additional points. Let's start over, and say the same situation occurs. Betsy and I meet at a conference, hit it off pretty well, and I get her phone number. That Tuesday I call, and we set the date for Saturday night at 7:00, and she gives me directions to her home. I know how forgetful I can be, so I photocopy the directions 10 times, putting one in my wallet, two in the car, one on my bathroom mirror, and the rest in my briefcase. No way will I forget how to get to this woman's house! Saturday arrives, and I make sure to have my work done so as not to be distracted prior to leaving. I realize Knoxville's on eastern time, so leaving at 3:00 puts me there by 7:00 her time. But I want to leave some extra room in case of road delays or direction problems, so I leave instead at 2:30.

I'm cruising east on I-40 and when I see the "Welcome to Eastern Standard Time" sign I have no problems, just pop in another CD and continue on. I get to the exit clearly indicated on one of the three sets of directions I have with me and notice that I've got a little time. I find a flower shop and pick up a dozen roses. Back in the car and I arrive at her house at one minute before 7:00. There I am, on the front porch, on time, flowers in hand, big smile on my face, and she answers the doorbell.

Now, what's going on for her? What are some of her internal conversations at this moment? Maybe they're more like:

- "Excellent"
- "He's too good to be true"
- "He likes me"

- "I like this guy"
- "This is gonna be a great night"
- "Wonderful"
- "Flowers on the first date. What does he want?!"

You can probably think of others. And how about me? What am I thinking? Very similar internal conversations. These are very different from the ones we each had in the earlier scenario. The *one fact here is that we had a promise, and I kept it.*

Back to our chart, we can see that each of the four key elements listed—trust, relationship, success, and self-esteem—are now moving in the positive direction. Her trust in me, as well as my trust in myself, both moving up. This relationship is now "moving" in a positive direction. The success of this first date, at least, seems to be supported. Her self-esteem—especially if three previous guys stood her up—is definitely moving up. And what about mine—I kept that promise, right on time, big smile on her face? Absolutely moving up as well.

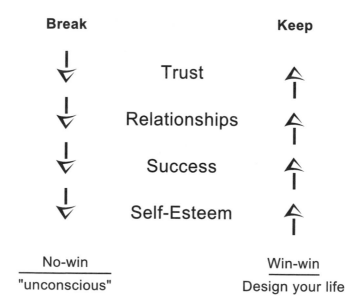

# Agreements

| **Break** | | **Keep** |
|:---:|:---:|:---:|
| ↓ | Trust | ↑ |
| ↓ | Relationships | ↑ |
| ↓ | Success | ↑ |
| ↓ | Self-Esteem | ↑ |
| No-win | | Win-win |
| "unconscious" | | Design your life |

We say keeping agreements is a win-win proposition. And this, of course, is not new. For ages people have talked about the importance of keeping commitments and whether or not people are "as good as their word." How committed are we to sticking with it, to making it happen? This has to do with integrity, and with our ability to build solid relationships. Many of us have seen this quote from Aristotle before, and there are many instances in which it is valuable to think about: ***We are what we repeatedly do. Excellence, then, is not an act, but a habit.*** [2] And in our way of thinking, a great deal of what we "repeatedly *do*" is actually what we "repeatedly *say*". It has to do with the connection with our later actions (including our later words) with our past and present actions (including our past and present words).

A key question is: *What side of the chart do you want to be on?* You get to choose. We all do. On the "break" side we produce certain results, and on the "keep" side we produce certain results. One way we close this topic in our workshops is to share a simple analogy. We say that for all of us, an angle exists. This angle (see below) represents the difference between what we say we're going to do and what we actually do:

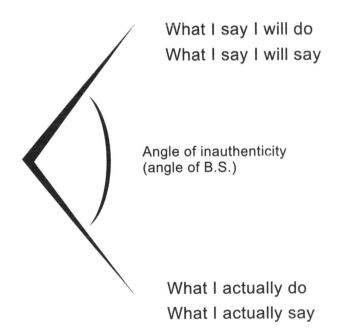

What I say I will do
What I say I will say

Angle of inauthenticity
(angle of B.S.)

What I actually do
What I actually say

We call the angle between the two the angle of inauthenticity, or in layman's terms, the angle of BS. We can reframe our question, in light of this angle, in this way: *How much BS are you producing?* This matters. Because, whether or not we know it, other people "smell" it! Most of us have pretty good BS-detectors. And in some cases, we've also gotten a lot of practice using them.

❊ ❊ ❊

Let's continue to deepen this distinction. And as we've said, distinctions allow us to see what we couldn't see before. We can then do what we couldn't do before. The whole point of noticing is to be *more at choice* about future actions and future results. Let's take a look at *three types of promises* and how they show up in our lives and in the world:

- *Strong* promises: Promises that I am absolutely committed to keeping. You can count on me.
- *Shallow* promises: These look like a strong promise, but what I *don't say out loud* is "unless X or Y happens." For example, I may say "Yes, I'll be at the reunion on Saturday" but what I *don't say* out loud is "unless it rains." Or "unless I have other work to do." Here, we reserve a private "out" for ourselves, but we don't let the other person know.
- *Criminal* promises: These are promises that at the moment of making, we know we have no intention of keeping.

As related to these types of promises, an interesting exercise for many of us is to take a look at the major domains of our lives:

- family/spouse
- work/career
- social/friends–relationships
- play
- body/health
- spiritual/religious
- mood/attitude
- money/finance
- learning/education

- dignity
- world/larger connection.

and see if *any patterns* emerge related to the types of promises we make. Take a look at the promises you make to your significant other, your family members, yourself, your friends, your co-workers, your boss and see what shows up (big eye).

Many of us find that we make criminal promises to ourselves. Or that we tend to make shallow promises with family members, that we somehow take them for granted, that they'll be there for us. Others have different patterns. But in our experience, our way of making and keeping promises *is tightly connected to our relationships and well-being*. What's possible is to clean up relationships containing broken promises; but of course this is *not* possible without first noticing and then accepting what we've been up to. From here, we can declare the current situation to be a "breakdown" for us—to be "not working" for us—and move into new action.

Promises change the world <u>now</u>—right when they're made—not only through the act of completing them. If you promise that you'll take care of the Jones account, the world is different now—not just after you take care of the account! If I promise my wife that I'll buy the peanut oil for the fried turkey, that changes her day now. She makes different choices, has different options now, does different things today. When we make a promise, the world is different because language conveys commitment—not just information.

While "a man is only as good as his word" may be a familiar expression, what may not have been so clear for many of us is the way in which we use promises to *design who we are* in the world. The promises we choose to make, as well as the manner in which we make and manage them, have a tremendous impact on our *public identity*. They also have a direct impact on the *types of relationships* we're able to form. Our results are often directly connected to the types of promises we make, as well as to our ability to *manage multiple promises* to different people or groups. We see this clearly in businesses, organizations, and families of all types. We can even see this at the individual level, where our personal declarations—which can be seen as promises we make to ourselves—provide the *launching pad*, the context for bringing about some change or improvement.

Speaking of this, let's return to self-esteem. Who is it that we often break the most promises to? We say it's *ourselves*. Anyone who's ever had self-esteem issues knows this is true. And even though we make up many stories and rationalize and have great excuses for why we didn't keep the criminal private promises we've made to ourselves, our bodies know. The broken promises "live" in our bones and our bodies, and over time this impacts our mood, our actions, and our results. Our moods and our bodies and our language are definitely connected.

Does it ever happen occasionally that we make a promise in good faith, and then events occur that prevent us from being able to keep it? Yes, it does. It happens to all of us, at one time or another. Here, we now speak about *managing our commitments* or *managing our promises*. What advice would you give if people asked you what to do in situations in which they made a promise, and then realized they wouldn't be able to fulfill it? Most of us would reply with "Let the person on the other end know." And does it matter *when* you'd let the other person know? Most of us would say Yes, it matters a lot when you let them know. Earlier is way better than later. As soon as you're aware that you won't be able to keep your promise is the time to let the other person know. And we all know this, yet it still shows up as an issue in many relationships and organizations.

*Being impeccable here doesn't mean that I keep every single commitment I make. It does mean, however, that I take full responsibility for actively managing them.* What's possible here is to *re-negotiate the commitment.* For example, when I call you to let you know that I won't be able to deliver X by Y, we can have a conversation in which I may commit to deliver it by Z date. Or maybe I can deliver W by Y. It's also possible, of course, that you absolutely positively need X by Y and no renegotiation is possible with me. In this case, we revoke the promise and you find somebody else to take care of it.

Renegotiating a promise now and then is one thing. However, should I notice that I'm *continually* having to renegotiate my promises, this is an area for me to look at. That is, *is this an event or is it a trend?* And if someone in your life is continually having to renegotiate his or her promises with you, this may be a valuable conversation to open up. As always, the mood and context for such a conversation will have a big impact on the results produced out of it.

Managing promises is an act of relationship building. If I don't care about my relationship with you, I let my promise to you go unfulfilled without talking to you. That action will have the predictable effect, on your end, of not wanting to deal with me in the future. I begin avoiding you anyway, the next time I see you coming, and so we both are moving in the direction of no future relationship with each other.

The only reason we do actively manage our commitments is because we *do* care about the relationship. And for the great majority of us, of course, our relationships are directly connected to our happiness, to our sense of well-being, as well as to our ability to actually accomplish anything.

Single promises are often *linked with other people and other promises*, of course, and this is especially visible in organizations as well as in family situations. Have you noticed, for example, that Bubba's falling down on a certain promise to you means that you can't keep your promise to Ann? You were waiting for what Bubba was going to provide as input to something you were putting together for Ann. Because he didn't deliver on his end, you're now scrambling to try to meet your commitment to Ann. And what you may not be aware of is that Ann had to have what you promised her in order to compile what she had promised Sandy for the board meeting, and so on.

In a fundamental way, any organization can be seen as a network or series of linkages of "nested" promises. Understanding these *commitment cycles* can be the basis for extremely powerful and effective change within organizations. It's all about commitments and how they are connected with other commitments to form the foundation for *everything* that goes on within the organization.

Have you noticed also that, as individuals, we make commitments *not in isolation*, but on top of other commitments we've made? Anytime we say Yes to someone's request, we've just made a commitment. Of course, the other person doesn't know about the 27 other outstanding commitments we've got—all he or she knows is that we said Yes and that equals a promise. We spoke earlier of the phenomenon of "overwhelm," which we see as a fairly prevalent moodspace for many of us in this country. We see a great number of *time management* books and seminars and systems out in the marketplace, some of which are undoubtedly more effective than others. Many people have shared with us their experience of achieving some short-term gains out of selected time management programs, but for whatever reason not keeping those improvements over the longer term.

To repeat, we claim that *time management* is a misnomer. There's no such thing as time management. Looking at the clock, we see the second hand continuing its march around. Nobody I know has ever been able to find and add an additional 3 hours at the end of a busy 24-hour day. For us, time simply cannot be "managed" in that sense. To "manage" something implies some control or influence over it, and that is just not the case here. For us, the following illustration provides a more powerful interpretation of what we're up to in these cases:

We *can* manage our commitments. We cannot manage time. This simple shift in orientation—and shift in focus and emphasis—may be extremely valuable to us, as we seek to design more effectiveness and less overwhelm into our lives.

Let's return to the example of the 27 other promises I've already made, before I said Yes to your request. You're not aware of these other promises I made. All you know is that I said Yes to your request, so we have a promise. Here I am, all covered up with these commitments. This is the situation. And here's the kicker—out of this, *I get to be resentful* when you innocently ask me how things are progressing a few days later! What I forget is that I'm the one who made the promise. I'm the one who said Yes in the first place. Back to the big eye.

Remember our earlier conversation about No? Here is a key example of how learning how to say No (through time and practice) can serve us. It is a powerful tool to enable us to manage our commitments. Without it,

managing commitments is virtually impossible and we very quickly realize that others are running our lives. Whenever this has happened to me,
it's also been accompanied by a healthy dose of resentment on my part.

And as we've said before, the reason so many of us find it hard to say
No is that we're operating with interpretations of what No is that don't
serve us very well. I much prefer the notion that the request and the
requestor are separate, that I can decline your request without rejecting
you. No is not a rejection of you, it is simply a decline of your request. Just
as others have the right to decline our requests (in a great many situations), you and I (in a great many situations) have the right to decline others' requests of us.

Like anything, learning to say No takes time and practice. There is no
substitute. And I do not want to imply that this is easy, especially if we
have years and years of acting in different ways. We have a lot of practice
doing it differently, so we're very competent at not saying No in many situations. And in many situations, those around us may have gotten used to
our not saying No and have grown accustomed to it. But the payoff is
worth it. Being able to say No means being able to design your life, being
able to design priorities and take actions that support you in going toward
the goals you've declared to be important. Being able to say No means
being able to be a person of dignity, being able to "stand up" in some way
for your own life. Being able to say No means being able to be a full partner in a relationship, be it personal or professional. This is a wonderful
example of the power of our language and our conversations. It's another
great example of how not being able to *say* a certain thing, means not
being able to *be* a certain way. ***As human beings, we each have the
right to decline others' requests of us.***

Let's turn for a moment to saying No and managing commitments
*within organizations*. Many participants in our seminars have shared
with us situations at work in which they legitimately cannot say No.
Certain workplace requests, for example, are really demands or workplace requirements of the position. In some ways, by agreeing to be an
employee in a certain organization means that we agree to say Yes to certain requests made of us by appropriate people, and agree to perform
accordingly. What is possible, however, is to have *conversations to clarify
where the boundary is* between these "requirements" and those which
are really requests. Our experience, and the experience of many of our
seminar participants, is that these conversations can be truly revealing for

everyone involved. It's often the case that the person making certain requests has viewed them as requests (which by definition may be declined or counter-offered), while the person responding has historically viewed them as demands, with no leeway for declining or renegotiation. Such conversations can lead to redefining work roles, as well as building more healthy and productive employee relationships.

❋ ❋ ❋

Let's move away for a moment from discussing how we manage the promises *we've* made and consider possible "language moves" we can make when we're on the other end. Specifically, let's consider situations in which *other people* have made promises to us and for whatever reason *have not kept them*. Do other people sometimes fail to deliver on their promises, in both personal and workplace situations? We say yes, they do. We all do, from time to time. If someone does not deliver what was promised, we say that we've got at least three options:

- Do nothing. Ignore it.
- Blow up in a fit of anger and loudly blame the other person.
- Make a responsible complaint.

Let's take each one in turn. 1) *Doing nothing* is not the action we'd recommend because doing nothing usually produces assessments which lead us to indignation and resentment. We simmer in silent resentment, which has an impact not only on this relationship but many others as well. And it usually produces neither the result of ultimate fulfillment of what was initially promised, nor the experience of happiness. 2) *Blowing up in anger* also usually does not produce the result we're looking for. By blaming the other person we usually produce defensiveness on their part. How do you normally react when someone, in an angry tone, loudly blames you for something? I usually feel triggered to anger and to immediately try to defend myself and my position. This obviously isn't fertile ground for strengthening the relationship, nor for getting fulfillment of what was initially promised. To us, 3) a *responsible complaint* is a powerful and very under-used move in both organizational and personal situations. It is simply a move to make when you care about the relationship, *and* you also care about getting done what was promised. Think about it— if you don't care about the relationship, alternatives 1 and 2 may make sense. But in our view, the quality of our relationships is connected with the quality of our journey—our own happiness.

***The first step, perhaps, to bringing responsible complaints into your repertoire is a conversation about responsible complaints!*** That is, a conversation in which people who interact with each other discuss commitments and managing commitments, as well as the negative consequences of having promises go unkept and unmanaged. Here, these people give each other permission to "call each other on" commitments not kept. In this conversation, we can also share our concerns with being beginners and "not getting it right" and "hurting feelings" which are certainly valid concerns. *In these ways, we set the stage or create the context (now) in which a responsible complaint (future) has the best chance of producing the result it's intended to produce.*

A responsible complaint is a conversation in which a person on the "receiving" end of an unfulfilled promise initiates a particular conversation with the other person involved. The focus of this conversation is on taking care of the broken or un-managed commitment, and doing so in such a way that the relationship is maintained and even strengthened. Pay close attention to emotion and context here, especially when first starting out. In this conversation, we may talk about many things. But ultimately, we must take *certain language actions* for this to be a responsible complaint. We start with the facts—with some *assertions*. We clarify whether we *did* or *did not* have a promise in the first place and whether or not this promise actually *did* or *did not* get fulfilled.

If indeed the promise was made and not fulfilled—and not managed in any way—we then *declare* the unacceptability of this happening again. We can share our *assessments* of the negative consequences which occurred as a result. We *request* that in the future, promises will be managed by doing X or Y. We can make a *new request, with a new timeframe, and obtain a new commitment* to take care of what originally needed to be taken care of. Or we can cleanly revoke the initial promise. By making these moves, among other things, we're "teaching" those around us about the dance we do around promises or commitments. (Depending on the given situation, of course, there may be very different types of consequences for *continually* falling down on commitments: legal consequences, financial consequences, social and relationship consequences, consequences related to public identity and career, consequences related to the prevailing mood or atmosphere, and so on.)

Responsible complaints are *powerful language moves*, having a direct impact on:
- Our ability to achieve the results we want to achieve, with and through other people
- Our ability to be effective leaders and managers in organizations
- Our ability to be "assertive" and "stand up" for ourselves
- Our ability to create mutually respectful relationships
- Our ability to create and sustain a workplace atmosphere characterized by trust, accountability, personal responsibility and effectiveness
- Our dignity
- Our happiness.

By setting the context—and with practice—we can bring the *responsible complaint* into our own repertoire in both personal and workplace situations. Responsible complaints are only used in situations where a *promise—a commitment*—was not managed or fulfilled. This is an entirely different situation than one in which someone doesn't fulfill someone else's (usually unspoken) *expectation*. Make sense? This is a critical distinction to have:

### Promises unkept are NOT equal to expectations unmet.

I learned it this way: *Expectations are free!* You can have all the expectations you want. And what's amazing to notice is this: ***The world does not care about your expectations. Or mine.*** There's nothing wrong with having certain expectations, of course. We all have some. The problem is when they start to become more than expectations for us, when we don't see them as our own personal and private expectations anymore. The problems start when we begin treating our expectations as if they were promises that other people have made to us. These problems almost always include negative impacts on our relationships, our moodspace, our public identity, and our results.

Expectations live in language, as internal conversations and narratives. We often do what we do without really seeing them, without really being aware of them (big eye). And whether we call them expectations or assumptions, they can have a powerful—and often negative—impact on us.

Don Miguel Ruiz, in his book <u>*The Four Agreements*</u>, says it this way:

> *We have the tendency to make assumptions about everything. The problem with making assumptions is that we believe they are the truth. Whenever we make assumptions, we're asking for problems. We make an assumption, we misunderstand, we take it personally, and we end up creating a whole big drama for nothing. It is always better to ask questions than to make an assumption, because assumptions set us up for suffering.* [3]

For promises unkept, a responsible complaint is a very powerful move to make. For unspoken expectations unmet, different story. In these cases, nobody violated anything; nobody fell down on any agreement. They simply didn't spontaneously take the action I expected them to take. What's possible here, of course, is a conversation in which some *actual requests* may be made, and *actual promises* may be entered into.

### For Businesses and Organizations

*The entire world of business may be seen to be a world of promise-making, promise-keeping, and promise-managing.* That's what's going on, all around, at a very basic level. Making a promise to deliver a good or service in a certain way, at a certain price, under certain other conditions, and then putting the capacity together—and maintaining it over time—to actually deliver on that promise. And innovating and continuing to make new and powerful offers and promises. And learning/changing/being flexible enough to maintain the ability to deliver this new product or service, and so on and on.

We may not call them promises, especially in work settings, but they are *commitments* nonetheless. Internally, they may take the form of agreements made in employee or leadership meetings (or in the hallways, or restrooms, or anywhere else) about implementing new goals, programs or changes; in other words, *agreements and decisions about who's going to do what, when, and how*. Parts of job descriptions may also be viewed as a form of agreement or commitment, as may many elements of the new employee orientation process. In business-to-business settings, agreements are usually called contracts.

Once I started looking for promises in organizations, I saw them everywhere! They *are* everywhere, everywhere we non-hermits are found. They are the basic move, the basic action, which coordinates our actions and *allows us to accomplish things in groups of any size greater than 1.* What I have learned so far is this:

- In organizations, underneath all physical and information processes are "commitment processes."

- At the most basic level, organizations are composed of human beings, under the shared roof of common purpose, coordinating action with one another. This is depicted in the simple graphic below.

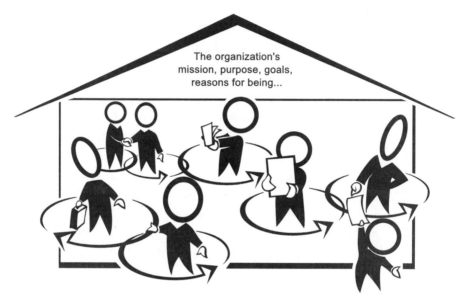

Human Beings Coordinating Action

- And the *way* we coordinate—internally and externally—is with promises, commitments, agreements. At a multitude of levels, in a multitude of ways.

- Organizations are, at their core, composed of *networks of commitments,* which are strongly connected to conversations and personal relationships.

Again, all organizations may be viewed as being composed of "nested" or "networked" promise cycles or commitment cycles, all connected to one another directly or indirectly. We know this already—we all know examples of how someone in one area failing to keep a commitment impacts others' ability to keep their deadlines and commitments, and how this can "ripple" through the organization.

These cycles are the very vehicle by which people make changes, do things differently, and do different things. They are the way in which new goals or priorities are "rolled out" and "implemented." They are the *actual mechanisms that are used* in order to reallocate resources, change directions, or undertake a particular set of tasks. It's all about people coordinating their action with the action of others. This has everything to do with the way in which we work together for a common objective.

We can do this well, or we can do this poorly—formally or informally, verbally or in writing, via email or smoke signals—but we <u>are</u> going to do this if we're a group of more than 1. This is *how we do what we do* in organizations.

Within every organization, right now, promises are being made and managed. Processes are being built, actions are being coordinated and taken for the purpose of achieving some goal—whatever was promised. People on the receiving end (internal or external customers) either are, or are not, satisfied with what was delivered. If satisfied, we close this "cycle" and make a new commitment, take a new step in whatever it is we're undertaking. And if not satisfied, we deal in some way with this situation and its aftermath.

Remember our discussion about Responsible Complaints? I support people in using responsible complaints in these situations, but let's be clear, whether or not a company's people are able to make responsible complaints, some commitments—at a variety of levels—*will* go unfulfilled. The only questions are about the particular "moves" people will make when promises are not fulfilled and about the collective impact, over time, of these interactions on the productivity, effectiveness and "culture" of the organization.

As people interact over time, and make promises to one another and work with others and coordinate action, inputs and outputs, a particular "culture" or "standard" evolves within the organization. Think about what it's like to be in an organization in which commitments are made publicly and clearly, the vast majority of people take their commitments seriously, and are personally responsible for owning and actively managing their commitments. In such an organization, they never are part of any unexpected, last-minute drops of the ball because they're always on top of things, always communicating with people and re-negotiating, modifying commitments in real-time. Here, everyone expects promises to be kept and to be actively managed in all cases. Here, anyone failing to manage a commitment *will* be "called" on it, even by peers and subordinates. (This is all agreed to ahead of time). Not in a super-negative, accusing way, but in a way that is consistent with a culture of trust, responsibility, personal accountability and teamwork.

Now think about what it's like to be in a company in which promises are allowed to slip and slide often, with many unspoken assumptions and misunderstandings, and with people not taking responsibility for managing their commitments. Think about the productivity impact as well as the "mood" impact. In this setting, people often blame others, or always have a ready reason or excuse as to why X or Y didn't get done. Real accountability is non-existent here, as gradually people at all levels slide into a kind of mild cynicism about virtually everything. People who've been on the receiving end of one too many broken commitment may begin to harbor a bit of resentment. It becomes much easier—and much more prevalent—to gossip and complain about others' broken promises behind their backs. It slowly becomes the standard, the norm. Yet no real action to improve is taken. No conversation for the sake of making this better is ever held. Promises simply keep getting broken, commitments continue to be unkept and not cleaned up, agreements are allowed to slip by unfulfilled. Often, it's as if this topic—which is at the heart of things—is considered to be *undiscussable*—undiscussable, at least, in conversations which could actually move things toward real change.

The conversations which organizations *require, prohibit,* and *allow* are strongly connected to that organization's culture, moodspace and success. The same applies for any relationship, for that matter. *What conversations will we absolutely engage in? In what situations? Who should initiate each given type of conversation? What mood will we aim for in these conversations? What conversations will we <u>not</u> engage in, no matter what? Instead of those, which ones will we have?*

And the starting point, of course, is a *conversation in which we discuss these conversations*, share our assessments about them and what they do to our organization or to our relationship. This is a wonderful starting point for redesigning "culture" or "mood" because we can get our arms around conversations. We can *make definite agreements* about conversations we *will* and *won't* engage in. We can declare an atmosphere of learning and set the stage such that we don't have to be experts right out of the gate. We can also request that others support us if we seem to be sliding back into old habits, sliding back into old conversations. For leaders at all levels, who get paid to have effective conversations, this can be a powerful approach for organization change. And for individuals in personal relationships, this can serve as a powerful tool for creating a context much more likely to lead to a mutually satisfying journey together.

Fernando Flores and others have developed a model which allows organizations to bring more awareness, rigor and purposefulness to the ways in which they interact and coordinate with each other. This model, known as the *Cycle of the Promise*, is an excellent tool for shifting toward what is called a "culture of commitment" and away from a culture of blame, excuses and non-accountability. In this model, the key actions involved in making an effective request leading to a solid commitment are learned by everyone. These key actions include:

- setting the context
- making an effective request (6 elements)
- obtaining a "valid" response (accept, decline, counter-offer, or commit to respond at a future time; see below)
- carrying out the actions needed to fulfill the commitment (which may include kicking off other promise cycles with others, which also must be managed)
- communicating status and declaring completion
- assessing finished results
- closing the cycle (or making a responsible complaint)

These are all highlighted and used as the primary levers of change. Intervening in order to improve results takes the form of creating a new context, introducing new distinctions and new ways of looking at the organization and its productivity. Here, improving at the level of "commitment management" is the focus.

This includes conversations in which new standards are declared and shared. It includes people making new agreements with each other, agreements to support each other in taking these new actions and being personally accountable. It includes people being beginners and learning to take new actions over time, and cultivating a new workplace culture of high-trust, high-accountability, and "clean" relationships.

Improving in this way includes an assumption that everyone is always at least partially responsible for things being like they are, and moving away from the "blame game." Organizational improvement here focuses directly on the underlying interactions out of which everything else flows—the way in which the people "coordinate action" with each other. *It's all about bringing some awareness and purposefulness to the ways that leaders and employees ongoingly make, keep, and manage commitments.*

*Viewed this way, the goal for organizations is "impeccable" coordination of action.* Again, this doesn't mean that every single person will always keep 100% of the commitments he/she makes, but it does mean that everyone will *actively manage* his or her commitments. It means that relationships will always be kept "clean." Actively managing commitments includes the ways in which we communicate with each other (and the ways that we don't), the types of discussions we have (and don't have) when it becomes apparent commitments will not be kept as originally planned. It includes the way we handle situations when commitments are not kept, and whether or not we make responsible complaints. It includes how clear we are when we make commitments. It also includes how much of our internal dialogue about this we share with others and in what manner the sharing occurs. How we manage commitments has everything to do with productivity, effectiveness, mood, and results.

Moving toward this *impeccable coordination* is very much supported by paying attention to our requests. It is also supported by paying attention to *how others are allowed to respond* to our requests. Just as not all requests are created equal (some are more effective than others), we can say that not all *responses* are created equal. Some responses will definitely support you in moving toward a culture of commitment, and some will definitely not.

Let's assume that we want to create such a culture, a culture of commitment and personal ownership of and responsibility for managing our promises. It's my direct experience that the following responses, over time, will NOT get us there:

- "I'll try."
- "Maybe"
- "Possibly"
- "Perhaps"

- "We'll see"
- Silence (no response)

Do these sound familiar? What has been your experience in cases in which many people respond to requests this way? Anytime you find yourself making a request, and the listener responds with one of these, we say get ready for sloppiness in coordinating, difficulties in working together, and frequent misunderstandings. We can also get ready for resentment and other "negative" emotions as misunderstandings lead to consequences that include ineffectiveness, inefficiency, and damage to public identity.

For those seeking to build a culture of commitment (for personal relationships as well as business environments), we say that there are *four valid responses* to others' requests. That is, we may talk a lot about the request and what it means, and we may have a lively discussion about many aspects of it, but at the end, we leave the conversation with one of these four in place:

- *"Yes"*—acceptance; now we have a promise.
- *"No"*—decline; we do not have a promise.
- *Commit-to-commit*—a promise to get back to the requestor with the answer at a specified time. *"I'll get back with you by Tuesday at noon with an answer, after I check my calendar and review the timeline for the other project—ok?"*
- *Counter-offer*—a decline of the initial request and initial conditions, coupled with an offer to accept if certain conditions are changed. *"No, looks like I won't be able to complete it by Friday... but I can commit to having it done by Monday at close of business. Will that work?"*

These four responses share one common trait—they are all clear. They are not fuzzy. They represent a much more "clean" interaction, so that all parties better understand *what's* really going to happen and *when* it's going to happen. They provide a much more solid foundation for working together and coordinating together. Shared understanding always comes before shared commitment. Coupled with the responsible complaint, these four responses are excellent tools for designing rigor and effectiveness into our organizations (and relationships).

Obviously, the culture of a company is strongly connected to its interactions and results. Pay attention to managing commitments, talk about them, emphasize them... and I promise a workplace mood of openness, respect, accountability and effectiveness is possible. Ignore commitments and allow sloppiness around managing commitments to become the "norm," and it's quite predictable—a sure bet, actually—that resentment and cynicism will take up residence.

❊ ❊ ❊

For leaders and managers: How would you characterize the way in which your organization coordinates action within itself? Consider convening conversations with supervisors and other direct reports in which the following questions are posed and discussed publicly:

- Consider how requests and promises are made; internally and externally; formally and informally; email and in person; at meetings and in the hallways. How effective are our requests? How effective are our responses?

- Are commitments ever misunderstood? Often? Never? In some areas more than others? Consider what happens to productivity and operational results when parties have not reached shared understanding of what is to be done. Consider what happens to the "mood" or "morale" also, particularly if these misunderstandings happen over time.

- To what extent are people personally responsible for actively managing their commitments? How does this play out in their actions?

- What has become the "standard" or the "norm" within the company regarding keeping and managing commitments? Are commitments broken frequently, infrequently, never? Consider what—if anything— happens when commitments are not kept; all levels.

- What percentage of people make responsible complaints when confronted with a promise not managed or not kept (positive impact)? What percentage of people gossip and complain to others (negative impact)?

- Are there some missing conversations here? What new conversations and new agreements are needed in order to begin improving?

**Footnotes:**

1. _Stopping by Woods on a Snowy Evening_, by Robert Frost; Dutton Books—Reissue Edition; 2001.

2. _Diogenes Laertius: Lives of Eminent Philosophers_, by Diogenes et. al.;Harvard University Press; 1938.

3. _The Four Agreements: A Practical Guide to Personal Freedom_; by Don Miguel Ruiz; Amber-Allen Publishing; 1997.

## SUMMARY—MAIN POINTS AND NEW INTERPRETATIONS

- *Promises (or commitments, or agreements)* are created when a request or an offer is followed by a declaration of Yes. They are seen as the *primary "move"* that we make in language, in order to do *anything and everything* we do with others. *Understanding promises is central* to understanding our relationships, our public identity (how others "see" us) and our results, for us as individuals as well as for our organizations.

- The *whole social fabric* around us is seen as being constructed, at a very basic level, of people (and the organizations they comprise) making promises with each other. We then go about the ongoing business of managing and fulfilling these commitments, as well as entering into new ones, in a wide variety of ways.

- Many of us are not very good observers of ourselves and how we make and manage *the web of commitments* that we each live in. Because of this, we often don't see the negative results we may be producing for ourselves by failing to take care of our commitments and the relationships that are at stake through them. Whenever a promise is made but then broken, we say that something is diminished in the relationship. Something is less than it was before. In many cases, not managing our promises well has a negative, downward effect on:
  - ➤ Trust
  - ➤ The relationship
  - ➤ The success of whatever is involved
  - ➤ The self-esteem—the emotional space—of those involved.

- It's not possible for us to keep 100% of the promises that we make, as originally promised. But it <u>is</u> possible for us to *actively manage* 100% of the promises we make. This is the key—*do we or do we not* operate with conscious awareness of the promises we enter into? *Do we or do we not* pay specific attention to what we say we'll do and when we say we'll do it... and then follow up actively should something happen that may prevent us from doing so?

- *When people break commitments to us*, we have effective options available to us. Not dealing with broken commitments almost always leads to resentment and a lessening of the relationship, as well as to a drop-off in productivity and effectiveness in accomplishing anything together. A powerful language move to make here is the *responsible complaint*.

- Other *tools for managing our commitments* include gaining more ability to *say No* and using *four "valid" responses* when answering requests: Yes, No, Commit-to-Commit, and Counter-Offer.

- Time management is a misnomer. What we really have is *commitment management*. It is here and with our declarations that we design our lives and bring about our own futures.

## HOW-TO: POSSIBILITIES FOR
## TAKING NEW ACTION

1. Refer back to your SAMPLE SITUATION and to the previous section on Requests. What *new promises* are needed? Think about promises *you* may need to make, as well as those *others* could make in order to start the process of bringing about better results. Consider the 6 Elements of Effective Requests, as well as the 4 Valid Responses to requests.

2. *Have a conversation* with others about the importance of *promises* and the importance of managing them and keeping them. *Share views* about how promises impact success, productivity, the relationships involved, the emotional space, the Results which are achieved. Discuss *responsible complaints* and their value, as well as ways in which our agreements with one another can be made clearly and understandably.

3. *Make new agreements* about how promises will be managed and relationships will be taken care of. *Put a context in place* such that you and others have permission to make responsible complaints, to decline requests, to make counter-offers and to commit-to-commit. *Put a context in place* of learning, of improving, of getting better with time and practice.

4. Big Eye: Are there situations you can think of in which *you* fell down on managing your commitments? If so, what steps *have you taken* to clean up those situations and take care of those relationships? And what steps *will you take?*

# *Chapter 8*

## HAPPINESS, LANGUAGE
## AND THE
## PRESENT MOMENT

*"If not now, when?"*

Zen question

What does it really mean to "live in the past"? To "live in the future"? To "live in the present"? *Do these have anything to do with language* and with the results we produce for ourselves? Does our orientation toward *time* have anything to do with our own happiness?

Many of us have a sense that spending too much time dwelling on and focusing on the past or the future is not productive. We have enough experience to say that it doesn't really help; in fact, that in many cases it seems to detract from our ability to create what we want to create. And on a deeper level, many traditions and cultures point to "being present" as a fundamental practice required for spiritual growth, awareness and development. What are we talking about here? And how might our understanding of language serve as a tool, as an entry point, as a lever, as we look for "ways of being" that bring us more peace and more effectiveness in our lives?

Most of us have, from time to time, found ourselves "living in the past" or "living in the future." These are metaphors, of course; we're actually always still living here, now, right where we are. But the metaphor points to *some action that we're taking* that produces the *result*—the experience—of somehow not being fully "present," fully conscious, fully aware of what's going on here and now. And this in turn diminishes our awareness, our ability to listen, to shift, and to take action. This is the key.

The actions which produce this result are, no surprise, *language actions*. They are recurring internal and external conversations, stories, assessments, interpretations that remain always focused on things past or things yet to come. These conversations, of course, may be conducted in and flow out of a number of *different moods*. (Remember our 3-circle model). And in circular fashion, different conversations, different assessments, different declarations, different language actions serve to *produce* different moodspaces. This is one of the major claims related to this way of understanding language.

By participating in certain conversations, we generate and help shift or sustain certain moods. By participating in other conversations, other emotional spaces are brought forth and supported. We like to make our moods "right"—we can observe this in our conversations. And moving forward in that mood, certain other interpretations are readily available and likely, while others are not. There is an undeniable connection which exists here. The mood provides the emotional flavor—the particular, subjective experience, the openness or closedness to possibilities—connected with being in the particular conversation. The mood matters.

Some conversations about the past may be seen as positive, helpful or enjoyable while others may be seen as negative, unhelpful and unenjoyable. The determining factor as to whether we experience a conversation as being "positive" or "negative" has to do with the particular mood the conversation lives in and produces. Also important are the length of time we stay in these conversations, and the results that come about because we stay in them as long as we do. We have found that better results come about when we spend the vast majority of our time right here, right now, in the present.

Let's take a look at some examples. We can say that we're living in the *past*, or "stuck" in the *past* when over time, lots of our conversations with ourselves and with others tend to be in the following moods. *(Note: We have all visited these moodspaces, at one time or another. As a human*

being, we say it's normal and natural and healthy to experience the full
range of emotions. To reinforce a point made earlier, this is NOT to say
that it's wrong to be resentful or sad or anxious, or that these moodspaces are inherently bad, or there's something we're not doing right if
we ever find ourselves here. To me, the keys are awareness, timeframe
and choice. Do we notice ourselves being here? Do we periodically visit
these emotional spaces, or live in them ongoingly? And once we stay
awhile, should we choose to move out of them, do we know what
"moves" are available?)

- A persistent mood of *resentment*. In this mood, conversations are full
  of assessments of unfairness, of blame, and of ascribing bad
  intentions to others related to something that has occurred. (Many of
  these assessments will not be seen as assessments, however; they'll be
  seen as the Truth.) They also include assessments of powerlessness, of
  not being able to do anything about the situation, of being victimized,
  as well as private promises to get even somehow. This mood supports
  recurring negative evaluations of other people and events, and
  assessments that we have been taken advantage of or greatly
  under-appreciated.

- A persistent mood of *guilt*. In this mood, conversations include lots of
  assessments about what I did or didn't do and how "bad" or "wrong"
  it was, how badly it violated my standards; recurring conversations in
  which I blame myself and "beat myself up". We may have these
  conversations in which we blame ourselves over and over again, over
  long periods of time, all connected to a single past event. We may
  promise not to forgive ourselves; we may even declare that nobody
  (not even God) can or will forgive us. These conversations include
  lots of negative assessments about myself, my general worthiness as a
  human being, and my possibilities, in a number of areas.

- A persistent mood of *sadness*. Sadness always has to do with loss and
  with a sense of having possibilities diminished. It is seen as a totally
  healthy, normal, natural emotional space, even to the degree that
  people who *never* visit sadness can be said to be missing out on quite
  a lot. Sadness reveals a lot about what we're concerned about, what
  we care about, in our lives. However, conversations in which we
  *recurrently* relive whatever events or circumstances surround the
  loss can, over long periods of time, make it difficult for us to see

possibilities and take action to move forward. Sadness *done well* ultimately includes a declaration of acceptance around certain "facts of life" (such as the fact that all of us, no matter what, will physically die), and assessments that some things happen in life and it's nobody's fault, it's just part of living in this kind of world.

The past is the past. We cannot intervene on past historical events. We can certainly always update our interpretations, update our assessments, make new declarations, open new possibilities, change our views on the events and people involved. In fact, that's one of the main benefits of understanding language this way.

But many of the conversations that keep us "stuck" in the past do so precisely because we are *not* updating our assessments or views. We are *not* making new declarations, ones that are different from our old ones. Instead, in these situations we recurrently make the *same* declarations and interpretations. And often it's the case that we live in them, defend them, justify them, all out of our commitment to make them—and ourselves—right.

Shifting our attention away from yesterday and toward tomorrow, we can say that we're living in the *future*—in a way that we see as negative or unhelpful—when our conversations tend to be in:

- A persistent mood of *anxiety* or *worry*. In these moods, our conversations include a great deal of concern about the uncertain nature of the future and what might happen. They include assessments about our inability to take any action that would clarify this uncertainty, and that the uncertainty itself is not good. There is a particular emphasis on the strong possibility of negative outcomes, even though we may not have any hard data (assertions) to back us up.

- A persistent mood of *dread*. This mood is connected to conversations similar to those in worry or anxiety, but with a more foreboding, doom-and-gloom tone. The same great concern and focus on uncertainty and negative possible outcomes exists, and it is coupled with a sort of resignation that there's probably nothing anyone can do about it anyway, so why not just give up.

- A persistent mood of *resignation*. Here, conversations include lots of assessments about how nothing makes a difference, no idea will work, and no action on our part can have any impact. It's as if the future's written in stone, and even though I want to change things, there's nothing you or I or anyone else can do that can change anything. So why even try.

In our way of thinking, the future doesn't exist as a pre-given "thing." It's not a thing—it's a distinction in language, pointing to our experience of the present that we'll have at a later time! Whatever the future holds for us, we'll get to it out of the *actions we take in the present*. Our predominant moodspace and its accompanying "background conversations" come before any actions we'll take, strongly influencing us and our interpretations, predisposing us to be open to certain possibilities and actions, and not others.

*What do all the "past" and "future" conversations above have in common?* By participating in them and staying in them a lot, our ability to take effective *action* is jeopardized. By staying too much in the past or the future, I take myself away from the present. And this is the key, for all of us: *The only place that we can take action is the present.* This includes both *physical and language actions*, actions of updating assessments, making new requests, making new declarations, entering into commitments, listening to others' perspectives, and many others.

Think about it—every action you ever took, when you took it, it was the present. It was happening "now" for you. Every action you will take in the future, when you do take that action, you will be taking it in the present. Said another way, the present moment is all we have. It's all we've ever had, and all we ever will have. Everything we do, we do in the present. It's always "now"! In one way, this is obvious and simplistic. In another way, at least to me, it's very deep and opens new possibilities, new ways of thinking, about us and our potential.

I like the analogy of the directory used in many shopping malls—you know the ones which are often positioned right at the intersection of corridors that show which stores are where. What do we find, what do we read, upon first walking up to the directory? Usually it's YOU ARE HERE. And what we can always add is: IT IS NOW. I highly recommend Eckhart Tolle's book *The Power of Now* for anybody wanting to explore more here. I found it to be a tremendously eye-opening read.

※ ※ ※

271

So let's talk about inventing some new conversations, updating and modifying our present conversations for the purpose of *moving toward the present*. Keeping in mind the strong relationship between language and moods allows us to "translate" moods into their major language elements. From here, we can more clearly begin to see the way our language serves to reinforce and keep us in a particular moodspace as well as the "language moves" which are available to us, should we choose to *purposefully move toward something different*.

First, we say that as human beings, you and I and everyone else are *always in one mood or another*. There's no such thing as a human being in no mood. As we've said before, whatever mood you're in, it's *not nothing!* When we're in a mood, it's also interesting to notice that we're usually not value-neutral about the mood. That is, instead we tend to be "champions" of our own mood, doing our best to enroll others in it with us. We become the poster child for whatever mood we're in, and we get very Right about being in the mood. It becomes the Right mood to be in, and we justify it by saying things such as "If you had happen to you what I had happen to me, you'd be in this mood, too!" I know from personal experience that for me, one requirement for moving forward is a willingness to get off the "I'm Right" conversation. It takes a willingness to *lessen my commitment to being Right,* and *increase my commitment to do what it takes* in order to create a good balance between my peacefulness and my productivity. This is worth repeating: *anyone who has ever successfully and purposefully moved out of one mood and into another has dealt with the "I'm Right" conversation, to one degree or another.* Get ready for it, because it will likely be one of the first internal conversations you'll have to deal with in this process.

This process starts with awareness, with observing, with noticing and requires time and practice, time and practice. With time and practice, this movement is absolutely possible. Without it, it is not. Below are some outlines of internal conversations which are connected to particular moodspaces, as well as suggested new internal conversations that serve to move us toward different moodspaces.

### *Moving out of the past (guilt) and into the present:*
### *Being In Guilt*

- I assert that I took—or didn't take—some action X which I now say violates my personal standards.

- I assess that I should—or should not—have done this.
- I greatly regret this, and assess that it's diminished my possibilities.
- I promise to not forgive myself.
- I'm right about this.
- Maybe nobody will forgive me if they know. Maybe I don't deserve to be forgiven at all, ever, by anyone.

## *Moving Out of Guilt and Into the Present*

- I have lived in these conversations for a long time. However, I'm beginning to see that they no longer serve me in taking me where I want to go.
- I declare that I have been blaming myself and living in these conversations long enough.
- I forgive myself.
- I accept myself.
- I love myself.
- I am a human being, I am still learning, and I am still growing.
- I am committed to not repeating that behavior.
- I will take the following steps to ensure that this does not happen again: xxx xxx xxx
- I will enroll the following people to support me in my new commitment: xxx xxx xxx
- I declare my gratitude to life for this opportunity to move forward.

  Note: depending on whether or not others are involved, and how they're involved in the situation, a sincere declaration of apology may also be extremely appropriate in reaching some closure and moving forward out of guilt and into the present. In many cases, though, the apology has long since occurred and the guilt is still strong because of the other internal conversations.

## *Moving out of the past (resentment) and into the present:*
### *Being In Resentment*

- I assess that I have been wronged unfairly.
- I assess that my life is full of these situations.

- I assess that I don't have the power or ability to improve the situation now.
- I declare that I do not accept how my life is.
- I promise that somehow, someway... I'll get even.
- I'm very right about this.

### *Moving Out of Resentment and Into the Present*

- I have lived in these conversations for a long time. However, I'm beginning to see that they no longer serve me in taking me where I want to go.
- I accept that in life, good things and bad things will happen to me. I accept that some possibilities have been closed to me.
- I declare that I accept my life.
- I declare that I'm always responsible for the choices I make.
- I declare that my promise to get even is hereby revoked.
- I declare that I forgive X.
- I request... (effective request, responsible complaint).
- I am still learning, and I am still growing.
- I am grateful to life for this opportunity to move forward.

### *Moving out of the future (anxiety and worry) and more into the present:*

### *Being In Anxiety and Worry*

- I assert that X event has occurred.
- Given this event, I predict that in the future something bad is likely to happen to me or someone close to me.
- I don't know what to do to avoid this "something bad."
- I assess that there's nothing I can do to remove this uncertainty.
- This uncertainty is very bad.
- I declare that I very much want the uncertainty to end.
- I'm right about this.

### *Moving Out of Anxiety and Worry and Into the Present*

- I have lived in these conversations for a long time. However, I'm beginning to see that they no longer serve me in taking me where I want to go.

- I accept that some uncertainty will always exist in my life, and in the lives of everyone.
- I accept that this uncertainty is a natural and permanent part of being alive.
- I declare my predisposition to take action in areas in which I have influence.
- I assess that if I somehow am not able to take action in a given moment, I can learn.
- I am grateful to life for this opportunity to move forward.

### *Moving out of the future (resignation) and into the present:*

### *Being In Resignation*

- I assert that X is happening.
- I assess that it will continue in this way regardless of my actions.
- I assess that I would like to change X.
- I declare that there's nothing I can do about this.
- I declare there are no possibilities for me here.
- I declare my predisposition to take no action.
- I'm very right about this.

### *Moving Out of Resignation and Into the Present*

- I have lived in these conversations for a long time. However, I'm beginning to see that they no longer serve me in taking me where I want to go.
- I assess that life contains many possibilities.
- I declare that I'm open to—and accept—new future possibilities.
- I assess the future as yet-to-be-written, and accept that my actions will impact it.
- I declare myself a learner in taking new action to deal with X.
- I am grateful to life for this opportunity to move forward.

❉ ❉ ❉

## Being Present and the Practice of Meditation

Being present involves all three of what we're calling aspects or parts of our predominant way of being:

- Language
- Body, biology and physical movement
- Moods/emotional space

We may move toward the present via any of these primary avenues. We've spent a bit of time with the language and emotional domains; now, let's turn for a moment to the physical, to the domain of our *body, biology and physical movement*.

The key question now is: *Is there any physical/body action we can purposefully take which will have the predictable result of bringing us more "into the present"?* Well, a great many people have already answered this question for themselves, with a great big Yes: there is a bodily practice which absolutely supports being in the present, and we call it *meditation*.

It is an ancient practice, of course, which has only recently (relatively speaking) been part of our mainstream Western understanding. There are now numerous scientific and medical studies which confirm the connection and results that millions of practitioners have experienced for thousands of years. There are a great many wonderful books and workshops which introduce this practice to those just learning as well as those which explore more deeply the many varied and different versions which may be practiced. It is an active element of many religious and spiritual traditions, in America and around the world.

Have you ever meditated? For many of us, it's a lot harder than it sounds. In fact, I heard this expression which I think sums it up well: *Don't just do something... sit there.* This points to the difficulty of "just sitting" and to our social addiction to "doing something." This is especially true in our time and in our country, in which change is ever-present and we are bombarded constantly with messages having to do with "doing more" and "being productive" and "achieving." Our "protestant work ethic" is celebrated everywhere, and being a workaholic isn't really viewed as a negative by large numbers of people. To not be always engaged, 100% of my waking day, with activities dedicated to directly producing financial or physical gain... is to somehow be "lazy" or "unmotivated" or "odd." To simply sit and relax, sit and center myself, sit and rejuvenate myself is viewed as "weak" and/or the epitome of wasting time. Sound familiar?

Of course, there is sitting meditation and walking meditation and standing meditation and even washing dishes meditation. Ultimately, it is taught, all of life can become a meditation, a purposeful and present moment exercise. That is, with time and practice, and with awareness and attention, we can accept fully and bring ourselves fully to every single endeavor of our lives, however "mundane" or "normal." And with this way of being we live our lives fully present, fully in acceptance of what is, and fully engaged. And even if we are not committed to the same degree of practice and the same degree of being present as masters or accomplished monks, sitting meditation can be a wonderful entre into a whole new way of understanding and using our bodies. It can serve as a wonderful space out of which new and more helpful internal conversations may spring. Here are the major claims underneath our focus on meditation and the body, and the connection to our peacefulness and productivity:

- *Our bodies, our language, and our emotional space are separate, yet braided together. Each strongly influences the others.*

- *Physical practices such as meditation absolutely support our ability to be present.*

- *Being present is where we want to be! The quality of our journey— in a variety of ways—is directly connected to our ability to be present.*

- *These time-honored physical practices can be a primary engine, a primary source of power for us, as we seek to invent new conversations and produce different moodspaces in our lives.*

There are many ways to meditate. Generally, practitioners start with a 10 or 15 minute period, and increase it with practice as they desire. Here is one suggested way to begin: *Find a comfortable place to sit, either in a firm straight-backed chair or on a cushion on the floor with your legs crossed. Your body should be erect, not slouched over, but relaxed—not tense or rigid. Find a position in which your body is centered, not leaning left or right, front or back. Relax your facial muscles, including your forehead, cheek and jaw muscles. Let your jaw drop a bit, just relaxing it softly. Let your tongue relax and not press the roof of your mouth.*

*Let your eyes shut, or partially shut with a "soft" gaze. Stay in the same position, breathing rhythmically. Notice your shoulder and neck muscles, and bring your attention to them as you let them relax. Let your back and stomach muscles relax, and your hips and leg muscles. Just breathe in and out, letting your muscles relax.*

*Begin breathing a bit more deeply, still rhythmically. Let the breathing be "low" in your tummy, rather than "high" in your chest. Feel your lower stomach pushing out and going in. Relax your stomach muscles all the way for this. You may have to loosen your belt or clothing. Keep the breathing regular and deep. Do this for a few moments, then check your posture again. Recenter yourself as needed. Notice if any areas of your body are tense. Relax these areas, and allow yourself to relax all over while maintaining the same posture.*

*Gently bring your attention to your breath. Pay full attention to it, having your attention come "in" on the in breath, and go "out" on the out breath. Simply have your attention on your breathing, nothing else. In and out. Don't judge your breathing, making it right or wrong or good or bad or too this or too that; simply observe it, have your awareness on it, and that's all.*

*Occasionally, you may be distracted by sounds outside of you, or thoughts or sensations inside of you. Without judging or blaming, simply allow your attention to fall from these things and return to your breathing. Be gentle with yourself—this is not a problem, it's normal and natural. At first, distractions are plentiful and seem very difficult to overcome. Internal thoughts about what I need to be doing, my to-do list, other commitments, other concerns, all seem to clamor and compete for my attention when I meditate. For me, these internal distractions are more of a challenge to move through than are the external ones.*

*Your mood or emotion may shift during this time. Again, without judging it, simply notice it and bring your attention back to your breathing. There will be plenty of time to deal with those things later on. Relax and breathe, in and out.*

*Keep doing this, breathing and noticing things, and coming back to the breathing in a non-judgmental way, until the time is up.*

❋ ❋ ❋

I found it very interesting, when I was first introduced to meditation in this way, that so much emphasis was placed on *breathing*, on awareness of our breath, of paying attention to it in such a way. We all breathe naturally, I thought. Breathing is breathing. What's the big deal? Well, as it turns out, it's a huge deal. Rhythmically breathing down low in the tummy is quite different from breathing up high in the chest. It produces a noticeably different mood, influences in a noticeably different way the internal conversations we have. Short breaths are very different from long ones, deep ones very different from shallow ones. (And of course, many of us are not very good observers of our breathing.)

One practice that meditating has taught me is to slow down and "lower" my breathing in preparation for any situation which might be difficult or emotionally charged. That is, to slow my breathing down, taking longer and deeper breaths, and to have the breath go down low, making my tummy go in and out as I breathe (vs. up high, which makes my chest go in and out). This tends to center me and, I believe, helps me to better deal with the situation and come up with more well-thought out ideas and solutions. I came to see this out of learning more about meditation, but for many people it's more in the realm of common sense. For example, in similar situations many of us have received–and given–the good advice "slow down and take a few deep breaths!" People on both sides of the Pacific have known about and experienced these connections for a long time. What may have been missing for many of us is seeing them in such a way that they can be used *purposefully* in our lives.

Somebody told me once that: ***Breathing—it's the secret to life.*** I agree–now, in more ways than one.

❊ ❊ ❊

I have found that meditating brings me face to face with myself, in a way that few other things I've been involved with do. It's a way of being *alone* with myself that in my life, is a bit unique. There's nothing else I'm involved in that has the same effect. Even prayer is significantly different, as prayer involves words and conversations in a way that meditating does not.

Of course, many of us haven't spent much time here, so we're not very practiced. We say we're not *comfortable,* and we're not–it's a new experience for us. Our bodies aren't used to it. We are all very familiar, very comfortable with two types of human consciousness:

- Being awake, alert and thinking; and
- Being asleep.

We're very comfortable in these two states. We have lots of practice here, and our bodies are familiar with these. To me, meditation can be viewed as a third type of human consciousness:

- Being awake, alert and *not* thinking.

In meditation, we are focused on *being*, on purposefully *not doing* anything. This whole book is centered around language–and in many ways, *meditation represents a direct attempt to take ourselves OUT of language*, to go beyond language, perhaps to a deeper way of being, to a more direct way of experiencing. And the practice of meditation can also be seen as one of stepping "back" a level, taking more the perspective of *observer* of ourselves–and doing so in a very non-judgmental, very accepting, very loving manner.

We rest in a different way here, not so much resting our physical body (though that certainly does occur) as we are resting our thoughts, our internal conversations, our internal judging and blaming. We're taking a break from participating in our anxiety, our resentment and our guilt. We are still awake, but we're purposefully <u>not</u> generating any conversations. Instead, the focus is more on observing. It is here that we can more clearly see what we're doing with many of our thoughts. We are also more able to see the sheer number of thoughts and judgments that we generate, ongoingly, on a wide variety of topics. For many of us, these seem to simply "spring" from us–unsolicited and uninvited.

This type of resting or renewing was never taught to me when I was growing up. I never even knew it existed–I didn't know that I didn't know how to meditate. It's a treasure, an ancient well of renewable strength and peace. There are fantastic resources available for those who want to begin practicing–and that's the key, to practice. *To learn to meditate, one must meditate!* We must declare our willingness to be beginners, and simply start to practice. The experience of meditating, and of gaining some practice and some competency here is fantastically different than reading about meditation.

To me, meditation is a practice that moves toward taking us out of language and slows us down a bit, renewing us on the physical, emotional and spiritual levels. It can give us an experience of peace and acceptance that serves as a great foundation for then taking action, making changes and moving forward. Always a key question: If you've never meditated before, what are the *internal conversations* that have kept you from doing so? What are the interpretations that have stopped you? This is not a right/wrong question... it's a big eye question. The opportunity is to notice your own stories and interpretations, and how they have historically had the end result of your not meditating (or not walking, or not jogging, or not having that conversation with so-and-so, or not doing whatever). From this noticing, new possibilities for purposefully inventing something new arise. Even when we're in the domain of the body and body practices, we find ourselves still dealing with language.

# *Chapter 9*

## Have-Do-Be
## or
## Be-Do-Have?

*"If you want to be somebody else, change your mind."* [1]

Song lyric from "Change Your Mind"
Sister Hazel

As we move toward the end of this volume, I'd like to return to our collective *pursuit of happiness*, and to the Dalai Lama's "great question that confronts us all": *How am I to be happy?* Let's begin with how many of us in the modern West appear to be answering this question. In many ways, our modern American and Western culture supports and encourages *consuming things*, and the term *consumer* is not used in a negative way when it's applied to us, either as individuals or groups. Today's advertising and marketing industries, in a great many fields, are actively courting potential consumers by consistently reinforcing and promoting a particular link between *having, doing and being.* It may be explicit or implicit, out loud or in the background, but the linkage can be summarized as:

283

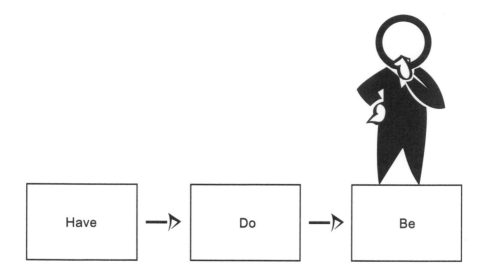

| Have | →▷ | Do | →▷ | Be |
|------|----|----|----|----|

**If you *have* this, you can then *do* that... which then causes or allows you to *be* whatever.**

If you *have* this beer, you can *do* things like hang out at upscale clubs surrounded by wonderful, ambitious, and exciting women and men, dancing and remembering exciting things you've done together, and then you'll *be* cool, self-assured, in the "in" crowd... and happy. If you *have* this car, you can *do* things like drive up mountains and across deserts, or on sleek super highways, which will then have you *be* rugged, independent, confident... and happy. If you *have* this kind of golf club, you can *do* things like drive it straight every time, and then you'll *be* a winner, confident, successful... and happy. If you *have* this particular vacation, you can *do* things like stroll the beach with your loved one and go out to tiki hut restaurants, which will leave you *being* rejuvenated, refreshed, satisfied... and happy. I could, you could, we all could go on and on here. Does this make sense? This promise may be out in the open or somewhere in the background, but in our culture, it is there. It's all around the central premise of *have—do—be*, in this direction.

This is ingrained in—and underneath—a steady stream of messages that we've gotten for many years. It's so pervasive and built-in that it moves to the background of our thinking as one of the "givens," one of the "facts." It's often totally taken for granted. And yet when we do acquire many of the things that we wanted to have, we find that we're still not happy, not peaceful, not enjoying the journey very much. Many of us have had this experience, where the *having* has not brought forth the *being,* where having X has <u>not</u> translated into being Y.

Having this experience, and having enough of these experiences over time, can often lead to a willingness to really re-think the whole equation. To really re-think the connections which exist between having, doing and being. *Of course, if we change our thinking around this it will change all sorts of things!* Can you see how this is so? New possibilities for taking action will show up, new ways of being purposeful about our own growth and learning will appear, new choices available for designing our own lives will show up.

❋ ❋ ❋

The more powerful interpretation, by far, reverses the direction and is summarized this way:

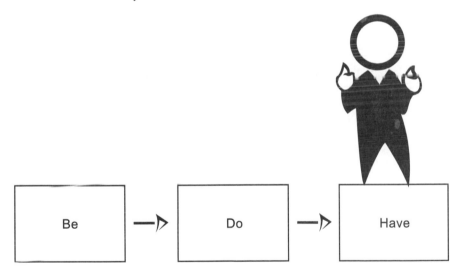

| Be | | Do | | Have |

Here, we start with *being*. This model, this interpretation, has us first *be* a certain way (including being in the present, as best we can). By then *doing* <u>whatever</u> we do from that way of being, over time we end up *having* what we want. And in more ways than one, seeming to also *want* what we *have*! With this model, as a byproduct somehow, the entire *have* portion of the model becomes less important. This is, obviously, a direct reversal from what many of us have grown up with, lived with, been bombarded with from all angles, and taken for granted.

So what are we really talking about here? How, exactly, do we take actions that = Be–Do–Have? How do we go about the business of consciously *being* one way, and not another? We have to start with language here, of course. We create out of what we speak. The actions required to *be* a certain way, and not another, absolutely include language actions.

*New declarations*. For example, new primary declarations of who I am and who I'm not. Declarations of love to those I love, including myself. New personal standards for being in relationship with others. Saying No and saying Yes differently than I used to. New declarations of trust. New declarations to open myself toward learning. Declarations of acceptance of my past, of others, of what is so. Declarations of forgiveness (and repeated declarations in the *process* of forgiveness). Declarations of gratitude. Declarations of apology.

*New requests and new promises*. In all areas. Requesting that others participate with me in my life, doing X, Y, or Z. When situations arise in which I'd like something to be different than it is, making an effective request, and interpreting it as a request and not a demand. Requesting that others keep their commitments to me (responsible complaints). Taking responsibility for managing my commitments, starting now. Holding others accountable for managing theirs to me, starting now.

*New assessments*. Examining and updating my assessments about myself. About others close to me in my life. About my job, my boss, and my colleagues. About groups of people. About the past and about the future. Sharing my assessments with others and listening to what they have to say about how they went from observation to belief in such a different way than I did. Checking my ability to ground my assessments.

Our ability to be one way and not another is strongly and directly connected to our willingness to begin generating, practicing and participating in new interpretations, new conversations, new stories. We are already the authors. We have the authority to write a new chapter or two. We start by being aware, by being willing to take a look, by being willing to take responsibility for the chapters we've written so far. And then we get to make a choice: knowing what we know about the power of language, what new stories and interpretations will we invent for ourselves? Of the infinite stories we could come up with, which particular ones will we create?

The notion of *being* one way and not another also includes our moods and emotional space. It includes our long-term, predominant mood, as well as our short-term emotions, our pattern of triggered reactions to events and circumstances. And as we've been discussing throughout, moods and emotions are strongly influencing—and influenced by—our language, our internal and external conversations, our assessments, declarations and stories.

We can also use our physical body and biology as starting points for *being* a certain way but not another. Our nutrition and exercise standards are opportunities, as are our sleep habits. Our posture and way of walking, sitting, and standing. Our willingness to do certain things with our bodies (like dancing, or yoga, or tae kwon do, or massage, or meditation, for example). Our ability to declare ourselves beginners and "put our body into" new learning situations—and to practice, over time.

These have everything to do with our *way of being*. The implication, of course, is that there's more than one way to be! And further, that your particular way of being and my particular way of being are not fixed and permanent, forever and always features of "who we each are." Rather, our ways of being are continuously dynamic and flexible, changing and growing and evolving with every experience we have—including everthing we learn, everthing we feel, everthing we say and everything we do.

For those interested in gaining support for making such a shift, resources are available. The practice of *ontological coaching* is the most powerful way I have ever experienced of shifting my way of being. It involves all three of our primary aspects—language, mood/emotions, and body. This type of personal coaching is, in my experience, the most direct way to bring what used to be invisible out to where I can see it, and do so in a way that I get to move forward in choice, acceptance, gratitude, and lightness. I highly recommend this type of coaching and am pleased to provide information about sources of such coaching in the appendix.

### A special note about gratitude and being

We've already touched on this earlier, but I see this as so important I'd like to bring it up again here, in the context of being—doing—having. *Being grateful* may be triggered by someone else fulfilling their promise to me or by their generous actions toward me. Many of us have had this experience. Gratitude may also be much deeper than that, as it can also be a pervasive way of living, a general moodspace in which we live our lives. Here, it's not triggered by an external event. This kind of gratitude is already there, as Rafael Echeverria says, as a "pervasive assessment that being alive is a privilege; that it's worthwhile being a part of this mystery." In this way of thinking, *gratitude is the emotion in which joy is built.* Here, a direct connection is made between a declaration of gratitude, and the *experience of joy.*

We claim that people who experience joy also have declared gratitude. That by acknowledging and declaring gratitude, we can consciously shift our moodspace, we can consciously improve the quality of our journey. To build joy, then, one needs gratitude. And gratitude can be declared into being. By you and by me, *at any time.* For *any reason.* And for *no reason at all.*

Do you believe that everyone has something to be grateful for? Have you ever been around people who are less fortunate than yourself? Are you aware of situations in which children and adults live in conditions far worse than those you're experiencing right now? **What are you grateful for?** The practice of purposefully engaging in this question and declaring gratitude has a *fantastic benefit-to-cost ratio.* What does it *really* cost us to do this? What do we *give up* in order to do this? And what are the *benefits* that come out of doing it? What do I get to *do*, or more importantly—what do I get to *be*—in return? We have the opportunity, every day of our lives, to simply notice. To acknowledge. And to declare.

**Footnotes:**

---

1. <u>*Fortress*</u>, by Sister Hazel; audio CD; 2000, Universal Studios.

# Chapter 10

## The Bigger Picture
### and
## Looking Ahead

---

*"Nothing endures but change."* [1]

Heraclitus (540BC–480BC)

*"The times, they are a-changing."* [2]

Bob Dylan

---

I agree with Heraclitus and Bob. I see the *shift in perspective* represented within these pages as being a part of a *larger shift* that seems to be
needed in order for us to get our arms —individually and collectively—
around some of the problems we face today. In my experience, a shift is
underway *already* in how many of us think and see the world, as well as
our place in it. Now, we may not describe this shift in the same way or
with the same words, but I believe many of us are already in it, are
already part of it.

This body of learning, this perspective that we've been sharing, is
absolutely consistent with this larger shift. I see this shift as positive and

289

as a natural part of our collective growth and learning. In fact, I see it as necessary in order for us to successfully and most ethically answer basic questions such as: ***How am I to be happy?*** and ***How are we—the collective "all of us" We—to be happy? How will we live together?*** Throughout human history, we human beings have changed how we answer these questions. This is directly related, of course, to the fact that over the years, human beings have dramatically changed how we "see things," in a variety of areas. We have changed our paradigms, we have become new observers. This is what is occurring here, now, today.

Willis Harmon's groundbreaking 1998 book <u>*Global Mind Change*</u> is one of my favorites on this subject. In it, he says: *"For the past 3 decades there have been ample indications of a change in values emphasis, and indeed of a shifting underlying picture of reality, among an expanding fraction of the populace. Similar changes have been noted in most of the modernized countries in the world. ... Key elements of this shift include:*

- *Increased emphasis on the connectedness of everything to everything—not only the "things" of the outer world, but also our inner, subjective experience*

- *A shift in how we see authority being situated, from external to internal. Whether in religion, politics, or science, we see growing disenchantment with external authorities and increasing reliance on intuitive, inner wisdom and authority*

- *A shift in the perception of cause from external to internal. The weak meaning of a statement like "We create our own reality" is that the way we perceive the world around us (and ourselves) is affected by the contents of our unconscious and preconscious minds. The stronger meaning of such statements (and the assertion that there are no coincidences, and that behind apparently accidental events may lie hidden meanings and patterns) is that we are indeed co-creators of that world and that ultimate cause is to be sought not in the physical, but in the mind, or consciousness.* [3]

I believe these shifts that Mr. Harmon speaks about are real and are occurring, and that they themselves may be connected to another big trend, another big shift: **We are collectively going from being *less aware*, to being *more aware*.** That is, over time, we human beings may be seen to be on a journey which takes us from being *less* conscious of our own creative power, *less* conscious of the ways in which we're connected and inter-dependent, *less* conscious of our own ability to guide our own development and bring forth our own experience... to being *more* conscious of it. And what seems to go hand in hand with more awareness, with being more conscious, is being more *responsible*, and less inclined to immediately point toward others for blame, whenever things don't go our way. What also seems to accompany this shift is an increase in our sphere of *compassion*; that is, we tend to become more compassionate to others, more accepting of different types of others, as we all are seen as doing the best we can, given how we see things. We're all seen as seeking to achieve many of the same sorts of things and to overcome many of the same sorts of challenges as we live our lives.

Something I read by Albert Einstein seems to also point in this direction as we look toward the future. He says: *"Our task must be to free ourselves... by widening our circle of compassion to embrace all living creatures and the whole of nature and its beauty."* [4]

Our big eye model is a perfect metaphor for this trend, for this movement into greater awareness. We're each unique observers, becoming more and more aware of *the particular ways* in which we each tend to observe. It's as if your big eye keeps going farther and farther back, first noticing and taking in just you, and then noticing and taking in you and your family, then you and your community, you and your country, you and your culture and traditions... and continuing still! Conscious growth and purposeful learning are directly connected to our ability to develop this capacity within ourselves. Everything we've said here about language is consistent with this. In a broad way, I believe that's what *everything* here is about. It's part of this larger process of becoming—becoming more aware, becoming more conscious, becoming more responsible, becoming new observers.

*I like to think of this as a possible scenario*: If indeed we're individually and collectively becoming more and more aware, more and more conscious in this way—and let's assume human beings keep this up for the next 100 or 1000 or 10,000 years—*what will we be like then?* How will we live? How will we see things? What will we have become? What will be possible? I don't know, of course. But somehow I like very much where this path seems to be going.

I have found Ken Wilber's 2001 book, <u>A Theory of Everything: An Integral Vision for Business, Politics, Science and Spirituality</u> to be a profoundly powerful look into the particular ways that we human beings—as individuals and collectively—continually change and evolve during the course of our lives. He builds on pioneering work done by Clare Graves and others, and shares a rather startling conclusion: the observer that we each are is indeed constantly changing... but the changes are not random! In other words, we are each indeed in an ongoing process of shifting how we "see things," and several particular and highly predictable levels of consciousness or levels of awareness have been identified across all known cultures and time zones. I highly and enthusiastically recommend this book to everyone.

## Looking Ahead

*"To find happiness for a lifetime, help the next generation."* To me, this ancient Chinese proverb points very clearly to the importance today of sharing the best of what we learn with our children. It also illuminates a key connection which exists for a great many of us: that between our *contributing* to others, *serving* others, *helping* others, *sharing* with others... and the quality of our own journey.

For example, would it have a positive impact if we learned—and then taught our *young people*—these distinctions, this way of understanding ourselves, our language, our relationships and our results? At the individual level, could this help them strike a more solid balance between peacefulness and productivity? Would this be an asset as they prepare for adulthood and all it brings? Could it help them form more healthy and satisfying relationships and careers for themselves? *I say yes.*

At a larger level, could this help them navigate in the world of tomorrow, a world in which change is everywhere? A world in which our ability to *continue learning* is key? A world in which our ability to form mutually beneficial, long-term relationships *with people from different countries and backgrounds* seems to be growing—not diminishing—in importance? *I say yes.*

Would it be a good thing if, over time, larger and larger numbers of people of different cultures came to understand each other as unique observers, necessarily "seeing things" in ways that reflect each particular set of beliefs, traditions and historical discourses? Would the world be a better place with fewer people going through life being terminally certain of their own "right-ness"? To have larger and larger numbers of people having the understanding that nobody sees things "like they are"... that everybody is interpreting? Would it be a plus to have more and more people aware of the ways in which our own internal and external conversations are creating and generating our experiences, our moodspaces, our results? To have larger numbers of us being aware of more choices, *as well as being more aware that we are indeed always choosing in the first place?* Would it be positive to have more people much more aware of the larger *social discourses* and "culture conversations" that we live in, as well as how these conversations shape us and are shaped by us? *I say yes to all.*

❋ ❋ ❋

It's my sincere hope that this has been time well spent for you and that you have found some real take-home value here. I am convinced that we *all* have the capacity to learn, to change, to bring about new results in our lives. It's been my intent from the start to keep us coming back to the big eye, to our ability to observe ourselves... and to observe the way we observe. This has to be the starting point—first we notice, we become aware—then we get to choose. Then we get to move into learning. It's only after we observe that we get to *consciously* change, design, update, build, create, bring about new results in our lives and in the world.

It's a privilege to share this with you. Even though I don't see myself as the best or most qualified person to be writing this book and sharing these distinctions with you, I'm very grateful for the chance to do so. For this I thank you, and I thank my wonderful family, teachers and friends who have been part of this journey with me. So until we meet again, my question to you is: *What do you notice?* And just as importantly:

*What are you committed to?*

*What do you choose?*

*What do you say?*

## Footnotes:

1. *Diogenes Laertius: Lives of Eminent Philosophers*, by Diogenes et. al.;Harvard University Press; 1938.

2. *The Times They Are A-Changin'*, by Bob Dylan; audio CD; Sony; original release 1964.

3. *Global Mind Change—The Promise of the 21$^{st}$ Century*, by Willis Harmon; Berrett-Koehler Publishers, Inc.; 1998.

4. *The Expanded Quotable Einstein;* by Alice Calaprice; Princeton University Press; 2000.

---

*"And God said 'let there be light' and there was light."*
                                                    *Bible, Book of Genesis*

*In the beginning there was the Word, and the Word was with God, and the Word is God."*
                                                    *Bible, Gospel of John*

I'd like to share with you a thought that you may have already found yourself thinking, a connection you may have already pointed to. The more I think about this, the more sense it seems to make:

***If we are indeed made in the image and likeness of God, and if God's word creates and generates, brings forth and manifests... why shouldn't ours?***

## Appendix A: References

*Ethics for the New Millennium,* by His Holiness the Dalai Lama, Riverhead Books/Penguin Putnam, Inc., 1999, p. 4.

*The Varieties of Religious Experience*—A Study in Human Nature, by William James; 1902.

*Remembrance of Things Past*, by Marcel Proust; Knopf Publishers; 1982.

*Global Mind Change—The Promise of the 21st Century*, by Willis Harmon; Berrett-Koehler Publishers, Inc.; 1998; p. 159.

*The Tree of Knowledge*, by Humberto Maturana, Francisco J. Varela and Robert Paolucci; Shambhala Publications; ISBN: 0877736421; 1987; p. 27.

*You Are What You Say: A Harvard Doctor's Six-Step Proven Program for Transforming Stress Through the Power of Language*; by Matthew Budd, MD and Larry Rothstein, Ed.D.; Crown Publishers; 2000, p. 137.

*The Four Agreements: A Practical Guide to Personal Freedom*; by Don Miguel Ruiz; Amber-Allen Publishing; ISBN 1-878424-31-9; 1997, p. 26, 63, 65, 69, 114.

*The Power of Now*, by Eckhart Tolle; New World Library, 1999, p. 128.

*Leading Minds: An Anatomy of Leadership*; by Howard Gardner; Basic Books/Harper Collins; 1995, p. 14.

*Conversations with God: An Uncommon Dialogue; Books 1, 2, and 3*; by Neale Donald Walsch; G.P. Putnam's Sons Publishing; 1996.

*The Fifth Discipline Fieldbook: Strategies and Tools for Building a Learning Organization*; by Peter Senge, Richard Ross, Bryan Smith, Charlotte Roberts, and Art Kleiner; Doubleday/Bantam Doubleday Dell; 1994. p. 242.

*Coaching to the Human Soul: Ontological Coaching and Deep Change*; *Volume 1—The Linguistic Basis of Ontological Coaching*; by Alan Sieler; Newfield Australia; 2003. p. 12.

*The Magic of Believing*, by Claude M. Bristol; Prentice-Hall, Inc., 1948, p. 29.

*The Expanded Quotable Einstein*; by Alice Calaprice; Princeton University Press; 2000.

*The Academic American Encyclopedia* - Hoffer, Eric; New York: Grolier Electronic Publishing, Inc., 1993.

*Of Human Interaction*; by Joseph Luft and Harry Ingham; Palo Alto, CA; National Press; 1969.

*Retooling On The Run: Real Change for Leaders With No Time*, by Stuart Heller, PhD; Frog, Ltd.; 1995.

*Reality Isn't What It Used To Be*; by Walter Truett Anderson; Harper & Row Publishers; 1990, ISBN 0-06-250017-1; p. 75.

*Diogenes Laertius: Lives of Eminent Philosophers*, by Diogenes et. al.;Harvard University Press; 1938.

*The Nature of Managerial Work*, by Henry Mintzberg; Harper Collins; 1973.

*Expression and Meaning*, by John Searle; Cambridge University Press; ISBN: 0521313937; November 1985

*Linking Language to Action*, by J.L. Austin; Cambridge University Press; 1962.

*Ceremony*, by Leslie Marmon Silko; Penguin USA; 1988.

*Anatomy of the Spirit: The Seven Stages of Power and Healing*; by Caroline Myss, Ph.D., Three Rivers Press, 1996, p. 215.

*Merriam Webster's Collegiate Dictionary*; Merriam Webster Editorial Staff; 1994.

*Stopping by Woods on a Snowy Evening*, by Robert Frost; Dutton Books—Reissue Edition; 2001.

*The End of the Innocence,* by Don Henley; audio CD; 1989; Geffen Records.

*Fortress*, by Sister Hazel; audio CD; 2000, Universal Studios.

*I Love You, You're Perfect, Now Change;* audio CD; Varese Records; 1996.

*The Times They Are A-Changin'*, by Bob Dylan; audio CD; Sony; original release 1964.

## Appendix B: Inspiration

The following books were not used directly as references in this project, but are works that have inspired me. I highly recommend them to you. To me, they are tremendous sources of wisdom, innovation and genuine optimism for tomorrow.

*A Brief History of Everything*, by Ken Wilber; Shambhala Press; 1996.

*A Theory of Everything: An Integral Vision for Business, Politics, Science and Spirituality*, by Ken Wilber; Shambhala Press; 2001.

*Integral Psychology: Consciousness, Spirit, Psychology, Therapy*; by Ken Wilber; Shambhala Press; 2000.

*Boomeritis: A Novel That Will Set You Free*, by Ken Wilber; Shambhala Press; 2003.

*Living Buddha, Living Christ*, by Thich Nhat Hanh; Riverhead Books/G.P. Putnam's Sons; 1995.

*Leadership and the New Science*, by Margaret J. Wheatley; Berrett-Koehler Publishers; 1992.

*Conscious Evolution*, by Barbara Marx Hubbard; New World Library; 1998.

*The Cosmic Serpent—DNA and the Origins of Knowledge*, by Jeremy Narby; Jeremy P. Tarcher/Penguin Putnam, NY; ISBN 0-87477-911-1; 1998.

*Unfolding Meaning*, by David Bohm; Routledge Publishing; 1985.

*Ontologia del Lenguaje* (*The Ontology of Language*), by Rafael Echeverria; Dolmen Edicion, Argentina.

*Building Trust: In Business, Politics, Relationships, and Life*, by Robert C. Solomon and Fernando Flores; Oxford University Press; 2001.

*Understanding Computers and Cognition*, by Terry Winograd and Fernando Flores; Addison Wesley Professional; ISBN: 0201112973; 1987.

*Overcoming Organizational Defenses;* by Chris Argyris; Allyn and Bacon; 1990.

*The Web of Life*, by Fritjof Capra; Doubleday; ISBN: 0385476760; 1997.

*Conscious Business—Transforming Your Workplace (and Yourself) by Changing the Way You Think, Act and Communicate,* by Fred Kofman; Sounds True Press; ISBN: 1564559319; 2000.

*Seven Habits of Highly Effective People*, by Stephen Covey; Simon & Schuster; 1989.

*Emotional Intelligence: Why It Can Matter More Than IQ*, by Dan Goleman; Bantam Books; ISBN 0-553-09503-X ; 1995.

# Appendix C: Organizations and Resources

*How to contact me:*

New Possibilities Press
8805 Tamiami Trail North, Suite # A-311, Naples, FL 34108
Phone: 239-514-5880 • Fax: 239-593-3275
Website: chalmersbrothers.com • Email: chalmersb@comcast.net

❋ ❋ ❋

I consider the following organizations to be *excellent sources* of professional coaching and outstanding educational workshops. They offer a wide variety of workshops, seminars, consulting and coaching–for individuals, groups and organizations. I have worked with many of these people in the past, and continue to work with several of them today.

These organizations provide short courses and long courses; introductory courses and advanced courses; courses specifically designed for men and those designed for women. They offer sessions with a business focus as well as those with a purely personal focus. They offer courses for couples and for relationships, sessions around moods and emotions, and workshops focusing directly on our body and on the whole physical domain.

On the business and organizational side, these organizations also bring teams of coaches and consultants together to support leaders and teams in a number of different ways, all having to do with bringing new distinctions and new practices into the workplace. *These are people I know personally, and I feel 100% confident in recommending them to you.*

- **Education for Living Seminars Southwest, Lake Charles, LA.** Contact: Ms. Laurie Riquelmy and Ms. Ellen Papania. Phone: 888 335 7952 (888 EFL SWLA). Email: EFLSWLA@aol.com. Website: EFLSW.com

- **Newfield Network, Boulder, CO.** Contact: Ms. Terrie Lupberger–75 Manhattan Drive, Suite 1 Boulder, CO 80303. Phone: 303-449-6117. Email: info@newfieldnetwork.com. Website: www.newfieldnetwork.com.

- **Coaching for Success, Lake Charles, LA**. Contact: Mr. Mike Papania—602 West Prien Lake Road, PMB 603, Lake Charles, LA 70602. Phone: 337 421 1481. Email: mpapania@suddenlinkmail.com. Website: coachingforsuccessinc.com

- **Personal Coaching: Mark Robertson, Nashville, TN**. Contact: Mr. Mark Robertson—2714 Linmar Ave., Nashville, TN 37215. Phone: 615-463-8458. Email: markrobertson@comcast.net.

- **Newfield Australia: Blackburn, Victoria, Australia**. Contact: Mr. Alan Sieler. Phone: 613 9878 5501. Fax: 613 9878 0394. Website: www.newfieldaus.com.au.

# A

**new**
**possibilities**
**press**

naples florida

# Quick Order Form

## *Language and the Pursuit of Happiness*

**FAX ORDERS TO:**
239-593-3275 • *Send this completed form.*

**EMAIL ORDERS TO:**
cb@chalmersbrothers.com • *Include information from this form.*

**SEND POSTAL ORDERS TO:**
**New Possibilities Press**
8805 Tamiami Trail North • Suite A-311 • Naples, FL 34108
*Include information from this form.*

**Please also contact me regarding:**
• Personal coaching
• Organization improvement/leadership/teambuilding/communication
• Speaking/seminars

Your Name: _____

Address: _____

City: _____State: _____Zip: _____

Telephone: _____Email: _____

**Price:** $24.95
**Sales tax:** Please add 6% ($1.50) for books shipped to Florida addresses.
***Please include $4.50 for Priority Shipping***
Total (non-FL addresses): $29.45 • Total (FL addresses): $30.95

Payment:     ❑ Visa        ❑ Mastercard

Card number: _____

Name on card: _____Exp. Date: _____